The Notebook of a New Clinical Neuropsychologist

Have you ever looked at a heavy volume on neuropsychology and wondered what it would actually be like to become a professional clinician, working every day with neurological patients in a busy hospital while simultaneously learning your craft? This book tells the story of that journey.

The Notebook of a New Clinical Neuropsychologist vividly details the experience of starting work in clinical neuropsychology, exploring early-career learning and development through an intimate, case-based approach. Topics include the learning of basic clinical skills and knowledge, counter-transference, the clinician's emotional experiences, ethical and moral dilemmas and the development of clinical reasoning. The book is structured around individual studies from the author's early caseload, with each vignette containing the relevant neuropathology, clinical presentation, history, neuropsychological test findings and other clinical data. Chapters are also organised around key neuropathological conditions, including traumatic brain injury, stroke and brain infections, which provide a broader context for the narrative focus of the book.

Few academic books explore the personal, intellectual and ethical dilemmas that face a new clinician working with patients in a neuropsychological setting. Tailored to facilitate experiential learning via case studies, reflective practice and problem-based learning, the book will be of interest to students and professionals working within the broad area of neuropsychology and brain injury services.

Rudi Coetzer qualified with distinction as a Clinical Psychologist in 1987. He is Consultant Neuropsychologist and Head of Service with the North Wales Brain Injury Service, Betsi Cadwaladr University Health Board NHS Wales and an Honorary Senior Lecturer in Clinical Neuropsychology in the School of Psychology, Bangor University.

The Notebook of a New Clinical Neuropsychologist

Stories from another world

Rudi Coetzer

Routledge
Taylor & Francis Group

LONDON AND NEW YORK

First published 2018
by Routledge
2 Park Square, Milton Park, Abingdon, Oxon OX14 4RN

and by Routledge
711 Third Avenue, New York, NY 10017

Routledge is an imprint of the Taylor & Francis Group, an informa business

© 2018 Rudi Coetzer

First published in German as *Professionelle Beziehungen: Theorie Praxis der
Baluntgruppenarbeit* by Springer 2012

British Library Cataloguing in Publication Data
A catalogue record for this book is available from the British Library

Library of Congress Cataloging in Publication Data
Names: Coetzer, Rudi, author.
Title: The notebook of a new clinical neuropsychologist: learning through
    experience / Rudi Coetzer.
Description: Abingdon, Oxon; New York, NY: Routledge, 2018. | Includes
    bibliographical references.
Identifiers: LCCN 2017033581 (print) | LCCN 2017036288 (ebook) | ISBN
    9781315122748 (Master e-book) | ISBN 9781138565012 (hardback) | ISBN
    9781138565043 (pbk.) | ISBN 9781315122748 (ebk)
Subjects: | MESH: Neuropsychology—methods | Brain Diseases—therapy |
    Clinical Competence | Personal Narratives
Classification: LCC QP360 (ebook) | LCC QP360 (print) | NLM WL 21 | DDC
    612.8—dc23
LC record available at https://lccn.loc.gov/2017033581

ISBN: 978-1-138-56501-2 (hbk)
ISBN: 978-1-138-56504-3 (pbk)
ISBN: 978-1-315-12274-8 (ebk)

Typeset in Univers LT Std and Sabon LT Std
by Swales & Willis Ltd, Exeter, Devon, UK

For my patients

Contents

About the author

Dr Rudi Coetzer is a Consultant Neuropsychologist and Head of Service with the North Wales Brain Injury Service, Betsi Cadwaladr University Health Board NHS Wales, and an Honorary Senior Lecturer in Clinical Neuropsychology in the School of Psychology, Bangor University. He qualified with distinction as a Clinical Psychologist from Stellenbosch University in 1987 and is on the Specialist Register of the Division of Neuropsychology, British Psychological Society. During 1995–1997 he studied Photography at Ruth Prowse College of Art and is a Licentiate of the Royal Photographic Society. A full-time NHS clinician, his clinical work is in the areas of assessment and rehabilitation of persons with acquired brain injury. His research and academic interests include psychotherapy approaches to brain injury rehabilitation, obsessive-compulsive disorder, neuropsychological assessment, anxiety and depression after brain injury, service development, psychological adjustment after acquired brain injury, cognitive rehabilitation and the delivery of rehabilitation services in under-resourced environments. *Working with Brain Injury*, by Rudi Coetzer and Ross Balchin (2014), won the British Psychological Society Practitioner Book of the Year award in 2016.

Foreword by Robert Jones

There is a problem with considering things to exist on a continuum and this book challenges those who like to classify the world into bi-polar opposites. Where on the continuum between therapeutic empathy and analytical detachment should clinical neuropsychologists position themselves? Where on the continuum between science and art should their work be classified? Where does your behaviour move from assessment into therapy? Where should we position ourselves between the poles of empiricism and intuition?

With typical humility Rudi explodes the myth of the continuum. We can be both scientists and artists, diagnosticians and therapists, clinicians and academics. But more than this, we can carry people in our memories and keep their stories safe as we remember how they touched our lives and found purchase in the small crevices of our souls.

Almost 40 years ago I was considering studying psychology and went to a talk by a psychologist who was approaching retirement. I remember him cautioning that the danger with this kind of work is that you 'leave little bits of your heart behind with everyone who is referred to you'. I think I have had the opposite experience and that the people I have seen have left little bits of themselves in my heart and that this accumulation seems more like a gift than a burden. This book strongly hints that Rudi has had the same experience. If there is a single word that sums up this book it is 'respect'. Respect for the patients he has seen, for the supervisors who have guided him and the colleagues who have watched his back. Like Joyce, this is a portrait of the artist as a young man, and contains important insights into the context of time and place. The growing pains of a new phase in the history of South Africa acts as a backdrop to the achingly sad stories of the people referred to Rudi. We see the emerging artist struggling 'to try and find a workable balance between remaining realistic, objective and professional, without losing too much humanity'.

Through the lens of Rudi's respectful gaze we, as readers, gain insight into the details of neurological functioning, psychometric testing and the relevance of anatomy. But we also see him cry at the sadness of the beautiful young woman whose fits have returned despite extensive neurosurgery and we see his helplessness in the face of the progressive onslaught of incurable disease. And always there is the uncomfortable knowledge that we are all subject to the fickle hands of fate. As Rudi writes: 'That could be me, or you, with a dementia or severe head injury, if fate randomised events slightly differently'.

The stories contained in this book are both interesting and emotional but, for me, it is Rudi's reflections on these stories that make this book of great importance. An early mentor once said to him that he should 'never stop imagining what life is like on the other side of the desk' and the real value of this book is that Rudi managed to heed this advice. There is much to learn in this book whatever the background of the reader.

Professor Robert Jones
Consultant Clinical Psychologist and Programme Director,
North Wales Clinical Psychology Programme,
Bangor University Wales

Preface

What's past is prologue.

(William Shakespeare, *The Tempest*)

'What is that?' she asks, looking straight at me.

'What is what?' I reply, staring at the beautiful Old Arts Building outside her window.

I look back at her. How annoying. She does not look away. Instead of breaking eye contact, a schoolteacher frown starts to form on her forehead. One eyebrow slightly up. I know the look well. Very well. It demands an answer. On the desk lies the receptacle of her curiosity. A small brown pocket notebook, worn and falling apart, with '*Republiek van Suid Afrika Republic of South Africa 81/140976 (B 39)*' printed in unfeeling bureaucratic font on the front. I did not want to leave it in my new office on the third floor.

'Come on, it's just an old notebook. You are obviously not keen on working today', I try to distract her from her curiosity.

Silence. Just her blue eyes staring at me. Try again.

'May I remind you, procrastination is just the avoidance of inevitable, and prolonged pain. We need to crack on and figure out this paper, Flo. I need to be back in my office by two'. Even though

I am on a teaching contract, I feel I need to show at least some commitment to research.

'You full well know I need to prove, that . . . that . . . uh . . . I'm sort of OK and don't want to be seen as just stealing bread off the academic table!' I blurt out in desperation, trying to fend off her question.

'Hmmm', she capitulates, giving me a perplexed, but slightly bemused look over her specs. I know that look all too well also. She'll be back!

My colleague Flo, or 'Dr Flo' as her patients refer to her, is curious about a little brown notebook I have brought with me, and put down on the desk where we are working on our paper. Flo and I come a long way. An established academic at the time, she decided to start from scratch again, and secured a place to do clinical psychology training. As a result, Flo was one of my very first clinical trainees shortly after I arrived in the UK. Later, after an earlier confession that what she really wanted to do was work in community-based clinical neuropsychology, she became a colleague in the hospital. Flo is retired now, but still does a bit of work at the university. Today we are meeting to work on a paper that is proving to be difficult to get back from the reviewers without yet more queries. Flo mutters something about 'nitpicking'. We agree, yes, writing this paper is like pulling teeth.

'Wisdom teeth', she rolls her eyes.

Recently I had been seconded to the university for a day a week, while remaining employed in my clinical job with the National Health Service for the remaining four days of the week. 'Do you think we should redo some of the stats to control for age in the control groups, and stratify by age groups, as the first reviewer suggested?' she asks looking less than enthusiastic.

'Are you trying to be funny, Flo? You know I am a clinician. Maybe we should ask someone who actually knows something about this stuff to have a look at it for us?'

Flo's gaze drifts back to the desk.

'Anyway, what *is* that little book?' she tries again, sounding just that tiny little bit too casual.

I should have packed it away, but have nothing with me to put it in.

'Flo, you are like a blood sucker!'

She is not giving up though. One of her strengths as a clinician! I am not going to escape, that's for sure. Time to give up.

'OK. It's, it's, I am not sure, Flo. Let's say maybe it's a love story'.

'Come on!'

'Flo, it is a little notebook, right? About damaged brains, if you have to know. The notes I made during my first chaotic year of working as a new clinical neuropsychologist. About 25 years ago. It is like a time capsule from the 1990s, which I recently rediscovered while moving house. There it was, still lying in a box, after moving country almost two decades ago. The essence of each case briefly summarised, a sticker neatly attached to the top of each page, ready to be referred back to at ward rounds. And some interesting data I have now decided to look at', I try to explain the impossible.

'And?'

'Flo, I had to learn to remember lots of stuff about my patients, about neuropathology, neuropsychological testing, neuro-anatomy and how to do case presentations', I try something more concrete, attempting to quell her curiosity.

I omit to tell her that these were the least challenging aspects. It was much, much more about the complexities of neuro-ethics, philosophy, existentialism, the role of society in disability, limits and counter-transference encountered on the path of becoming a clinical neuropsychologist.

Without any doubt I have been unsuccessful. Her curiosity is now really stimulated.

'Can I see it?' she pleads.

'OK, just a quick look, we've got work to do, Flo', I capitulate.

She gives it a cursory glance. Then looks up at me, mouth half open.

'Oh my god, your handwriting is still exactly the same!' she giggles.

I take the notebook back, and tell her one of the stories inside. Funny how this grabs her attention so much more than our research paper . . .

At the end of the short vignette, Flo ponders something for a few seconds. Then she gives her verdict.

'You must write a book about this, even if it's only a little one', she says in a serious, you-must-do-it-or-else tone of voice.

It is late Friday afternoon, with the cognitive colloquium for university faculty in full swing. I'm a bit lost, but trying my best to not look as if I am. The PowerPoint with all its tautological pixels refuses to link with any patients I've seen before. Is it Morse code from within someone's soul? Life at the university is proving to be hard, and very different from that in the hospital. For one day each week I feel like an imposter. I am convinced everybody can see I know nothing about cognitive neuroscience, and am relieved when any of my new colleagues asks me to contribute to their work, *anything*, for example, a lecture. I cannot yet speak the language of academia. In fact this is proving to be very similar to the way I felt many years ago. Back then, a few years after completing my clinical training and internship, I started a journey in hospital-based clinical neuropsychology. Then I did not speak the scientist-practitioner language of neurological disease, injury, signs, symptoms, scans and diagnoses. It is a long time ago. But now hospitals feel like home. Maybe with time academia will become another home also.

A couple of weeks after my meeting with Flo, I am in clinical supervision. I am presenting my cases. Some clinical dilemmas are universal and timeless. A vignette from the time of the little brown notebook helps me to illustrate a point I am trying to make about caring for my current patients. Ron, my clinical supervisor, is an excellent photographer. The walls in his office are colourful mosaics of his photographs. I always imagine he can 'see' what I am talking about when I present my cases during supervision. Ron is a very experienced clinician, as well as an accomplished academic. A black belt martial artist, he knows how to focus his attention. He has a lovely, expressive face, little muscles full of fun and sensitivity in equal measures. All tranquil now, leaving no doubt he is drawn in by listening to the vignette from the notebook. The story ends, and the room is suddenly quiet. Ron is smiling.

'You must write something about that time, young man! As an academic, you are free to write what you want to and also *how* you want to'.

For centuries storytelling has been a wonderful method for passing on knowledge. It may well be the earliest form of case-based teaching and problem-based learning. Stories have the capacity to captivate the listener, to draw them into another world, make them temporarily part of it. As regards the clinical sciences some of the best stories ever told are written up in the early classic case reports. These capture some of the timeless truths of brain injury, of being a clinician and what it means to be human in Charcot's 'sea of misery'. For stories to live, they need to be *told*. Here in this book a story is told 'from the other side of the desk' in the hospital consultation room, as seen through the eyes of the clinician. It is a story of how it *feels* to be a new clinical neuropsychologist. What you see, hear, learn and experience through your patients while working at the sharp end of the profession. Ever wondered what it is like to learn to be a clinical neuropsychologist? Read on. This book is not an academic textbook in the classic sense of the definition. There are much better books for learning the in-depth academic knowledge required to train as a clinical neuropsychologist. No, this book is about something altogether different. It depicts the journey of becoming, and continuing to be, a clinical neuropsychologist. The narratives of patients, and how it is subjectively experienced by the clinician, form the tapestry of broader, more universal stories. Stories about how brain injury change who our patients are, who they were, who they might have become but now will not. It also attempts to illuminate how their stories affect us in the ways we think and feel about what it means to be human. Every patient is different. Becoming a clinical neuropsychologist requires a commitment to not only meet the intellectual challenges involved, but also develop compassion, emotional resilience and toughness.

Every case vignette in this book is about a specific, numbered case from the little brown notebook Flo was so interested in. Some demographic details have been very slightly altered, and pseudonyms used throughout to make individual patients completely unrecognisable. Similarly, pseudonyms are also used for all colleagues, and the main characters are amalgams of some of the people intimately involved in my learning. Using narrative dialogue, metaphors and symbolism in the writing hopefully helps to bring experiential learning to the pages of the book, by giving a better voice to patients, colleagues and what is now history. After so many years, memory dictates that the narratives are of course not exactly as they were spoken at the time. Nevertheless, these narratives still hopefully very accurately reflect the nature and emotion of what was exchanged. Every event described in the book actually occurred, including, for example, the roof incident, imposter cleaner and protesting crowd. The clinical details of every numbered case in the book are presented here in this book exactly as they were captured in the notebook, factually correct and unedited. Included are the specific lesion locations, referral sources, clinical histories, clinical presentations, diagnoses, neuro-imaging findings and the psychometrics results. These are embedded in the text, rather than tables, to better illustrate the 'in-the-moment' hypothetico-deductive approach to assessment in clinical neuropsychology. Hopefully above all else though, through case-based storytelling, the humanity, tragedy and many riddles of an altered brain is partially captured for brief moments, and how it is, and feels, for some of us learning our clinical craft. I hope reading it helps to inspire those who themselves may be considering clinical training in a profession within the field of the broader clinical neurosciences, not only clinical neuropsychology. Clinical training in whatever specialty, by its nature is difficult to get into, and never quick. However, it is rare to find anything better to do with our time, than the privilege of helping our fellow human beings. Chapter 1 sets the context for the rest of the book. Keep going. The remaining chapters tell the story of learning to care for those who we could have been, if fate was randomised slightly differently.

Rudi Coetzer, June 2017
North Wales, UK

Acknowledgements

The story of writing a book usually has many characters. In this case for example, there is 'Ron', who is happy to be 'unmasked' as Professor Robert Jones. Robert has been my critical friend and clinical supervisor for many years, through good and bad times. Writing is a lonely job, and at times requires a bit of 'mothering' to succeed. Dear 'Flo', in real life Dr Frances Vaughan, has never failed in that area. Then there are people like Lucy Kennedy at Psychology Press, who believed in me as a writer, and her colleague Elliott Morsia, who took care of production. One cannot ever wish for a better team than Lucy and Elliott. Writing also requires a home filled with warmth and shared with the right occupants. The North Wales Brain Injury Service has now been my home for many years. All the people who work there with me, and those who come there for our help, have all had a profound effect on me. Life would be very difficult without them. I also cannot possibly express my gratitude to every single one of my new academic colleagues in the School of Psychology, Bangor University, for giving me another home, and their exceptional kindness welcoming a clinician in their midst. Finally, writing is set in historical context. The colleagues, patients and other persons featuring in this book are carried forever in my heart. Without them, and too many other people to mention, writing *The Notebook* would never have happened.

1

Birth

First days in neuropsychology

> Intellectual growth should commence at birth and cease only at death.
>
> (Albert Einstein)

Opportunity

Sometimes the best stories are the ones that are true. Or maybe they are just more memorable. It is the early 1990s. After 27 years of incarceration Nelson Mandela has recently been released from prison. As if in a dream, his long awaited steps towards freedom are beamed across the world, for all to see. The iconic black and white photo of him in his distant youth is instantaneously updated in millions of minds, brought to life, in full colour. What was static, is converted to motion. Wow, that's what he actually looks like! South Africa has temporarily stepped back from a nightmare, a deep cliff descending into unknown darkness and uncertainty. It is as if a collective breath is being held. Even though too often there is yet another return to the darkness of the past. Ready to explode again, hovering precariously close to the edge of the cliff. But, generally there is now optimism for a birth of something new. *Nkosi Sikelel' iAfrica*! [God bless Africa]. Nevertheless, violence remains at epidemic levels. There has not yet been a free and fair democratic election for all citizens of the country. In among all this chaos, optimism and fear, ordinary people go about their normal daily lives and jobs. Hope is the medicine that keeps everyone going. Waiting for opportunity to arrive, something new and embrace what's on offer.

It is a beautiful morning, with a sky so blue it seems to have swallowed the universe and all its troubles, grasping every ray of light the sun has on offer today. I am at work. It is my first day here. A chance meeting while putting out the bins a few months earlier, brought me to this ward round today. I am back at the university teaching hospital where I completed my internship at the end of my clinical training in the late 1980s.

'Hey Tomas, is that you, or am I dreaming?'

'It is indeed me, Rudi! And how are you, my man?'

Tomas is a psychiatrist who was a registrar I worked with while an intern. He has recently returned from doing locums in Canada. Tomas and I got on very well, and I am pleased to see him back. In particular I valued his loyalty, compassion and truthfulness while we were working together.

'Why have you come back?'

Tomas tells me why he is back in the country. He jokes and says contrary to popular rumour the weather was not so bad in Canada. And that people's troubles are the same everywhere in the world. It also transpires that his master plan is to develop a neuropsychology and neuropsychiatry clinic for the hospital where we met. Although it is a bit rough around the edges, it is one of the two big university teaching hospitals in the city. While he is talking, I read between the lines that he is out on an informal recruitment drive. Anyway, that was his story on that Sunday evening the bins had to go out. If ever there was an unglamorous meeting trying to attract someone into the profession of clinical neuropsychology, this must surely be it.

The din of chairs creaking and people talking at the ward round is somewhere in the background. My mind is still with the bin evening. Tomas tells me more about his time in Canada and working with clinical neuropsychologists, neurologists and neuropsychiatrists. It sounds fascinating. Psychiatrist that he is, he must have sensed my interest.

'What would you think about the possibility to specialise in clinical neuropsychology, and join the team in the new clinic I am planning to develop?' he asks with his typical poker face.

I look at him blankly.

'What?'

'We really need a specialist clinic to look after patients with brain injuries and other neurological problems. Nobody takes care of them. There are no magic drugs to cure brain injury. I am sure the department of psychiatry will be supportive of us if we said we wanted to develop a new clinic', Tomas continues, suddenly sounding very enthusiastic.

It sounds like one of those opportunities where your gut instinct is that this does not need thinking through, or consideration of minutiae such as remuneration. Forget logic, accept now, or regret forever.

'I'd be very interested, definitely count me in', I say without thinking.

Is this the *coup de foudre*?

Confusion

The sounds of the ward round wrestle themselves back to consciousness and put an end to my mulling over of how I got to this place.

It really is like being in another world here. Things are a bit confusing, to say the least. Everyone appears to be talking in a foreign language, as if it is their mother tongue. Fluently. Full of emotion. And fast. Anxiety provoking. People come into the ward round. Some on their own steam, others in a wheelchair, one or two with a drip in the arm. Many say nothing, some a lot, a few others look frightened and cry. Sometimes they say things so funny, it would be inappropriate *not* to laugh, if it were not so incongruous with their immediate surroundings. A kaleidoscope of the human condition. But I have already figured out that they all have one thing in common. They either have, or are suspected to have suffered an injury or illness of the brain. It's a new world they enter, similar to my own journey. Can they detect my anxiety, spot the imposter in the audience? It is impossible to imagine what this new world might feel like for them. Do they even remember the old? Some persons have absolutely no physical signs of a brain injury, and walk, talk and interact just like you or me. Others the average man in the street would be able to instantly detect something is obviously wrong. Nothing makes sense to me. The first week is a blur of images, voices and smells. But above all of emotions. While I suspected the demands on the head would be significant, it dawns on me that I have been totally unprepared for what this world does to the heart. Learning the methodology of clinical reasoning will be one thing, living to live with the absence of a recipe to bring order to inner emotions quite another.

Week two brings more confusion. Everything happens too fast. How on earth can these people be helped? *Patiens*, Latin for patient, is a person who is suffering, a human being who is not well. Increasingly it is this 'who is well, and who is not', and for those who are 'not', having an idea of what 'it' is that is wrong. It is this that is most confusing to me. Disorientating, like fog when a walker is temporarily lost in the mountains. A *tabula rasa* being suddenly deposited in a science library. Inscriptions are needed, and soon. The broad goal is to through clinical exposure and learning gradually emerge from the fog with the skills and knowledge required to speak the

4

language of my colleagues in this new world. But not only speak the language, also the corresponding ability to, like them, actually do something useful for the never-ending conveyor belt of patients we see every day. To reduce their suffering. That's what is needed. Intellectually it's not that difficult to figure out, emotionally not so easy. A feeling of helplessness, and at times panic, overwhelms me every time I find it hard to keep up with the sheer volume of human suffering and new information I am supposed to absorb on a daily basis. Which is all the time. I need to figure out something, very quickly, or I am going to badly flounder. It's an apprenticeship yes, but not like you would have thought. There is no protected time to learn. It really is the deep end. It's impossible not to feel. Thanks to exhaustion, the nights bring a short soundtrack of lifts stopping on floors, ward doors creaking, voices, call bells, the sound of cutlery, followed by instant deep sleep.

Early one evening I go for a run with Tomas. Breath is precious when running in the heat of an African sunset. I try to surreptitiously prod him for tips as to how he thinks I would best learn the stuff I need to know for this new role, a little bit faster than is the case at the moment. In other words, how to resemble a clinical neuropsychologist, just a tiny little bit more as I go along. He asks what I have done so far. Fortunately we have started going up a steep hill. There is a bit more time to think about an answer. At the top of the short incline I mention that I did have a fair amount of training in neuropsychology while doing my clinical training, and that as he full well knows, I have done a lot of cognitive testing while an intern. I tell him that I am trying to revise what I already know, and learn new stuff through seeing patients every day. He seems pleased with that, but then says there will be a lot more to learn. Something about the Canadian neuropsychologists he worked with being able to 'take apart the frontal lobe and then put it back together again'. Or something to that effect. Only he knows exactly what he means. He suggests a plan involving systematically reading key texts. Targeted reading, to develop specific areas. No point in over-reading, he says. He will help me to identify the best ones. The classics. We have started to run downhill now. The air suddenly feels a little bit cooler, more forgiving of fatigue.

Plans

Books, the right ones, should of course be at the centre of my developmental plan. Why did I not think of that on day one? It is the early 1990s, long before Dr Google could quell your anxiety by instantaneously answering all your questions. The books eventually include those by Oliver Sacks, Kevin Walsh, Alexander. R. Luria, and a couple of years later, what was then the new edition (1995) of Muriel Lezak's 'bible' of neuropsychology. We did cover the previous edition (1983) of said 'bible' in great detail during my clinical training. Thanks to cramming at the time, now in my new job the contents of the book are, when I need it most, unfortunately too vague to confidently apply in the moment while seeing patients. Studying during the evenings helps me learn and re-learn some of the essentials of clinical neuropsychology. My apprehension starts to slightly decline as I gradually connect neuro-anatomy, psychometrics, neuropathology and clinical assessment skills to the patients I see. The plan is working reasonably well. The sheer volume of information to be absorbed makes progress achingly slow, but some things start to make more sense. In particular once I have seen it in a patient's presentation. Things are looking up. There's even more free time in the evenings now. A bit of a social life returns. I go out for supper with a friend one night. She is an artist and writer. I secretly admire anyone working in the arts. My first choice at university, but second choice clinical training came my way instead. Seeing Suzie will be a nice break from studying neuroscience texts.

The restaurant sounds drone on in the background. Plates clanging, people chatting about nothing, everything, life. Smiling waiters are crossing the floor like scissors, probably cursing when out of sight.

'How are things in your new job?' Suzie asks.

'Love it. We saw someone today who presented with memory problems. You should have seen the scan! His medial temporal lobes were necrotic. And we know the medial temporal lobes are involved in human memory. In fact more than that, we've known since the 1930s that something called the limbic system is involved in memory', I mercilessly rattle off most of what I had recently read. I bet she'll be impressed.

'What does necrotic mean?'

Oh, diseased, basically wasted, like a scar, you know', I casually answer, as if she should know that.

'Was he OK?' Suzie asks, looking concerned and puzzled.

I don't quite know what she is asking and am a bit surprised.

'What do you mean Suzie, was he OK?'

'What happened to him, does he have kids, what will become of him?' she asks.

Her concern is now obvious. She looks at me in a distracted way, and slowly lights a cigarette.

'You have a lot of knowledge, but you *know* nothing', she spits out, and exhales a white plume of dismissal.

'Absolutely nothing. Zero. Zilch. *Niks. Lutho.* Can you ask for the bill please, I have to go', she says in a cold voice.

Life at work goes on after the 'ice bucket supper date disaster' with Suzie. I muddle my way through ward rounds, referral allocations and seeing patients. My artist friend's observation does, however, linger with me, like a constant sound of nagging in the background. Tiny fragments of doubt crackle their question, occasionally piercing the background din. Like static. *You know nothing.* Correct, perhaps I was naive, and this impulsive venture will soon be too much for me. I don't make a real, valuable contribution to the work of the clinical team. Suzie is right. What hope have I to make better the incurable, I cannot even reliably figure out what is wrong with them. A regular 'supervision' walk one evening on the promenade by the sea with one of my close friends, Sam Murray whom I know from clinical training, does not resolve anything. Sam, like me also works at a state hospital in a deprived area. When I ask him what he thinks he contributes to *his* patients' lives, in the darkness his answer is clearly audible over the sounds of the crashing waves.

'What do I do for my patients? I take bread off their tables. They pay ten Rand for a taxi, and then I cannot fix any of their terrible problems', he says looking out over the dark sea.

'Don't give up too soon. Otherwise all hope dies too. Maybe that is all we can offer, Sam?' is the best I can come up with.

We continue walking in silence. Despite my words of not giving up too soon, Sam is a braver man than I, to speak the unspeakable truth in this socially broken and disabled country.

Then, one day not too long after the walk by the sea, there is a breakthrough of sorts. Perhaps not everything is futile. Having completed my clinical psychology training and subsequent internship only five years earlier, my psychopathology knowledge after a few more years of practice is still OK. I can with reasonable confidence assess and recognise when someone is clinically depressed, or suffers from say an anxiety disorder, as opposed to transiently being emotionally not as well as can be. This morning proves there to be at least one genuinely useful contribution I can make at the ward round. A patient referred from the psychiatric inpatient ward located at the block next to us requires neuropsychological testing. Bedside cognitive testing on the ward suggested she was 'slow in her thinking abilities', and there is a suspicion that she might have a learning difficulty. There is some uncertainty about this diagnosis, though, which is whys she has been referred for testing. Mrs Jackobson (case # 16 in my notebook) arrives at our unit with one of the ward sisters to accompany her, and her husband. I introduce myself to Mrs Jackobson and her husband who has come to visit her. I explain that I would be performing a neuropsychological assessment, and what that entails. She looks at me with an expressionless face, like wax, the disinterest in what I had just said etched in sharp lines around her mouth. Mr Jackobson looks anxious and grateful. Mrs Jackobson silently nods her agreement to be assessed.

8

We do the history, and clinical assessment. Her voice is quiet, as if holding something terrible down. Mrs Jackobson had a head injury, was unconscious for a whole day and can remember nothing of the following week. She has since then been unable to return to her job in a shop. Clinical assessment of her psychological status reveals that she is apathetic, suffers from early morning awakening, hypersomnia during the day and has no energy. She overeats, has gained weight, lost her libido and feels irritable and sad. I give her a break, and have a word with her husband. He tells me her problems started after the head injury. Sobs while he tells me how life, which was already not particularly comfortable for them, imploded since her injury. I call Mrs Jackobson back and proceed to test her. The ward staff were right. Her total IQ on the Wechsler Adult Scale of Intelligence is 52, and the rest of the neuropsychological tests all at or below the second percentile. But I follow my gut feeling (or perhaps I am still haunted by the parting remarks of Suzie . . .). Yes, Mrs Jackobson has severe cognitive impairment, and yes, she is very slow. The head injury caused some of that, I suspect. But the scores are too low to on their own explain her presentation. And additionally I think she also meets most of the diagnostic criteria for a major depressive episode. It feels good to be reasonably sure of someone's presentation for a change. Though not nearly as good as the feeling of being helpful to someone, when she later pours her heart out to a stranger willing to listen to her story. Mrs Jackobson is trying to understand and process how she finds herself in this place rather than at home with her kids. Maybe I can help her and her husband develop some understanding of why she feels so terrible, and why, plus how, her brain does not work as well as it used to.

Help

It's been several weeks since I saw Mrs Jackobson, but the huge, imposing face-brick hospital I enter each morning remains as psychologically impenetrable as before. I am walking towards our unit, negotiating the oncoming and passing human traffic. Navigating the corridors and the wards they eventually spit you out into, is easy to learn. Settling comfortably into this vast space of human pain and suffering, is quite something else. Being a visitor you get absolutely no sense of the emotional demands involved in being *part* of the machine that is a hospital. The long corridors with their exposed wiring and tubing in the ceiling grab you by the scuff, unceremoniously dumping you in a ward. Only the faint echoes of your footsteps are left behind. A referral note in your hand, which usually reveals almost nothing of what really awaits you. There you stand, thinking, what on earth am I supposed to *do*. Looking around for clues, there is only vinyl, green or yellow vinyl on the walls. In our own unit, on the floor of the lounge where we meet for case discussions and new referrals, there are acres of scratchy nylon carpet tiles, of an indeterminable colour. Possibly an as yet unidentified hue of illness green. All rounded off on the outside with brown face-brick. God, the bricks look baked rock hard, not only by the African sun, but by all the human misery and death they stoically contain within their multitude of inner spaces. And the referral in your hand still says nothing, but then suddenly whispers, 'sink, or swim'.

A neurologist, and my friend the 'bins episode' psychiatrist, have on their own accord taken me under their wings. And so the 'bin man' should, it was his master plan after all. The 'bin doc', Dr Tomas Burger, and the neurologist, Dr Johan Carstens will with time prove to be the very best teachers one could ever hope for. First they help me with the generics, the basic algorithm of survival as a hospital-based clinical neuropsychologist. Or put differently, not looking like a complete fool while the nurse is watching what you are doing by a patient's bedside. They will with time teach me the structure of how neurological patients are assessed, how things fit together. Ask this, look for that, ask them to do such and such, then interview a relative. They also help me with understanding the basics of neuro-imaging. And of course, the dreaded neuro-anatomy. A bit more about that later. Much later. One important thing I figure out early on for myself by watching others presenting their patients is that there is no time for fumbling with patient files, hopelessly lost in pages, or sometimes, volumes of information. No, everyone who presents has some form of memory aid, and invariably, a 'recipe'. Some, for example, write on their hands, others stick patient stickers to the sleeves of their white coats. I will have to learn how to remember my patients, the facts of their illnesses, injuries, lives and what it all means.

I decide that a notebook that can fit in a pocket of a white coat would be perfect. Yes, at the time it was considered a mortal sin in this formal environment of titles and attire not wearing a white coat, or in summer, a white short sleeve safari shirt. A standard government-issue little brown notebook becomes my aide-memoire for ward rounds. Furthermore, it also becomes a portable collection of summaries to gradually build up a better overall picture and understanding of neuro-pathology, its symptoms and signs, related neuro-imaging, and clinical neuropsychology findings. Each with a patient sticker at the top, to avoid confusion. The stickers are also a token of having done something, *something* to evidence another patient has been seen. If only it were as simple as just looking at them. The questions you ask, the tasks you ask patients to do, make your own brain hurt, what must it do to them? There is very little time though to ponder these thoughts. Ward rounds. Will they see that I am a fraud, my knowledge base uncomfortably thin? However, there is no possibility at all of avoiding presenting your patients, and what your conclusions were. Every day. Very quickly the anxiety of presenting patients to a peer audience is gone, thanks to flooding. The little notebook steadily provides a tangible measure of my slow progress. But most importantly, very early on I see that effective presentation and understanding a patient's history, neuropathology and symptoms, in essence entails 'storytelling'.

Storytelling

Dr Burger and Dr Carstens know their stuff. *Really* know their stuff. They never use the medical file of a patient when they present at rounds.

Dr Burger and Dr Carstens own, and carry in their heads, all their patients' stories. Gradually I begin to understand why they can remember large amounts of information, and seemingly effortlessly. It is so much easier to remember stories. The patients' stories feel as if they are 'carried in one's heart', rather than a part of a cognitive process of learning. Through the impact of hearing persons' stories, their fears, their madness, humour, perplexity, their loss and much more, the associated neuropathology becomes a lot easier to understand and remember. One becomes the keeper of their precious stories, enough to fill the whole wing of a hospital. Look after these, because patients die, but hopefully not fully if fragments of their life stories live on in someone else's mind, or brain. It all feels like a huge responsibility, acting like a vault for other people's lives, ensuring their stories don't die. Maybe that is one of the additional reasons why it is crucial to develop strategies for remembering patients' stories. It is also something that is much more important to the doctor–patient relationship than we always realise. With time I discover that remembering someone's story, why they came to hospital, what they told you, when summarised at follow-up *sans* a medical file is powerful. In the big ugly machinery of the hospital, another human being has been interested enough in my problems to remember me, me specifically, among hundreds of other patients.

To perform a responsible job one needs the right tools. This is no different for a scientist-practitioner. The tool for eliciting and structuring patients' stories through the process of the clinical interview is the glue that holds everything together. It is not a particularly difficult algorithm, or recipe, to learn. Provided we accept its imperfections, and that it requires practice. The bedside assessment in clinical neuropsychology shares several similarities with the same process used in behavioural neurology and neuropsychiatry. No wonder the universal language of applied clinical neuroscience is composed of a few 'dialects', by profession, but with the main version of the language remaining the common thread through all these disciplines. In this world of the hospital the rule of membership is simple: no language proficiency – no citizenship. Learning the skills underpinning clinical assessment has many benefits for testing hypotheses and developing diagnostic formulations, but one is often overlooked. It is that this is also the structure, although much more compressed and focused on the 'highlights' of a specific case, of the basic process of presenting during ward rounds, writing case reports or engaging in case-based academic teaching. Let's now take a slight detour to have a closer look at the broad approach of how to perform and structure assessments. Remember that the case vignettes in the remainder of this book will follow the same structure.

So where do we start when seeing a patient for the first time? The answer is very concrete: find the patient's file. Sometimes easier said than done, especially in huge, busy, chaotic hospitals. Don't automatically ask a nurse to find it for you, Dr Burger counsels me. They have their own work to do. Find the file yourself, learn the mechanics of your hospital's patient administration system. You might need this skill one day. Usually late on a Friday afternoon, during a crisis! Anyway, never let anyone, least of all the nursing staff get even a whiff that you think mundane tasks such as locating a file is beneath you. *Find* the file. Read the clinical notes. Identify what is relevant. It is not always straightforward. Handwriting is often illegible, old faxes faded into oblivion. Medical terms used incomprehensible. Sometimes more than one volume of notes to trawl for information. Which section of the file would contain the relevant stuff? The truth is it depends on the type of neuropathology. It could be any section, or even any combination of sections. But emergency room attendance is a good place to start, especially for acute onset pathologies such as head trauma and cerebrovascular accidents (strokes). For slowly evolving neuropathology read over the family medicine or internal medicine notes. Have a look at GP letters. Radiology is obviously a section never to be skipped. More generally, scattered throughout the file, the medical record can also be a good place to learn a little bit more about the social history of a patient.

Dr Burger is on a roll. It's obvious he believes in, owns, what he is sharing with me. He tells me the next step is to try and systematically, in a short space of time work through the rest of the medical file. Be prepared that these can be mountainous, especially where diagnostic uncertainty exists. Check the special investigations section for results on CT or MRI brain findings, as well as blood test results for infections that could potentially have involved the brain. Look at the surgery section, which might contain information about any brain surgery, but also surgery gone wrong where patients arrested on the table or became anoxic. Never skip the neurology section, as most clues will be found there. Read carefully over the psychiatry section. Many neurological illnesses and injuries can have as first presentation subtle (or frank) changes in behaviour or personality. Try to make a summary, and then compare it with what is described in the referral letter. Finally, take a spare sticker from the file, so you don't get mixed up with who is who halfway through the day, or heaven forbid, the end of the day. It is exactly these stickers that at the end of each day went into the little notebook containing the cases described throughout this book.

Besides managing caseloads, using hospital stickers also helps to correctly identify patients. This also allows you to introduce yourself in a respectful way, by knowing a new patient's name, age and gender in advance. With time, I learn the importance of telling patients who you are, what you are there for and explain what you intend to do. If it looks like they forgot, help them by telling them again, before they have to ask you. Indicate how they should address you, and ask how they would prefer you to address them. Ask for permission to continue. Then don't make protracted small talk and delay the inevitable. Doing so can increase their apprehension. Instead, get going and ask if they have anything bothering them that they would like to tell you about. If they know that they are in hospital, ask what brought them here. Crucially, ask about the onset of any of their difficulties. Ask if there has been a change from before. Observe all the time for anything striking in the way they look, emotion expressed, ability to tell their story and so forth. Next take a history, concentrating on the bits you don't yet know from having read the medical file.

A few important landmarks or epochs to cover include birth process, complications, developmental milestones, schooling, hospital admissions, medication prescribed, mental health problems, substance misuse, forensic history, major surgery and family history.

The next step is to perform bedside cognitive testing. Much of this is new to me, and here Dr Burger's patient teaching proves to be invaluable. The main areas to cover include noting the patient's handedness, level of arousal, speed and effort of information processing, orientation to time, place, person and situation. Next up are the main language functions, including reading, writing, comprehension, word generation, object naming and repetition. Language functions are followed by assessing new learning and retention, or 'short-term memory'. After that, we assess constructional ability, visual-spatial functions, and finally executive control function. As regards executive functions, watch out for problems related to lack of initiation, planning, perseveration, impaired set-shifting, poor problem solving, inability to learn from errors, impulsivity, concreteness and lack of strategy, among others. More broadly, consider input and output when testing. For example, someone with a hemiplegia has an impaired motor output, someone with hearing loss, an impaired auditory input. Accordingly adjust how you test (input) these patients. In conclusion, one of the main functions of the bedside cognitive testing when performed by a clinical neuropsychologist is that it helps to determine if formal neuropsychological testing will actually be necessary. Sometimes it becomes clear during this early screening that it would be unnecessary to put a patient through an exhausting and anxiety provoking testing. What is obvious on bedside testing does not need to be formally tested. The bedside cognitive testing can also help identify early hypotheses about cognition, to be examined more closely later, and updated as required.

The mental status examination, as a psychiatrist Dr Burger's *forte* of course, comes next. Most of what he tells me I already know from clinical training. While perhaps less didactic than the bedside cognitive testing, it similarly relies heavily upon good observation skills.

Note the patient's appearance, self-care, expression of affect, eye contact and their insight or understanding of their problems, he guides me. Most data are gathered from attentively listening to their narratives. Nevertheless, there are also important questions to ask. The more straightforward questions are about sleeping pattern, appetite, changes in weight, energy, libido and other somatic issues such as headaches, dizziness or double vision. To assess someone's mood for signs of depression or mania requires more in-depth, but subtle questioning and simultaneous observation. These tend to explore how someone has been feeling most of the time, do they feel sad, what does the future look like, feelings of guilt, inability to enjoy anything or even failure to experience *any* emotions. Look if the narrative of the patient is congruent with their (facial, body language) expression of affect. Always cover suicide risk and any thoughts or plans to harm someone else. Ask about anxiety, for example 'Is there anything that worries you, or frightens you?' and look for signs of generalised anxiety, as well as specific phobias. Try to gain an impression of the person's perceptual experiences (for example, hallucinations or illusions) and thought processes (for example, paranoia, tangential thinking). Finally, try to get some sense of the patient's insight or self-awareness, their ability to weigh up and reflect on these to form a judgement as regards their own illness or injury, or put differently, their mental capacity for decision-making.

With the passage of time, and Dr Burger's constant help, I learn a crucial skill. This skill gradually gets cemented down through intermittent failures to remember it. When performing any clinical assessment it is essential to distinguish between what is objective, and subjective. In other words, what patients tell us (their narrative) versus our own observations, or their measured performance on tasks. What patients tell us is a symptom, what we can measure or objectively observe, a sign. For example, a patient who reports a severely depressed mood, but who's self-care is immaculate and speaks about their depression while expressing objectively positive affect, is different from someone who is so depressed they can hardly speak, is tearful, unkempt and looks exhausted. Similarly, a subjective report of a 'terrible memory' needs to be evidenced with objective performance on testing of memory functions, and their effort. Specify in clinical notes, or ward round presentations what type of data are being referred to. For example, 'Mr Kriel subjectively reports very poor memory, but on objective testing while he could only recall one out five words after five minutes, with multiple choice this improved to five out of five'. Mr Kriel's symptom is of experiencing memory problems. However, objectively he has poor spontaneous recall, but preserved recognition memory. This is much more meaningful than simply documenting patients' narratives – sometimes slightly dismissively, perhaps somewhat unfairly, referred to by Dr Carstens as 'journalism'. But there is a point in there.

What happens to all the data, all the information gleaned from the patient? How is it *organised*? Generally, everything is put together in the following order, shorter or longer, depending on the audience, to construct the crucial 'story'. First demographics (who is the patient), complaints or symptoms (what is troubling them), course (since when), history (their background), clinical presentation (bedside cognitive testing and mental status evaluation), collateral information (what do relatives or significant others make of their presentation) and finally, special investigations such as brain scan findings and formal neuropsychological test results. All these data combine to make a differential diagnosis. Differential diagnosis means listing the most likely diagnoses, in order of probability. For the clinical neuropsychologist mostly this is not so difficult. Often the diagnosis is already available in the medical file or referral, for example, traumatic brain injury, or middle cerebral artery stroke. The more difficult part for the clinical neuropsychologist is the formulation. This is the process whereby the diagnosis is 'explained', meaning how, and for what unique reasons is the presentation like this, in this particular patient, at this time. It takes no leap of insight to see that formulation is the gateway to the main purpose of assessment in the first place – to help formulate a management or rehabilitation plan for the individual patient. After mastering the basic underpinning neurosciences, clinical assessment, neuropsychological testing and formulation start to comprise the basic 'scaffolding' enabling the clinical neuropsychologist to learn and grow as a clinician in an experiential fashion. Let's have a look how.

Growth

It's been several months. The winter storms have come and gone. Things are going quite well. This morning I am seeing Mr Pietersen (case # 91) for neuropsychological assessment. He is 20 years old, skinny, with shoulders drooping downwards, his eyes downcast. Mr Pietersen sustained a severe head injury. He was unconscious for three days. He was recently admitted following an overdose. While being treated for depression, a psychiatry registrar became aware of a history of a serious head injury two years before. Although I already know his formal diagnosis (of a traumatic brain injury) from the referral letter, I ask him what had happened.

Mr Pietersen looks up for the first time, and says, *'Die skollies het dit gedoen, dokter'* ['Some thugs did this to me doctor'], the bitterness in his voice unmistakable.

'I am sorry to hear that, Mr Pietersen'.

I ask more questions. What are his main problems since the injury? What bothers him most?

'Sal self nie kan se nie', he replies ['I have no idea, really'].

We cover his pre-injury history. His early development seems OK in as much as his milestones were normal. Mr Pietersen grew up in poverty. Mr Pietersen completed seven years of formal schooling. He has tried to find work but could never get anything more than temporary manual labour. I enquire about substance misuse, rife in these sprawling areas of socio-economic deprivation hemming in our hospital. He confirms smoking *'wit dagga pype'* – a mix of cannabis and a street drug called mandrax. It is smoked through a broken bottle top, with the silver paper from a packet of cigarettes rolled up to make a filter in the neck of the bottle.

After vacillating for a minute or two if I should in view of his poor schooling actually perform formal neuropsychological testing, I decide to do it anyway. Despite his poor schooling, his Wechsler Adult Intelligence Scale IQ score is 101, which is average. There is some subtest scatter, on block design with a standard score of 7.5, suggesting possible visual-spatial problems. Mr Pietersen's Wechsler Memory Scale performance is in the normal range. Trail Making Test trails A and B are both fine, percentile 75 and 74 respectively. The Rey Complex Figure Test performance is also normal. I begin to doubt the hypothesis of visual-spatial problems. The next test, the Hooper Visual Organisation Test, confirms that my doubt was justified. He scores near normal (23), but with subtle qualitative signs of possible executive difficulties. And then he completely flunks the Porteus Maze Test, a simple test of executive function. I got it right! The profile fits traumatic brain injury to a T, so to speak. Everything adds up: presenting problems, clinical picture, neuro-imaging, history and psychometrics confirming executive difficulties. I am very pleased I tested Mr Pietersen, and in doing so gave him the best possible neuropsychological input. What I will do next, is see him later and go over his results with him. That should help him understand where his problems come from, and make sense of things. Going over the results could also help with rehabilitation strategies to try and minimise some of the effects of his impairment on his daily life.

That afternoon I see Mr Pietersen to go over my findings with him. I explain the diagnosis and resulting cognitive impairments to him. He does not look particularly impressed.

'*Weet jy wat die skollies aan my gedoen het dokter, en hoe dit voel vir my nou?*' ['Do you have any idea what the thugs did to me doctor, and how I feel now?'] Mr Pietersen whispers to me.

He is right. I know his diagnosis and cognitive profile. But that still does not tell me much about how it feels to have suffered a brain injury or illness. To him personally. He has taught me a valuable lesson. Only one way to do my job a bit better. Ask. He answers.

'*Alles is verlore. My kindertjies het niks te ete nie. Niemand wil vir my werk gee nie. My lewe is verby. Ek wens ek kan vrek*' ['Everything has been lost. My little children have nothing to eat. My life is gone. I wish I could die'], he says in a quivering voice.

I am stunned, and look down at his file to break eye contact with him. When I look up from the file, Mr Pietersen is looking at me expectantly. He has just bared his soul and told me that his life has gone to hell. There are two tiny shiny paths findings their way down over his way too thin cheeks. I am sure he is hungry too. I can hardly swallow, never mind say anything to him. What's the point of neuropsychological testing when you cannot feed your kids? Increasingly I realise that I will have to see many, many patients before I can hope to have a deeper level of knowledge and skill. It's a brutally hard school of learning. Oh my god, this is going to be much more demanding emotionally than I ever thought, and require a lot of help! What does one say to such patients? I have no idea.

'I will come and check on you in the ward tomorrow, Mr Pietersen. Just to see how you are', is the best I can come up with.

There will be many more days like these, too many to count.

Counting

Very briefly, before concluding this chapter let's now look just a bit more closely at the data captured in the little notebook. These data provide a more general sense of the clinical work at our unit in the hospital at the time. It should also help to give a broader context to the individual case vignettes that make up the remainder of this book. Excluding a couple of re-tests, there are 125 cases summarised in the notebook, spanning a period of approximately one year. These were, however, not the total number of patients for neuropsychology during the period, only those presented or of relevance to my learning. Nevertheless the wide range of neuropathology is striking. Unlike say a 'head injury clinic' or a stroke service, our unit accepted referrals of most of the major pathologies. The 125 cases broadly fitted into the following general diagnostic categories. Definite traumatic brain injury, head injury (concussion or suspected mild traumatic brain injury), cerebro-vascular events (stroke, haemorrhage, infarcts, aneurysms and so forth), brain infections such as encephalitis, epilepsy, dementia, alcohol or substance abuse, hydrocephalus, brain tumours, anoxia or hypoxia, visual hallucinations, Huntington's chorea, and neuropsychiatric illness. These diagnostic groupings accounted for 106 of the 125 patients. The remaining 19 patients had diagnoses including sleep apnoea, Pick's disease, Sydenham's chorea, electric shock injury, Friedreich's ataxia, sarcoidosis, Wilson's disease, and progressive supranuclear palsy, among others. Of the 125 patients, 64 had a co-morbidity of some sort, for example diabetes, or substance abuse and 42 out 125 were female. The average age of the group (N = 125) was 39.72 (SD = 13.42, range = 14 – 71) years. Table 1.1 displays the number of patients by main diagnostic grouping.

Table 1.1 Diagnostic group and number of patients (N = 106)

Primary diagnosis	N	%
Traumatic brain injury	41	38.7
Head injury	6	5.7
Cerebrovascular event	16	15.1
Epilepsy	8	7.5
Brain infection	5	4.7
Dementia	5	4.7
Alcohol/substance abuse	5	4.7
Psychiatric illness	5	4.7
Hydrocephalus	3	2.8
Brain tumour	3	2.8
Anoxia/hypoxia	3	2.8
Visual hallucinations	4	3.8
Huntington's chorea	2	1.9

These broad diagnostic groupings obscure some of the interesting data contained within each category. For example, the patients with brain infections included (perhaps today less frequently encountered) diagnoses of neurocysticercosis, and neurosyphilis. Looking more closely at the group of patients with traumatic brain injury, the majority were males (32 out of 41). The average age of the traumatic brain injury group (N = 41) was 33.41 (SD = 11.82) years. Males and females were of a similar age, with males on average 33.25 years old (SD = 11.37) and females 34 (SD = 14.04). Of the 41 patients with traumatic brain injury, 35 had a full or short-form Wechsler Adult Intelligence Scale as part of their neuropsychological assessment, with an average score of 92.01 (SD = 18.59), considered to be in the average range. There was also substantial co-morbidity in this group, with 19 of 41 patients having other diagnoses as well, 10 out of 19 being substance abuse. Some of these trends probably continue to mirror what we see in populations with traumatic brain injury today also. The cerebro-vascular accident subgroup of patients had, perhaps as expected, even higher co-morbidity (10 out of 16 patients) and were a bit older on average (45.88 years, SD = 10.68) than those with traumatic brain injury. Co-morbidity also possibly obscured the prevalence of some diagnoses. For example, while there were only 5 patients with a primary diagnosis of alcohol and/or substance abuse, when those with a secondary diagnosis (of substance or/and alcohol abuse) were added, the number increased to 26. Most of the referrals came from either a psychiatrist (53 out of 125 referrals) or a neurologist (47 out of 125 referrals). As regards the primary reason for referral, 109 patients received formal neuropsychological testing. These data perhaps provide a brief glimpse of the more technical side of the work.

What are the other, more 'hidden' implications of numerical data such as the above? How does it *feel* for clinicians to work in such hospitals? The large numbers of patients seen day in day out, can obviously be physically draining. But the emotional demands are sometimes swept under the carpet, as part of the culture of being a clinician. The almost hopeless social situation of many of our patients, the tragedy of their individual stories, not often talked about by us. Sometimes we experience burnout, blunting, anxiety, feelings of hopelessness or even despair. One of many personal challenges is to try and find a workable balance between remaining realistic, objective and professional, without losing too much humanity. Maybe there is value in the point made during the 'seaside supervision stroll' with Sam, described earlier in this chapter. Don't give up, because with that hope might die. For now, just get to the next hour, the end of this day, and things will be fine. Ploughing through the numbers, I gradually started to believe our patients can subconsciously detect who are loyal, and not give up on them too soon. But perhaps this is just a self-preservative rationalisation to protect us from losing our minds in these settings of utter human despair. Whatever the case may be (who knows for sure anyway?) surviving this first drawn out storm of doubt, nemesis of numbers, and crisis of confidence hopefully gradually opens the door to becoming a clinician. In the remainder of this book, selected patients among the 125 in the notebook are at the heart of the broader story of a tough journey to learn more about caring for our patients.

2

Toughness

Traumatic brain injury

Toughness is in the soul and spirit, not in muscles.

(Alex Karras)

Seeing

How on earth is this possible? We've been asked to see Mr Sarel Van Vuuren (case # 5), an inpatient on the neurosurgery ward. I look again, in disbelief at the referral form we received this morning. I blink. The message written in an obviously hasty handwriting is utterly incongruous, almost humorous, were it not about such a serious matter. The curvy flow of the penned message contrasts with the humourless referral form designed by the dull mind of a bored bureaucrat somewhere in central government – Department of Health, of course. Forms kill all flexibility in an attempt to enforce rules and structure. So surely then this referral must be some kind of administrative mistake? I look around. Dr Burger is of no help, he is chatting with one of the nurses. He looks very interested in whatever she has to say. OK then, so be it. Very, very occasionally patient labels are erroneously mixed up, most commonly if two patients have exactly the same names and surnames. Then in a moment of rushing, the wrong sticker can be attached to the correct notes, or referral form in this case. But then when the clinician goes and sees the patient, the date of birth usually gives it all away and inevitably the mistake is corrected in good time. So what's up today?

I have another look at the form. The person referred to us, Mr Van Vuuren, must be too impaired to be able to undergo a neuropsychology and neuropsychiatry assessment? Why refer, if we assume it's not an incorrect label? I ponder this question for a minute or so. Ah, now I get it. The referral was probably written by one of the medical students, on behalf of the registrar. Someone in the same situation as my own, new to the job and lacking in knowledge. I guess the registrar, busy and harassed, signed a pile of these forms without looking at the details. Head injury – refer to the new neuropsychology and neuropsychiatry clinic – good, sign, next form. Before we go into the side room where Mr Van Vuuren is, I have a quick read over his medical notes, to check if it tallies up with the referral. The notes report, among other things, the helicopter landing at the hospital, transporting a patient in an 'unsatisfactory' condition. The patient shot himself through the head with a large calibre revolver. There is mention of an entry wound to the left temple, a large exit wound on the right temple, where 'brain tissue and blood are pouring out'. This is difficult for me to process and fully comprehend. Dr Burger returns, his face expressionless. I continue to reflect on the medical notes I have just read. How could this shocking wound not have been enough to kill him, any person, however tough and strong he or she may be? Or at the very least leave him so disabled that he would be fully dependent on others for all bodily functions. Maybe in this case, seeing is believing, after all.

Dr Burger and I open the door and enter Mr Van Vuuren's side room, located slightly off the noisy main ward. Here in his room it is quiet and everything seems very white and clinical. Also much cooler than on the main ward, where the sun is blazing through the large windows, making it uncomfortably warm inside the building. It is like entering a different world. Mr Van Vuuren's head is bandaged. Before we can introduce ourselves, he raises slowly but purposefully in his bed so that he sits upright, then looks towards us, and greets. Dr Burger looks puzzled, which for me is a worrying sign. If he has no clue, I am toast.

'Good morning, doctors', Mr Van Vuuren says in a completely normal tone and volume. As if we are talking about the weather.

His lips are dry, looking like bits of old cling film are sticking to the pale pink skin. Floating invisibly, somewhere, everywhere in the room, I can faintly smell his waterless breath.

'How are you today, Mr Van Vuuren?' Dr Burger opens with his usual line.

'I am fine, doc', Mr Van Vuuren immediately replies.

OK then, no gross language processing problems here, I observe.

'Any pain or discomfort, Mr Van Vuuren?' Dr Burger asks with a subtle tone of perplexity in his voice.

No, I am fine, doc', comes the answer.

'Any pain in the head, or headaches?' Dr Burger starts to probe a bit more into the obvious.

Mr Van Vuuren does not bat an eyelid before he replies, 'Nothing at all, doc'.

'How is your head feeling, does it ache?' Dr Burger tries again.

'My head's fine, doctor', Mr Van Vuuren replies, with a little bit more emphasis on the 'doctor'.

Was there an ever so slight sharpness, or irritation, in Mr Van Vuuren's voice when he answered Dr Burger's question?

A slightly uncomfortable silence briefly replaces the questioning. Dr Burger now looks more puzzled than when we entered the room and Mr Van Vuuren greeted us. What is he thinking? I am suddenly aware of a palpitation. Please, don't let Tomas ask me a question in front of Mr Van Vuuren, to find out what do *I* think. Nothing of the sort happens. Dr Burger in his usual calm and methodical manner continues his bedside assessment.

'How are you feeling inside, Mr Van Vuuren, are you worried about anything, or perhaps feeling sad?' He tries to open up another line of enquiry.

'I am fine, doc'.

'Are you sleeping OK?'

'Like a log, doc', he replies with a slight smile.

Dr Burger, one eyebrow slightly raised, asks, 'How is your appetite, Mr Van Vuuren?'

'The food's good here, and they give me loads doc', followed by a pensive pause, and then continues, 'I don't even have to ask them for a second helping. It arrives with the second helping included!' before he starts laughing.

I also almost laugh, the food in the hospital is terrible. Mostly brown, soggy, but always meaty, its exact identity indeterminable.

Dr Burger does not find anything funny, and seems deep in thought now.

From my own observation thus far, it appears that Mr Van Vuuren is not depressed or anxious. But something is not quite right. He is a powerfully built man in his forties. Big hands. His face is suntanned, and in sharp contrast with the incongruous pristine white bandage around his head. In the V of the neck of his pyjamas, a forest of untidy chest hair makes a little informal garden. He seems unconcerned for someone who has suffered such a devastating injury to his brain. The other thing I notice, is that he initiates very little spontaneous conversation. Mr Van Vuuren, unlike most patients thus far, does not ask us anything about his injury, when he can go home, or even if he might be able to go outside for a cigarette.

He is strangely incurious. Unless Dr Burger asks something, he does not say a word. But at the same time he seems not bothered by anything at all, almost as if he would be happy to wait patiently for minutes, no, *hours* for another question. Something else catches my eye. Mr Van Vuuren has dark blue eyes, but something about them I find quite disconcerting. He looks at us, yes for sure, but I also feel that he isn't really watching us, or fully engaged with what is happening. Almost like I imagine a recently deceased person's eyes would look if you were able to look them in the eye shortly after the moment of death. Maybe I am seeing too much into it. Perhaps he is by now bored by all the clinical staff coming to see him after his miraculous escape from death. Anyway, if it were me, I also would not particularly want to talk to strangers about having shot myself. Even if they were clinical staff. Some things are private.

Dr Burger's voice draws my thoughts back to the room. He is finished with his examination. It is time for us to go. We thank Mr Van Vuuren and leave his room, to go and make a file note. While we walk back to our unit, I ask Dr Burger how it is possible that Mr Van Vuuren appeared to be so mentally unscathed following a massive wound to his brain, and why he seemed so emotionally disconnected from us. Almost as if he were looking not at us, but 'through' us.

'It made me feel really uneasy the way he looked at us, although I cannot put my finger on what it was. Did you also feel that he was staring at us?' I ask Dr Burger.

He frowns, and looks at me for a few seconds, then speaks.

'Well, he looked at us, and he didn't. It initially threw me also, but let me explain. The first part of your question. In this job you will learn that humans are much tougher, but also infinitely more fragile than you ever thought. They can survive catastrophic levels of poly-trauma, but on the other hand be killed outright by a well-aimed sharpened bicycle spoke to the heart. Trust me, I am a doctor', he concludes, with a wry smile.

We continue walking in silence. Oh, I believe you doctor, that's why you said it in the second person. I do wonder if all that exposure to human trauma has left you with a spike in your heart also, my thoughts whirl around in my head. Trust me, I may not yet know much about the brain, but let us remind ourselves, I'm still the psychologist here.

As we continue walking, Dr Burger looks at me sideways, a second too long, as if he read my thoughts. He then returns to my question.

'The second part of your question, about Mr Van Vuuren appearing to have stared at us', Dr Burger continues.

He then explains to me that from looking at the scan, and also speaking to the nurse in charge, the bullet appears to have destroyed large parts of Mr Van Vuuren's lateral and medial frontal lobes. Furthermore, the bullet also severed the optic chiasm, leaving Mr Van Vuuren blind. The penny drops. I can suddenly *see* everything in a different light. Mr Van Vuuren is of course totally blind. He simply responded to sound. When we walked in he must have heard the door open, or when questions were being asked, he turned his head towards the sounds. He could not actually see us. His other main problem was that of apathy. That's why he initiated nothing spontaneously and appeared so incomprehensibly unconcerned about his very obvious catastrophic situation. Dr Burger tells me a bit more about the frontal lobes, and that they mediate many human behaviours as well as the cognitive functions underpinning them. One of these concerns problems with initiation, or volition, commonly affected after traumatic brain injury. My hands-on learning about what happens during serious head injuries, or put more formally, the neuropathology of traumatic brain injury, has today started in earnest. It is also unfortunately the beginning of a relentless exposure to the tragic effects of sudden, violent force to the brain. Including through guns.

Forces

What exactly is a traumatic brain injury, with its many invisible symptoms? I ask, and Dr Burger explains to me that traumatic brain injury, also referred to as 'head injury' sometimes, occurs when the brain is injured through a transfer of external force.

'This usually involves rapid acceleration or deceleration. Another way of understanding it, is to think of momentum. Momentum is simply mass multiplied by velocity. Momentum involves energy, and in the case of sudden deceleration, a transfer of energy, in this case to the brain', he makes the basics very understandable.

Dr Burger's explanation also makes me think. The term 'head injury' is a bit of a misnomer then. I ask Dr Burger if this is true.

'Yes, that's correct. An injury to the head does not automatically imply a traumatic brain injury has occurred. It is only when the actual brain tissue is injured through bruising, bleeding and shearing, that we would make the diagnosis. The most common examples of how a traumatic brain injury might be sustained include car accidents, falls, fights, firearms, industrial accidents and sports injuries among many others. As regards the actual injury to brain tissue, besides the bruising and bleeding through the immediate transfer of force, shortly after, other problems such as swelling and infection evolve. Most traumatic brain injuries have a distinct pattern of injury, involving the front of the temporal and frontal lobe, plus also some widespread general damage to the neurons', Dr Burger continues.

'And forgive me for asking, but if there is this pattern of damage, do all patients present like Mr Van Vuuren?' I ask.

Dr Burger greets a passing colleague, and then continues talking.

'Common impairments include behavioural or personality changes, cognitive problems and emotional difficulties. The most frequent cognitive problems are poor information processing, new learning and retention, or short-term memory as it is sometimes called, and impairment of executive control function. But no, although there is a similar pattern of pathology among patients with traumatic brain injury, each presents differently, sometimes very subtly. It's like this for many reasons, for example their pre-injury personality, general intellectual ability, pre-existing psychiatric illness, substance abuse, you name it'.

30

'How do we know one traumatic brain injury is more serious than the next?' I wonder out aloud.

'Well, first of all the severity of traumatic brain injury is generally classified as mild, moderate or severe. The rating of severity basically depends on three things: How long the patient was unconscious for, how deeply unconscious, and for what length of time after the injury they have no recall. The acute care staff use things like the Glasgow Coma Scale to determine depth of unconsciousness, and the inability to remember events immediately after the injury is called post-traumatic amnesia. As opposed to retrograde amnesia, the forgetting of events immediately preceding the injury. And remember, as a general useful rule of thumb for the clinician, post-traumatic amnesia is almost invariably longer than retrograde amnesia in traumatic brain injury', he explains.

Never mind amnesia, I catch myself thinking. To me Mr Van Vuuren looks pretty badly injured, at least from a physical point of view. He must have been precariously close to dying. How can memory loss be such a big determinant of severity of injury? The more physical damage, the more serious the injury? A bit like when your leg gets caught under a bus, as opposed to a bicycle? This does not make sense, I can almost hear our footsteps echo out the words as we walk towards the hospital canteen now.

'But surely if you have a hole in your head, your skull, it's worse?'

'Not always. There are different types of traumatic brain injury. The broadest distinction is between penetrating and closed. In a penetrating brain injury, the coverings, or dura, are breached, and the brain damaged by whatever enters it. But it is then also exposed to air, which brings its own problems. Anyway, as you can surely figure out, Mr Van Vuuren suffered a penetrating injury. But severity does not always equate to symptoms. I remember a man who sustained a very severe traumatic brain injury, made a complete physical recovery, but had subtle cognitive problems. He also presented with disinhibition, more specifically a complete inability to control his sudden inappropriate laughter in social situations. More disabling than a hemiplegia', he concludes appearing distant.

I decide to go back up to the ward where Mr Van Vuuren is after lunch, and re-read his medical file armed with my new-found knowledge about traumatic brain injury still fresh in my mind. In the canteen I am reminded by the unidentifiable brown matter in front of me on my plate, why I almost laughed when Mr Van Vuuren commented on the good food.

Laughter

It is going to be a busy day. Mr Van der Merwe (case # 53), aged 22, is attending for neuropsychological assessment. He is the first patient of the day. Mr Van der Merwe was referred to us by a clinical psychologist in private practice. The referral states that Mr Van der Merwe suffered a severe traumatic brain injury. He has been unable to get his life back on track, despite making a reasonable physical recovery. Before I decide if I should test him, I perform a basic clinical assessment. He is just a whisker under six feet tall, of athletic build, slender, blonde hair and green eyes. But my first, overwhelming impression, is how *alive*, full of boundless energy he is. Despite a slight left-sided weakness.

'Hello Mr Van der Merwe. My name is Rudi Coetzer, you can call me Rudi if you'd like to. I am the neuropsychologist here in the hospital. Please take a seat, Mr Van der Merwe'.

Hey, is it free then, Rudi?' he says with a wink.

I almost choke, quickly inhale, and ask, 'What? No, of course you don't have to pay me. This is a state hospital'.

Mr Van der Merwe laughs at my obvious surprise. He seems beside himself, like someone who has heard a really great joke.

'You said take a seat. If I could carry two or maybe even three, I'd take more!' he roars with laughter.

'OK, Mr Van der Merwe, I get it now. I am a bit slow today. Let's get on with it', I smile back at him.

'Sorry Rudi, I've got a girlfriend, my man! Your loss, my *bra* [brother]!'

More laughter.

Well, this is going to make a good change. Thus far none of my patients were this happy and full of fun.

Mr Van der Merwe jokes almost non-stop. I notice his speech is slightly dysarthric. And he is very familiar. Maybe I should not have asked him to call me by my first name? Nevertheless, he is able to give the full history of what happened to him, which is consistent with the referral and medical notes. A year ago he had a motorcycle accident. Came off his bike. No other vehicles were involved. Twisty road it was, he tells me. In fact I know the road, including the spot where he had the accident. I ask if he was rendered unconscious. He was. Two days, he tells me. What was his last memory? He describes seeing a road sign of a turnoff to another town. I know the sign. If he travelled somewhere between 100 and 120 kilometres per hour, that leaves a period of retrograde amnesia of between 10 and 15 minutes. He said he did wear a crash helmet. He tells me he has no memory of the flight to hospital in the helicopter.

'I missed all that excitement, mate! What a pity. I love flying. That's why I had two wheels rather than four. What do you drive, Rudi?' he leans forward, appearing genuinely interested.

'We need to crack on Mr Van der Merwe, I need to do some tests with you. To check out your memory and so forth', I say sounding possibly a bit too businesslike.

Mr Van der Merwe becomes a bit more frosty. Gives me a challenging look. Important to keep things nice and cool here, I think.

'OK, if you *have* to', Mr Van der Merwe agrees with a sour tone to his voice.

'See, Mr Van der Merwe, I told you it won't be nearly as bad as you thought', it is now my turn to be a bit more light-hearted.

Mr Van der Merwe has just completed the Wechsler Adult Intelligence Scale, and scored a total IQ score of 114, flying through the subtests. He also looks as if he is enjoying himself.

'Too easy for me! Try another one, sonny boy', he giggles.

We continue.

On the Word Naming Test he achieves a score of 22, which is not too bad, considering his slight language difficulty. But I am intrigued by his executive functions, and administer the Austin Maze. Mr Van der Merwe scores 17; 6; 6; 8; 9; 5; 5; 3; 4; 4; 3; 1; 5; 0; 1; 0; 0; and clearly struggles, becoming very irritable and frustrated.

'This is a rubbish test!'

Time to change tactic.

We complete the Trail Making Test, which goes a bit better, with trail A equalling a performance on the 38th percentile, and trail B 54.

His mood improves. Perhaps a good time now to do what many patients in my limited experience thus far find the most frustrating and anxiety provoking about the formal neuropsychological assessment: testing of their memory functions. This is going to be hard work.

I let out a silent inner sigh of relief. Besides a modest underperformance on visual memory, Mr Van der Merwe's Wechsler Memory Scale performance is actually normal throughout. Next, I administer the Rey Complex Figure Test. Mr Van der Merwe's copy score is equal to percentile 80. However, he displays very poor planning when considering his sequencing, as captured by handing him successive colour pens during copying. He finds it all hilarious, and draws a 'smiley face' instead of the circle and three dots in the upper right quadrant of the figure.

'Beautiful, I could have been Leonardo, don't you think!' he mocks the test.

I can't help but smile.

The next test reveals more problems. His Hooper Visual Organisation Test performance is impaired, scoring 21½ out of 30, but even more telling are his qualitative signs indicative of executive problems such as concreteness. His crippling problems with executive functions become even more obvious as testing goes on. The Porteus Maze is too much for Mr Van der Merwe, and he makes eight mistakes. Suddenly he becomes more irritable again. He is also unable to reflect on his own performance, or utilise error feedback from his own performance.

'These tests are for kiddies, why are you using them on me? When I was 10 I would have done it easy peasy. I am 22 now, for heaven's sake! I have forgotten how to play these little games. Anyway, can you do them?' he asks looking me up and down.

I keep quiet for a good minute before responding.

'Tell you what, Mr Van der Merwe, I'll score all your tests, and then next week you come back and I'll tell you about your results. I think we've done enough for today'.

Mr Van der Merwe's test profile provides a reasonably consistent theme of problems with executive function. His scores provide evidence of poor planning, impulsivity and an inability to learn from his mistakes. Reflecting on the actual testing session, I recall that his behavioural problems only became much more pronounced and observable during this more structured situation as time went on. In fact, do these observations potentially mean a lot more than the actual scores? I wonder, while looking at the profile. The scores don't really neatly translate into his everyday difficulties. I ponder whether maybe at times we are possibly too easily seduced by numbers? Maybe numbers make us think we know something, something tangible, or real? While what we are probably looking for is right there in front of our eyes through qualitative observation, mirroring more realistically than numbers the everyday problems in the world out there where our patients live their daily lives? In Mr Van der Merwe's case, why he is socially so crippled by his deficits, and will probably struggle to hold down a job, or form successful long-term interpersonal relationships. It's not only in the test scores. I look at his medical notes, in particular the imaging report. It says the CT of his brain shows a right parietal area of 4.5 × 1.75 cm tissue loss, extending down to the temporo parietal junction.

A week later I see Mr Van der Merwe, and give him feedback about his results.

'So my memory is fine, you are saying?'

'I think so, Mr Van der Merwe, in as much as that it should not give you big problems. But I did wonder if solving problems, or learning from mistakes you make may be a bit more difficult. Have you noticed anything?' I gently ask him.

'Pah, those kiddies tests! Who cares about them?' he says dismissively.

'Well, just for what it's worth, Mr Van der Merwe, to help your recovery, try to pause before you do stuff, or speak too quickly in company. Almost like counting to 10, you know? Come on, it can do no harm, and may help with your rehabilitation', I almost plead.

A long silence follows.

'Anyway, will I get better?' his answer suddenly comes, in the form of a question.

I pause a while, before responding. 'A bit more over the next year, I think. Time will tell, Mr Van der Merwe'.

He seems to chew over my prediction and advice.

'Thanks for your time, it was good meeting you. Hopefully I'll never see you again!' he thunders with laughter.

Who knows, I think. Science a bit, but ultimately only time knows. Time will one day tell us the final outcome.

Time

The season is starting to change into another. Mr Van Vuuren ends up spending two months as a patient in our hospital. He requires further surgery, including fixing the couple of holes in his skull. Our turf becomes his temporary home. He does not seem to mind. Never asks the universal question of, 'when can I go home?' I end up seeing him several times more over this period, and get to know him a little bit better. Or rather, a bit more about his cognitive functioning. Given his visual impairment, I can only do rough and ready adapted bedside tests, coupled with clinical observation, to develop some sense of understanding of his thinking and reasoning skills. It transpires that he is actually remarkably preserved in this area. His processing speed and efficiency is indeed fine, as is his short-term memory. He has no problems with performing calculations. But his executive abilities, unsurprisingly, are compromised. Mr Van Vuuren's planning is poor, and a rather interesting sign is that he cannot judge heights of landmarks he is familiar with, like the mountain looming over the city. Inability to judge the height of landmark buildings, other structures or mountains is a sign of frontal dysfunction, Dr Burger tells me when I ask him about it later. I also increasingly observe Mr Van Vuuren's emotional immaturity, or simply coming across as being emotionally superficial. He makes jokes fairly frequently, and clearly struggles to read social contexts. Later I find out that this has also been described as a sign of frontal problems, sometimes called *witzelsucht*.

During these two months I also meet Mr Van Vuuren's wife. She puts on a brave face when we talk, or may just be very stoical. I am seeing her for support and psychotherapy. At times I wonder if she can sense my inexperience. She does not mention anything though, and over time instead helps me form a more complete picture of her husband. Mr Van Vuuren can remember nothing of his injury, how or why he sustained it, and when I asked him about it, he cracked a joke. I have to ask Mrs Van Vuuren what happened. She is not quite sure, but thinks it was a combination of financial problems, and possibly also with hindsight, stress in the relationship. She says she feels responsible. I try to alleviate her feelings of guilt by saying that it would be entirely understandable if they experienced stress in the marriage, in view of the financial difficulties. But nobody is sure if that was indeed the root of the problem, and she does not want to dwell on it.

In our psychotherapy sessions, we explore the past, and how things are for her now. She is often very quiet. During one of these spells, I break the silence, by asking the inevitable question, 'Do you have any plans or thoughts about after he is discharged from hospital, Mrs Van Vuuren?'

Her expression makes me feel like I have punched her, and winded her.

After a brief silence, which to me feels like a week, she replies, 'We will find a way to look after him at home'.

Then Mrs Van Vuuren goes quiet again. Looks at me with sadness, and fear, before she tells me what really worries her.

'He is not the same person. It is my husband's body, it is him, Sarel, but it is not him inside. Someone else is in there. It is awful. He is a different man. The Sarel of old has left. Always quiet before, reserved, people thought he was shy, but I think he was just a bit of a worrier. Now as you can see for yourself he is crass, makes inappropriate sexual comments or jokes all the time. The other day in front of a young nurse! I was so ashamed, I wished the floor would swallow me', Mrs Van Vuuren blurts out, before continuing.

'Will it get better? Will he be the same man again, and how long will it take? I don't mind the blindness, it should not be a major problem, but will I get my husband back? Will he improve a lot more?' she asks, now with a frantic tone in her voice.

Mrs Van Vuuren tucks a stray curl of her shiny auburn hair behind her left ear. The pale blue dress with little white daisies she is wearing today does not belong in a hospital. Her dark, almost black eyes are infused with the colourless pain of losing the life-giving warmth of being loved by another human. They are waiting for an answer.

I know I don't know.

'Please tell me the truth'.

What I do know is that cognitive therapy won't be the answer.

'I don't know for sure, Mrs Van Vuuren'.

I have read a lot more about traumatic brain injury over the past two months, but I am not sure I can confidently answer all her questions, and this one least of all. I wonder if I ever will be.

The trajectory of recovery after traumatic brain injury varies, is complex, and is determined by many factors. As Dr Burger pointed out to me a couple of months ago, some of these factors include injury severity, pre-morbid abilities and problems including psychiatric, family support, post-injury social problems or support, access to rehabilitation, age, education and problems with substance misuse, among many others. Most of the spontaneous, and also the most dramatic, recovery occurs during the first 6–12 months. During the second year things slow down, and from year three onwards there is thought to be a plateau. But individuals vary in their psychological makeup, and motivation to do well and engage with rehabilitation ranges from none to stubbornness. For these reasons, and because we are scientists not politicians, we don't predict the future when we don't have at least some data to back up what we are saying. My intellectual reasoning is suddenly interrupted.

'But can you just give me some indication what will happen to him? Please?' Mrs Van Vuuren pleads.

'I honestly don't know what will happen to him long term. He should have further gains for about a year, say a year and a half, but to what degree I do not know. He is likely to remain blind. I understand that's not your main worry. Like you, Mrs Van Vuuren, I am worried that his personality may have changed forever, but we cannot be 100 per cent sure. I wish I knew more, so that I could tell you, but I really don't', I try to weave together an answer that is truthful, while remaining sensitive to her situation.

Mrs Van Vuuren looks at me, her dark eyes glistening. She has traces of a faint smile around her mouth.

'Thank you for telling me, thank you so much', she finally says.

I don't know what to say. I offer her a tissue. The only helpful thing I can do today is to help her dry her tears.

Tears

Four months ago I tested someone who's only child shares a birthday with me. Mrs Naidoo (case # 85) did not remember it though. I remember this bit of clinical information affecting my heart, and head. The sadness of her not remembering the birth of her child, and because it meant that her retrograde amnesia was more than four years in duration at that early stage post-injury. Mrs Naidoo suffered a very serious traumatic brain injury in a car crash three and a half months earlier. Other than that her history was unremarkable, and in particular no episodes of substance misuse or psychiatric illness. Left school just before the equivalent of A levels (matric). Mrs Naidoo sustained a skull base fracture in the accident and was rendered unconscious. She remained in a coma for two weeks. Mrs Naidoo was also a bit unusual from a neuropsychological perspective because she is left-handed. I remember this, because as I tested her I kept on passing test material to her 'wrong hand'. I also recall that she was very disorientated for time. On reflection now, she was obviously at that time still in post-traumatic amnesia. Baseline neuropsychological testing was performed, against which to chart her progress, and figure out how to help her with her future rehabilitation. However, what I remember most clearly is her tears. Every time she could not do a test, and there were many she struggled with, she would burst out sobbing. At first I was very taken aback, and almost discontinued testing her. I would later learn from Dr Burger, and the books he suggested I study, that this was most likely the well-described catastrophic reactions seen not infrequently in patients with severe head trauma.

Mrs Naidoo is back to see me for follow-up today. She looks so much better than when I met her, and I can barely hide my pleasure seeing her in clinic today. God, the human body is so tough.

I smile at her, and say, 'Hey Mrs Naidoo, it's great to see you again. You look a thousand times better than when we met last time!'

Mrs Naidoo looks surprised, then blushes. She looks away and does not respond. For a brief moment I wonder if I might have been a bit too forward, but then put two and two together. She has no memory of meeting me four months ago. I look down at her file, and notice her date of birth. It is her birthday next week.

'Happy birthday for next week, Mrs Naidoo, I know it's a bit early to wish you, but I hope you have a nice day'.

Mrs Naidoo smiles at me, looking delighted, and asks, 'How did you know that? It is on Wednesday'.

She has beautiful even white teeth, framed by purple-pink lips and a magnificent cappuccino complexion.

'I can see it on your file, Mrs Naidoo', I say, thinking that I can also see that her disorientation for time has passed since I last saw her.

I explain to Mrs Naidoo that today I will do some tests and compare these with her results when she was still in hospital. She thinks very deeply, and I realise she can obviously not remember doing the baseline neuropsychological assessment four months ago. Oh yes, the human body is so very tough, but at the same time the mind so exquisitely fragile.

I encourage Mrs Naidoo during the testing. My heart is getting the better of me. I really, really want her to do well. She is young, her child needs a 'fixed' mama. At times I catch myself holding my breath. It's feels like watching a ferocious rugby match, wishing there would be a breakthrough and that she would pass just one more item. I *need* her to do well. Her performance today will be key to the next stage of her rehabilitation. As Mrs Naidoo progresses with the testing, it gradually becomes clearer that she has indeed made gains in some areas of neuropsychological functioning over the past four months. For example, her attention and processing has improved, from scores of 6.0 on digit symbol and 7.5 on digit span (Wechsler Adult Intelligence Scale), to 7.0 and 10.0 respectively. Her Hooper Visual Organisation Test performance improves from 12 to 16, and whereas four months ago she made 14 errors on the Porteus Mazes, she now makes only 2. In other areas her performance is bit more variable, modestly up on some, the same on others, including the Wechsler Memory Scales. Her Rey Complex Figure copy performance increases from 23½ to 24½, but much more tellingly she can at least now after 30 minutes recall a few details (score of 8) of the figure, as opposed to none before. Mrs Naidoo is exhausted when we finish. I tell her she has done well today. I also observe that today there were less tears than four months ago, but I do not share this with her. Instead I tell her that in view of her progress that I will be referring her to a private specialist inpatient neuropsychological rehabilitation unit to the north-east of the country. For once the financial Sword of Damocles is not ominously hanging above us. There is likely to be significant motor vehicle insurance funds available for her ongoing care.

It is the end of the day. Finally time to go home. The face-brick monolith where some people come to die, others to live, now unceremoniously releases me through the glass doors that expressionlessly ignore me from the opposite direction in the mornings. Autumn is coming, it is the month of April. I wonder what winter will bring for all of us in this strange world behind me. Today was a full day. Maybe even a good day. At least as regards Mrs Naidoo. A silence creeps up on my thoughts, and I refocus on my immediate environment. The car park suddenly seems more empty than usual. My watch tries to tell me that given the time, it is unusual. I don't make any connection, and leave. Somehow the roads also seem quieter. Where are all the cars, this time of day is always busy? And am I imagining it, or are the pavements a bit too quiet also? Something is not right and intuitively I immediately pay more attention to my surroundings. Switch on the radio in the pickup, just in time for the news headlines. I've not seen a paper or any news since last night. The aerial outside the vehicle grabs modulated frequencies from the sky, and with a static splutter posturing as a human voice spits the news out. Chris Hani has been assassinated. Shot through the head from close range. Why? I feel ill. I close the window. There is a chill, winter must be coming early. Does anybody know how many times brains, lives, minds, peace, love, hope and trust have been permanently destroyed by guns, ending in the tears of tragedy? And always to be followed by even more. Life here is unbearably fragile at the moment.

3

Fragility

Cerebro-vascular pathologies

Life is fragile and absurd.

(Leo Tolstoy)

Bending

'Can you remember what happened on the day you came to hospital, Mr Stevens?' I ask, while trying to simultaneously have another quick look at the sparse information on the referral form.

Mr John Stevens (case # 82) is attending for a neuropsychological assessment. I am trying to determine what exactly happened to him that resulted in his recent hospitalisation. This should help me to decide which neuropsychological tests to administer. Also, and perhaps more importantly from a psychological perspective, I would like to find out how much he knows about his brain injury, or is aware of.

'I went to the beach on the Saturday. A couple of weeks ago it was, I think. Anyway, it was a hot, wind-still day. I was collecting mussels, rock oysters and *allekrik* [a type of local shellfish], there were loads that day. The rocks were covered in them. I remember bending down, straining like mad to dislodge a particularly big one stuck to a wet rock. Then nothing, everything went black. I don't know what happened on the beach. Next thing I wake up in the hospital', Mr Stevens tells me, sounding almost as if he is still somewhat surprised to find himself here in the hospital.

As if he should still be on the beach, under the sun, rather than the faintly humming strip lighting fixed to an alien white ceiling above us.

There is more information contained in Mr Stevens' medical file. Reading over the notes, the background history is as follows. A fortnight ago Mr Stevens collapsed at the beach. By sheer chance a bystander saw Mr Stevens fall over while on the rocks near the waves, and then fail to get up. She went to see what exactly happened. When Mr Stevens remained motionless on the rocks, she thought he must have fallen on his head, or had a heart attack. In a panic she then ran to the nearby beach shop, asked the owner if she could use the phone to call an ambulance. An ambulance arrived, and after a short delay given the terrain, Mr Stevens was taken to the nearest university teaching hospital (ours) and admitted for emergency treatment. Some of this was documented in the ambulance crew's notes, now kept at the back of the medical file. In particular they noted that he had in fact not hit his head. There were no visible wounds to his head. Instead, he seemed to have collapsed. Initially the paramedics thought he may have fainted, but realised that this was not the case when they could not rouse their patient. Mr Stevens is now an inpatient on the neurology ward. The referral indicates that from a purely physical point of view he is doing well, but one of the neurologists thought it would be sensible to obtain an assessment of his cognitive functions.

Mr Stevens is sitting in the chair on the other side of my desk, his arms folded. Mr Stevens is in his early forties. He is not wearing hospital pyjamas, but his own clothes. He is tall, with dark brown hair and pale blue eyes. The striking thing talking to Mr Stevens is that one would never suspect anything is wrong, never mind a neurological problem. Mr Stevens looks so *normal*. He makes good eye contact, and is fully engaged with the assessment process. In fact the clinical bedside examination of cognition and mental status reveals nothing of note. Similarly his previous medical and social history is fairly unremarkable. He has never had any medical problems, nor any mental health issues. He has had no head injuries requiring medical attention in the past. He tells me he has never used any illicit substances, he doesn't smoke or drink. No family history of medical problems either, or for that matter any other clues to his current presentation. After successfully completing his schooling, he went to college and completed his technical training in engineering without experiencing any academic problems. A keen fisherman, he was on the beach the day he collapsed. After we have finished the clinical assessment, I give him a rest break. Mr Stevens is to come back for the formal neuropsychological testing half an hour later.

Mr Stevens arrives back, on time, and tells me he went to the hospital canteen for a cup of coffee. We start the testing after I explained to him the nature of what I will be doing. He seems perfectly happy and unconcerned about undergoing an assessment of his cognitive functions. I make a mental note that this is slightly unusual. Many patients are, understandably, apprehensive about being tested. Often patients have some awareness that something about their cognition is 'not quite right', but would rather not have someone delve too deeply. Mr Stevens' neuropsychological testing proceeds uneventfully. He is right-handed and finds the tasks relatively easy. In fact, similar to the initial bedside testing, the formal test results also fail to show any striking quantitative signs of possible significant impairment of cognition.

His Wechsler Adult Intelligence Scale short form prorated IQ score is 109. This is likely the expected range for him given his background. The Wechsler Memory Scales yields percentiles of 64 for associative learning, 87 for logical memory, and 70 for visual recall. The Rey Complex Figure Test copy trial produces a percentile score of 90, with good organisation and planning evident. Delayed recall on the Rey is at the 40th percentile. The Benton Visual Retention test shows a normal performance also, with 8 correct and 3 errors, within the expected range for him.

Interpreting Mr Stevens' test profile provides evidence of preserved general intellectual ability, no obvious memory problems, and other cognitive functions such as construction and language also are unimpaired. What is going on? Looking more closely at executive control function, while he has a numerically almost normal performance on the Austin Maze, achieving two consecutive error-free trials on attempts 11 and 12, it is striking how after immediately reducing his errors on these trials, he thereafter really struggles to consistently eliminate the last couple or so of errors after trial 12. Mr Stevens perseverates with making the same errors, and quickly becomes frustrated by his performance on this test. While doing this test, he says he knows he should turn left here, but then actually almost immediately makes an error by turning right. Reflecting on the neuropsychological mechanics of such a presentation, I ask myself if it represents, metaphorically speaking, 'talking the talk, but not walking the walk'? In more technical language, we might formulate that his verbal self-direction of behaviour has to some extent become disconnected from his actions. It's an interesting test profile, and I feel I need to read up to find out more about his neurological diagnosis documented in the medical notes. It should help to better understand how his neuropathology adds up with his neuropsychological test findings. According to the medical file, Mr Stevens had a type of stroke, known as a Circle of Willis bleed, in his case more specifically of the anterior communicating artery.

Disruption

At the medical school library I find a lot more information on stroke, or as I soon learn, is sometimes also referred to as cerebrovascular accidents (shortened to 'CVA' in some notes I later encounter). First, that unlike traumatic brain injury, a stroke is a condition more likely to be seen in older patients, although not exclusively so. Basically, a stroke occurs when the blood supply of the cerebral vascular system is disrupted in a specific place, adversely affecting the neuronal tissue irrigated by that specific vascular area. Broadly speaking there are two mechanisms by which a stroke may happen. A blood vessel can rupture, bleeding into the surrounding tissue and neurons, irritating it and also causing starvation of oxygen and glucose through disrupted blood flow. This is called a haemorrhage. The other main mechanism of stroke is when a blood vessel becomes blocked or constricted, starving the immediate surrounding brain area of life-giving blood carrying oxygen and glucose. These events are known as infarcts. Often the blood vessel becomes blocked in a place where it is already constricted and dislodged debris from the walls of the vessel further upstream may then become stuck in this downstream area of narrowing. Most strokes are infarcts, or ischemic infarcts, meaning that the damage results from poor or stopped blood flow to the specific region in the brain affected by the reduction or cessation of irrigation.

As a specific example of how strokes can affect patients, I decide to look at the case of Mr Stevens again, and why his neuropsychology findings were most likely compatible with his neurological diagnosis. To understand Mr Stevens' case, I realise I first need some very basic knowledge of the blood supply to the brain. The Circle of Willis essentially consists of the anterior communicating artery and the posterior communicating artery, supplied inferiorly (from the direction of the neck) by the two internal carotids and the basilar artery, which itself is supplied by the two vertebral arteries. This explains why humans have four big vessels in their necks, supplying the brain with blood. From the Circle of Willis, on each side (left and right) three important blood vessels travel superiorly (upwards) to irrigate relatively specific regions of the brain. These vessels are the anterior, middle and posterior cerebral arteries respectively. Another, but entirely different type of bleed for the neuropsychologist to be aware of is subarachnoid haemorrhages. These occur when there is a bleed underneath the coverings of the brain, onto the underlying cortical surface, in any area of the brain. Later on I learn from Dr Carstens that new bleeds show up as white on a CT scan because of the iron in our blood, while old strokes show up as black because of water filling the space left by dead tissue.

Leaving aside subarachnoid haemorrhages, most strokes coming to the attention of a neuropsychologist probably occur as a result of middle cerebral artery pathology, as well as also those involving the anterior and posterior cerebral arteries. Add a patient's handedness, and how localising language functions are in right-handers, plus the fact that the associated signs (for example, weakness) of these strokes tend to present contra-lateral (opposite side to) to the lesion, and the average clinical psychologist new to neuropsychology has a reasonable working knowledge to start to build upon when seeing stroke patients on the ward. While reading, reflecting on some of the patients I have so far seen presented at ward rounds, this basic algorithm appears to work reasonably well to try and 'neuropsychologically triage' a fair proportion of stroke referrals. But not all . . . Returning now to Mr Stevens, sometimes Circle of Willis aneurysms or haemorrhages, given its location in the brain, can effectively disrupt pathways from the basal ganglia region around the Circle of Willis, to the frontal cortex. These are sometimes referred to as cortico-striatal-frontal circuits, and are thought to underpin some of the executive functions. Mr Stevens would probably fit this picture, I decide. At other times structures (part of the limbic system) neighbouring the Circle of Willis that are more closely involved in memory functions may indirectly be affected through these strokes. I am beginning to understand how sudden restricted flow, and at other

48

times, sudden flooding of blood to neurons can bring death to the brain cells of these areas. Or indeed the person.

Floods

The violence is still haemorrhaging out of the country's remaining factions, feuds and fears. Big atrocities come in waves, standing out against a steady flood of the other background non-stop low-level violence occurring on a daily basis. Most of the latter don't even make it to the papers anymore. The former do. There are some attempts to stop the madness, to bring stability and justice. But the bleeding continues, and nobody has a functioning tourniquet to hand. Today the Boipatong Massacre hearing started, to try and bring the perpetrators to justice. In the confusion and chaos it is not always clear who is who, or what lies behind these unimaginable events. In the shadowy world of violence often sides are switched, new masters served. Anxiety for the future has become part of life, and visits me when I am not actively busy with something. It has just gone after midday, and I am navigating my way through the myriad of hospital passages. Some are blocked with grey metal trolleys and people, while in others the never-ending floods of human misfortune and those who support them are flowing fine. I am on my way to a psychiatry ward on the other side of the hospital. There I meet Mrs Sandra Goossen (case # 113), brightly dressed and waiting for me. I am a bit late. I have a guilty, fleeting thought that the luxury of being late relies on inconveniencing others. Or perhaps it's not my own thought but a memory of a consultant's cutting comment during a ward round.

Mrs Goossen is 38 years old, and was referred to me a few months ago by a psychiatry registrar. At that time, the referrer wanted some testing done after the patient's stroke. I recall that a CT of her brain showed a fronto-parietal lesion. My testing revealed low-average general intellectual ability on a short Wechsler Adult Intelligence Scale and some noticeable visual memory problems on the remainder of the tests.

I remember Mrs Goossen as being a bit apathetic during testing. Not today. Today she is very talkative. The referral says she is now in a manic phase. Which actually looks to be the case, as becomes apparent when I start the assessment. She is easily excitable and answers my questions in an impulsive, almost random fashion. Mrs Goossen is emotionally superficial, for example, when I ask her about her mood. She perseverates, finds it difficult to disengage from a topic once we have started. It is also possible to elicit perseveration on bedside cognitive testing. Her language functions are fine on bedside testing. In fact she just talks nonstop, and is almost unstoppable. After a bit of vacillation, I decide to try and do formal testing anyway, despite her obviously elevated mood. An interesting case, with such a clear change in mood in the presence of a circumscribed lesion after a stroke a few months ago. Plus I have a baseline neuropsychological test profile to compare today's results with, provided I succeed in administering a few tests today.

Despite the heat in the small office off the ward, Mrs Goossen flies through the testing. Much too fast in fact. At times I find it difficult to keep up with her. Nevertheless I manage to score the tests as we go along, albeit not as easily as is usually the case. Interestingly, briefly looking at her baseline profile, I see today her IQ score is 9 points higher than a few months ago. Admittedly, nothing much, but still given her mental state today, I feel it is of potential significance. I am able to do a Wechsler Memory Scale with a bit more ease, almost as if the effort of remembering stuff slows her down just a tad. Looking at her scores again, I see that this time visual reproduction is still below average for her. But I can now actually administer logical memory and associative learning, whereas at baseline I could not. Mrs Goossen's performance on both of these are well into the normal range. We do the next test. She struggles with the Porteus Maze, and makes six mistakes. To be expected, given that her lesion extends to the frontal lobe, I silently update my hypotheses about her presentation. Mrs Goossen once again does a perfect copy of the Rey Complex Figure, but her delayed recall is, though slightly better, still lower than would have been expected for her.

With the neuropsychological testing completed, I think the picture is becoming clearer to me. Everything fits nicely with a couple of my hypotheses. First, the cognitive profile broadly fits with a right-sided fronto-parietal stroke in a right-handed person. Second, comparing today's results with the baseline, the results show the typical modest improvements we tend to see in our patients after the first six months post-stroke have passed. As Dr Carstens said to me not too long ago, we know much earlier in stroke what the long-term impairments are likely going to be, than in traumatic brain injury. Looking at Mrs Goossen sitting in the chair on the other side of my desk, I am not so sure about the diagnosis of mania, but then again that is in the domain of psychiatry. I find myself briefly actually feeling quite pleased, thinking I am now after only a few months in this job almost reasoning like an 'old hand' in clinical neuropsychology. Furthermore, Mrs Goossen has been so fast during testing that there is time to have a chat with her, possibly about the more interesting aspects about her as an individual person, rather than just a neurological patient with a lesion. I relax, lean back in my chair and ask her to tell me about her stroke, what happened, if can she remember anything, and how it affected her.

What follows is an unexpected flood of words, a torrent of emotion. It suddenly overwhelms the atmosphere in the room, and both of us also, I think. The room feels hotter and smaller than a few minutes ago. Mrs Goossen tells me, laughing first, then crying, then both, that she had been expecting a baby. She says it was a bit of a shock.

'The baby was a gift, you know', she tells me with a quivering voice.

'You did not expect to be pregnant?'

'No, I was not in my twenties anymore. But you never know, babies move in mysterious ways. Do you know about babies?'

'Not much really, I am sorry', I say not knowing what on earth to say.

'Well, everything seemed fine. But then I lost him . . .'.

'Lost him?' I wonder out loud, caught by surprise.

Did she misplace him somewhere in the house, or maybe a shop?

'Yes, he was a little boy. My special one. But born too early, dead', she sobs like a mortally wounded animal about to die.

It's impossible to stop her now. Mrs Goossen's story is pouring out. I don't know what to say to her and wonder anxiously if my role is to be someone who will hold her story, preserve it for eternity. And that perhaps in this way her son will somehow live on.

Mrs Goossen's story continues to flow into the uncomfortable air of the room. After his death, Mrs Goossen tells me, she had a 'nervous breakdown'. Then things went from bad to worse. Mrs Goossen suffered a stroke. How brutal when she had lost her baby, suffered a breakdown, then a stroke. She is sobbing. I notice the rough hospital paper tissue I gave her is just a small soggy ball in her hand now. There is a knock at the door. The porters are here to escort her back to the psychiatry ward.

Mrs Goossen's story still hangs heavily in the stuffy room smelling of other people's suffering. I certainly found out more about her than merely her neuropathology and neuropsychological test performance today. I catch myself thinking that while this place is exponentially increasing my life experience, and that by now I have even occasionally been challenged to try and understand what death is, I still fail dismally to figure out life. Why was what was, and is, so precious to Mrs Goossen, new life, taken away before it even started? There is no rational answer. This is one for the hospital vicar. But reflecting on her case, at least I think I do have a third hypothesis to add to the neuropsychological examination of Mrs Goossen. While hypotheses one and two in my view almost definitely hold up, I do wonder if it is entirely correct to say that she is manic, or even hypo-manic. The third hypothesis? I suspect she is broken by the loss of her baby, and that her cognitive impairments, especially the executive impairment associated with frontal lobe involvement, is just not able to block the flood of emotions since his death. We need our frontal lobes to keep a lid on things, or thinking about clinical training, 'our Superegos to contain our Ids'. Otherwise we could go mad? Is this possibly who Mrs Goossen is?

Who?

Monday morning, the start of another week. There is a new consultant psychiatrist at our clinic. She sits with her back to the door, in the little dark office, left, immediately after the reception area to our unit. There is no name on the door. I ask who she is, and am told she is Dr Ana Sharkova. What sort of a name is that, Russian, I ask. No, just arrived from the UK, so she doesn't think she is Russian, the nurse tells me. The first patient for the day has also just arrived. But not from as far afield, the nurse looking at me with a slightly tilted head informs me. Did I see just the merest twitch in the corner of the nurse's mouth, just a milligram of sarcasm in her tone of voice? I ask her who the patient is. She tells me he is Mr Rolf Stander, and I must not mess with him. Now it's my turn to smile. I can see that I am being led up the garden path. The nursing staff, who have seen it all, and use their demonic sense of humour without any mercy to regularly remind newbies like me that we know *nothing*. Not today. I suspect she has forgotten I have now worked here more than four months, and that I don't confuse narrative with fact anymore. Attempted to distract me with trying to suggest very subtly that I am more interested in who the new consultant is (who *was* she again?) and then exploit my gullibility by telling me Mr Stander, my first patient, might be a handful. I casually lean out of the door of the nurses' office and call Mr Stander, as if to say to the nurse, see, there is nothing to worry about – I know who he is.

I don't know who Mr Stander is. But for some peculiar reason I try to make small talk with him as we walk to my office. He says nothing all the way, so halfway there I stop talking. After he is sat down, I read the referral. Mr Stander (case # 15) is aged 34, and has been referred by neurology. The history is that he was a boxer for two years when he was at school. The current problem is that he suffered a right parietal lobe stroke five months ago. His presenting problems are listed as not being able to recognise familiar people, and that he has significant difficulties with anger and aggression. I immediately change from being quite casual up to now in my approach to Mr Stander, to being a bit more formal. I explain to Mr Stander that if it is OK with him, I shall be asking him some questions, and a give him a few tasks to perform for me. Hopefully nothing too taxing, I try to reassure him (or myself?). This will help me better understand his symptoms, I continue to explain. He still does not say a word, and just stares at me blankly. As if I am speaking a foreign language. I don't, not for him at least. I did check on the patient sticker what his first language was coded as. Same as mine, it was. I make a mental note to from now on pay attention to every word the nurses tell me. Some narratives may later prove to be fact.

I ask Mr Stander what his 'best' (dominant) hand is, upon which he duly lifts his right hand. It's now clear that he at least has comprehension of basic verbal commands and questions. But something is not quite right. His left hand has remained firmly in the pocket of his loosely fitting khaki trousers since I first noticed him in the waiting area. And he has still not said a word.

'Would you mind walking to the wall and back for me, Mr Stander?' I ask, with a preliminary hypothesis in mind.

Mr Stander walks, slightly clumsily to his right, left hand still in his pocket, to the wall and back, and stops at the other side of my desk.

'Please sit down, Mr Stander. What troubles you?' I ask him.

Mr Stander finally speaks. He has noticeable difficulties with articulating, or *making*, words. He tells me that since he had a stroke a few months earlier, his life has been a bit different. He can't remember who is who, everybody looks more or less the same, speaking is a bit harder, but on the whole things are not too bad really.

Really, is that true? I wonder.

Instead I ask, 'Please show me your left hand, Mr Stander'.

He leans to the right in his chair, before slowly pulling his left hand out of his pocket, and then almost imperceptibly uses his right hand to 'help', place it on the table in front of me. Has Mr Stander has been 'hiding' a hemiplegia?

Despite the problem with his non-dominant hand, Mr Stander engages well with formal neuropsychological testing. He has already learned to partially compensate for his motor problems. He scores 121 on the performance scale of the Wechsler Adult Intelligence Scale, 109 on Total and 96 on Verbal. But with such high non-verbal performance, I start to wonder if his performance does not quite fit with a right hemisphere stroke? The Wechsler Memory Scale Revised sheds some light on his presentation. Mr Stander obtains a verbal memory score of 93, visual memory 109, and general memory 97, which to some extent mirror his IQ scores. However, he scores 74 on attention and 86 on delayed recall. Which means there is a new hypothesis to test – his processing of information might well be the problem. I administer a Hooper Visual Organisation Test and Mr Stander scores 23½, raising further my suspicion that he has difficulties with specific aspects of visual processing. We continue with the testing. Tests of executive function show nothing remarkable. I decide to have another look at his visual memory and give him the Benton Visual Retention Test. Mr Stander scores 3 correct and makes 8 errors. All the errors are to the right side of the designs, and looking more closely, in the lower right quadrant of his visual field. Now I am more confused.

While the testing has provided useful information about his visual perceptual deficits, the subtle language difficulties remain a bit trickier to interpret in view of his handedness. Looking again at the Wechsler Adult Intelligence Scale subtest scores, it shows that his lowest score is on comprehension. Perhaps his language difficulties represent subtle executive problems dating back to his boxing, coupled with the mild motor problems affecting his speech? Or maybe he has mixed dominance for handedness, being more ambidextrous than meets the eye? Is his 'best' hand really his dominant hand? Or maybe his lesion is 'bigger' than the lesion seen on scan? I go over his results with him later, and explain how the problem with visual perceptual integration may account for his problem recognising people. He looks at me blankly.

'What do you think of that, Mr Stander?' I ask.

'I think I am just a bit forgetful with names, but it is not a huge problem', he says with clear irritation.

Ah, now the light goes on. I failed to also see, right in front of me throughout the clinical assessment and formal neuropsychological testing, the difficulties with self-awareness and insight some patients with right-parietal lesions sometimes present with. How embarrassing. It reminds me that in this trade reading, no, studying facts, count for very little before being internalised through observation in patients. And seen repeatedly, if you want to know your stuff half as well as Dr Carstens and colleagues.

Notice

It is still early morning and work has just started. Walking from the car park towards the hospital, the rain reflects off the huge, looming structure in front of me. Through the main entrance to the hospital, past the Red Cross lady sitting behind her table, writing, always writing, with her pile of pamphlets to her left as they always are. Upon arrival at our unit, there is call waiting for me in the Sister's office.

'Can you come up to the ninth floor sometime today?'

It is Dr Carstens' registrar. The ninth floor is where the neurology inpatient ward is located. Our unit is on the ground floor, where there is not the panoramic views to be appreciated from the ninth floor. Apparently something to do with the pecking order of the different medical specialities in the hospital. There is only one floor above neurology: the neurosurgery department. Dr Carstens' registrar continues.

'Dr Carstens would like you to see a Mr Piet Moolman (case # 46). He said he would be interested to hear your thoughts on Mr Moolman's neuropsychological presentation. Unfortunately Mr Moolman will only be on the ward for a couple of days. He apologises for the short notice and absence of a written referral, but on Wednesday Mr Moolman goes back home', Dr Carstens' registrar continues in an accent broadcasting confidently that English is not his first language.

Upon arrival in the neurology ward later in the day, Mr Moolman is sitting on his bed. I introduce myself, and we start the assessment with Mr Moolman telling me why he is in hospital. He is well educated, in his mid-forties and holds a responsible position in the agricultural retail industry. Mr Moolman is a good historian. He provides me with all I need to know within a few minutes. Tells me he had a 'funny turn' at work, of which he could not remember much. He 'blacked out' and 'shook, plus 'wet himself'.

Mr Moolman continues, 'To cut a long story short, the company doctor saw me, and thought I had a seizure. But he felt he could not be entirely sure without further special tests'.

'What happened next, Mr Moolman?'

The company doctor referred him to the university hospital where he now finds himself, under the care of Dr Carstens. According to Mr Moolman, Dr Carstens examined him, and then requested some 'scans'. Later when I read over the notes, I see that there are indeed requests for a CT and an EEG, but no reports outlining the findings.

'Dr Carstens said I have a cyst on the right side of my brain, that's what caused the seizure', Mr Moolman continues.

He also informs me that Dr Carstens said the cyst was 'benign', and there was no need for a 'brain operation' to remove it.

In fact, since he was started on medication (carbamazepine) everything settled down. That's why he is going home tomorrow. He is well enough.

From what Mr Moolman has told me, everything seems quite straightforward. I decide to do a quick bedside neuropsychological examination, and also ask Mr Moolman if he'd come for formal neuropsychological testing first thing the next morning. The bedside examination reveals the following. Mr Moolman is right-handed, and fully orientated. His speech is normal, there are no obvious language difficulties. Mr Moolman's new learning and retention are also fine. Testing reveals no problems with executive control functions.

Mr Moolman copes well with construction tasks and is able to copy the Necker cube. While drawing, I notice he is a little bit clumsy on the left, and that it looks like he has a smaller left hand. When I look a bit closer, I also see that his left leg, casually swung over the side of the bed, looks a bit less muscular than the right. I wonder if he had polio as a child? It used to be a common problem at around the time he was young. But then I quickly discard this hypothesis. He has been diagnosed with having a right-sided cyst in his brain. Perhaps this explains why he has a bit of a weakness and corresponding slight muscle waste. My clinical examination concludes with a brief bed-side review of mental functioning, which reveals nothing of note. Mr Moolman is neither depressed, nor anxious.

The next morning Mr Moolman is brought down to our clinic by a porter. I go to collect his file. In the meantime the porter wheels Mr Moolman to my office. Mr Moolman is already seated at the desk when I return to my office. I explain what the neuropsychological testing will entail, and by what time I think we should be done.

'It should not take very long, Mr Moolman. I will do a shortened test battery', I reassuringly tell him.

Mr Moolman is going home today. I assume Dr Carstens would specifically be interested in neuropsychological testing, to have a baseline of cognition, in case there is a future deterioration in his condition. I'll ask him later when I go up to the ward. But then, according to Mr Moolman, Dr Carstens did say the cyst was 'benign' and should 'cause no further mischief, as long as you take your medication'? The testing proceeds uneventfully. His left arm I now notice more clearly is quite a bit smaller than his right. Nevertheless he compensates well with his right hand, for example, during tests such a block design. Mr Moolman also appears a bit sluggish, or apathetic. Furthermore, at times his answers are possibly a bit long-winded. The general impression though is that Mr Moolman performs considerably better on language-based tests. Which makes sense given his robust level of educational achievement, and the presence of a right-sided lesion in a right-handed patient.

As predicted, the testing is completed before too long. The hypothesis was that that he would struggle with nonverbal functions. From qualitative observation of his test behaviour, I can already see he has greater difficulty with constructional and visual-spatial tasks. The few tests administered provide further evidence to confirm the hypothesis. Mr Moolman's shortened Wechsler Adult Intelligence Scale rather dramatically shows the expected pattern, with a verbal IQ score of 122, and a performance IQ score of 72. His Wechsler Memory Scale performance provides more proof of the presence of subtle problems with right brain functions, Mr Moolman scoring 14 on associative learning, 11.5 on logical memory, and 9 for visual memory. His Hooper Visual Organisation Test yields a score of 22 out of 30, also impaired. Particularly in view of his likely pre-morbid intellectual functioning, this would be a low performance for him. The remainder of the neuropsychological test profile is unremarkable. Neuropsychological tests results strongly suggest a right hemisphere lesion. The behavioural observation of being a bit sluggish or slow is probably due to the side effects of the anti-seizure medication he has just been started on. The other factor to consider is that most brain disorders affect attention or processing speed to a greater or lesser degree. I decide I'll go up to Neurology and tell Dr Carstens about my findings before Mr Moolman is discharged.

The only problem is that Dr Carstens is nowhere to be found. He is a busy man. Always in the wards, on his own, or surrounded by an entourage of medical students in their new white coats, stethoscopes dangling around their necks or peering out from pockets. The students struggle to keep up with him, he does everything fast, including walking between wards. He is 'old school' and believes in 'see one, do one, teach one'. Which reminds me, I need to present the neuropsychological test results of another patient, Mrs Lahotle, at Dr Carstens' neurology academic round on Friday, where everyone from medical students to consultants are present. I better prepare well. Another Dr Carstens truism is that 'cognitive signs disappear like mist in front of the moon' when you call in your patient at the academic round, to demonstrate your findings. By that time they have had say the Mini Mental State Examination performed by a steady stream of interns, medical students, clinical psychology trainees and of course the consultants also. No wonder they can remember the date and recall three words by the time of the academic round, or copy the design, do most of the items in fact . . . suddenly Dr Carstens appears from a side office.

'Oh, there you are, Rudi. I have something interesting to show you', he blurts out.

From a brown X-ray folder, Dr Carstens takes a CT scan film, inserts it into the embracing silver arms of the viewing box and switches the backlight on. The image first flickers, stutters a bit and then comes into sharp focus. About the same thing appears to happen in my head. I focus on a light area, then a dark *nothing* area, then back to the light area, then the nothing area again in the image. Only I seem unable to focus. Something is desperately wrong here and my cortical cogs struggle to turn.

'Hey, where are the other slices?' I ask, completely puzzled.

The room is starting to feel under-ventilated.

'Something's missing man, you need to show me more slices', I try again.

I keep on looking, but I don't know what I am supposed to notice.

'What do you think?' Dr Carstens asks.

'Well, well, um, let me think, um I'm not sure. Actually to be frank with you I don't know where to look and cannot find my way around the usual landmarks. Looks like a chunk of the image on the right did not develop on the film?'

Ah, that must be it!

'Did the technician mess up the film? Where is the rest'?

The room is definitely lacking air.

'Sorry Johan, I am stuck, actually, I'm totally lost', I admit as I feel myself going red in the face.

'Relax! Look closely, did you notice this? There is just about no right hemisphere so speak of, remarkable, isn't it Rudi?' Dr Carstens says, pointing to the dark half of the scan.

I look again. It's hard to believe my eyes, but now that he has 'opened' them for me, it is actually near impossible not to notice the absence of virtually one half of the patient's brain.

I feel myself take a small breath, pluck up the courage, and ask 'How is it possible for someone to function, no, what I mean, is to be alive, with such a catastrophic brain lesion?'

The airless room is now silent, the X-ray box like a solitary painting in a minimalist room.

'By the way, who's scan is it? Are you going to present him or her this Friday, Johan? I've never, ever, in my life seen a patient like this', I say, genuinely surprised.

'It is Mr Moolman's scan', comes Dr Carstens' reply.

I don't manage to really process the answer.

'Sorry, say that again?' I manage to stutter.

'It's Mr Moolman's scan, the chap you saw on Monday, and tested this morning, remember', Dr Carstens replies while continuing to look intently at the image still illuminated on the X-ray viewing box.

'Are you sure it is his scan?' I ask in disbelief.

Come on, focus now, I remind myself. Stand back, think it through.

'My understanding was that Mr Moolman had a diagnosis of a right hemisphere cyst?' I finally manage to say.

'Oh that, yes you are right. Look, here it is. But much more unusual is this black space here, in fact 80 per cent gone according to the radiologists I had a chat with this morning. Of course now just fluid, where the bulk of his right hemisphere should have been', Dr Carstens explains.

'How . . .', but I don't get any further.

'Now here's the interesting bit. The history is that at age 3 he had a fall, which resulted in a hemiplegia. The hemiplegia did improve a bit with time, and interestingly he had no problems at school. Passed matric at school without any problems. As I take it you know, he is successfully employed. We did some further investigations in view of the truly remarkable CT, and putting together the neurological findings, radiology and history, found out that he had an occlusion of his right internal carotid when he fell at age 3. A stroke, if you wish. His right hemisphere simply died. You are very unlikely to see many of these cases, my young friend. I needed to have his neuropsychology documented, to try and confirm my own impressions of his cognition. And it's good to have a baseline in case we need it for another day in the future', Dr Carstens concludes.

Tomorrow

As I walk back to my office, I feel overwhelming doubt regarding my clinical abilities. Yes, I can now see how things fit together, but only after Dr Carstens explained it to me. The cyst was the cause of Mr Moolman's later life onset of a first seizure. This prompted referral to hospital, where routine CT scan as part of the diagnostic workup revealed a right hemisphere cyst. But of much greater relevance, was the coincidental finding of an obliterated right hemisphere in a high-functioning adult. Is this an extreme case of neuro-plasticity? The size of a brain lesion is not necessarily always the primary determinant of neuropsychological test performance. Reflecting on what I learned today, I ask myself why I got things so horribly wrong. Too much confidence, too early, I beat myself up. However, Dr Carstens did say that these cases are rare. And failure is part of becoming a clinician. Maybe I should be a bit more forgiving of myself? Nevertheless, I could have done things better. Why did I simply listen to the patient's narrative, and take his report of the diagnosis as fact? Why did I not look properly when I did the bedside examination, or when I tested Mr Moolman, in particular at his dexterity and walking? Especially because I know that motor performance is very important in clinical neuropsychology, due to its sensitivity to acquired brain injury. Why did I not consider time since brain injury? Taken together, maybe it was the fact that Mr Moolman provided me with an instant solution to the problem I was about to embark on solving. One of several things I have learned today is that provided we look long enough at a problem, the solution should become more noticeable.

The rest of the day is spent doing outpatient follow-up appointments. Afterwards, I write the notes, catch up with some colleagues, and check what is scheduled for tomorrow. Despite being busy, somehow Mr Moolman's case lingers on in my mind, colouring the day. I realise that I still feel a bit humiliated and bruised after my failure to notice what now seems so obvious. But I reassure myself that while today was bad, tomorrow is another day. Tomorrow will hopefully bring another 'life' in clinical neuropsychology. Through today's mistakes, tomorrow I will hopefully be a bit better at what I do. On the positive side, I did learn a lot today. Not least how the brain is much more complex than depicted on the pages of books, a timely reminder how we should be careful not to equate lesion size to expected magnitude of neuropsychological impairment. Most important though is that I learnt the hard way not to be too confident too soon. Becoming a clinician also entails to learn from, and live with, inevitable failure and setbacks. The route back to the parking lot outside the hospital takes me past now increasingly familiar wards and passages. On my way out through the main entrance, I pass the Red Cross lady. Outside the rain has stopped. The air fresh and sky clear, the hospital complex looks a bit less imposing than this morning. Perhaps it feels like that if you can forgive yourself for not being perfect. Arriving at my car, while starting to unlock the door, a thought, no, a visual image stops me in my tracks. Did I just imagine that, or was the Red Cross lady's pile of leaflets on her right? Was she writing with her left hand? That's bad of me not to notice, I must definitely have a better look tomorrow morning.

4

Badness

Infections in the brain

Badness is only spoiled goodness.

(C. S. Lewis)

Perception

The admin and nursing staff here in our unit in the basement of the hospital take no prisoners. Even though admittedly for some who *have* to visit, the basement can become a prison of sorts. It is Thursday morning. Mrs Esterhuizen is in charge of admin, and assisted by her sidekick, Mrs Brown in reception. Mrs Esterhuizen has the presence of an annoyed heavyweight boxer, whereas Mrs Brown strikes one as a nervous bird-like figure, scrawny and delicate. Most days they are helped by Sister Jantjies. Reception is where our patients announce their arrival when attending outpatient appointments. Mrs Brown checks their identification, updates their attendance record and sends them down the passage to the waiting area. It's not really a waiting area as such, just some, once black, now dark grey plastic chairs next to each other, randomly placed in a recess midway down the passage. Mrs Esterhuizen and Mrs Brown have been doing this initial sorting and checking in of patients for many, many years, and rule the ward with an iron fist to make sure that everything runs smoothly. Without them the unit is finished, dead. They are super-efficient, never late for work, able to bring order to any amount of chaos. Sometimes requiring just a mere raise of the eyebrow, or a slightly too long icy look. Mrs Esterhuizen and her lieutenants will stand up to anyone to ensure the hundreds of patients that come through our unit each year, are seen to and cared for by the clinical staff. They are greatly respected for that, and accordingly their word is law.

The hissing sounds of a hushed conversation in full flight greets me as I walk into the nursing staff's office where everyone is congregating this morning. Seamlessly Mrs Esterhuizen disengages from the social chit chat, and tells me, no, instructs me, 'The medical students are here for you'.

She pauses just that little bit too long, and gives me a look to check if I have remembered.

'Yes, Mrs Esterhuizen, thanks, I have not forgotten about them', I reassure her.

I do have a memory, albeit very vague, that a few weeks ago I promised Dr Burger that I would spend an hour or so with the medical students to introduce them to the basics of neuropsychological assessment. Returning a favour for his time spent with the clinical psychology interns, teaching them basic psychopharmacology.

'And you have a patient straight after that, a Mr Mkosi from ninth floor'.

'That I definitely haven't forgotten about, Mrs Esterhuizen'.

A slightly tilted head, and am I imagining it, a raised eyebrow meets my gaze.

'So you did forget about the medical students?' her one eyebrow lifting a millimetre higher as part of the inquisition.

Mrs Esterhuizen must have heard, and processed in a flash, that I was sure of the patient's appointment, but not entirely so about the students. No point ever trying to dodge her.

'Maybe. Sort of, but actually not quite. I did know about it. Let me crack on with them, it's going to be a busy day', I try to save some face.

Did Mrs Esterhuizen look bemused when I left, or am I just being a bit sensitive this morning I wonder while walking towards the small group of medical students.

'Hello, I am Rudi, the clinical neuropsychologist here in the neuropsychiatry and neuropsychology clinic. Dr Burger asked if I would take you through the basics of the bedside cognitive testing of patients', I introduce myself to them.

Did I say something wrong? They all recoiled when I opened my mouth. Surely they cannot read my private thoughts that it is a bit disingenuous for me to say in a formal, pretentious voice that 'I am the clinical neuropsychologist', whereas I should probably say 'Hello, I am the imposter here in the unit, I am still learning to be a clinical neuropsychologist, but let me tell you anyway about the basics I have learnt thus far?'

No, they won't know that. Time to increase the authoritarianism. They are after all students, that part of my life I finished five years ago. They have not yet.

'Follow me'.

There is not a sound. They are starting to annoy me. I turn around, now facing the students, and say 'Come on, let's go now'.

Still they don't budge. And they don't make any eye contact either.

Something is wrong here.

Suddenly there is hysterical high-pitched laughter behind me. I swing around. I have an audience. Mrs Esterhuizen and her whole roost are standing outside the office, bent double, howling with laughter. I look back at the students. They are as stunned as I am. The one's mouth is open. Something's not right. I look around again. Mrs Esterhuizen is marching towards the students.

'Relax, he is not the strange cleaner. He *is* the neuropsychologist!' She starts laughing again.

'He is just a bit new, and we thought he's much too serious and needed to relax. Otherwise sooner or later his nerves will snap in this place', she says, turning towards me, and winks.

'Isn't that true, Mr Serious, you need to chill, son?'

Aaargh, Mrs Esterhuizen has struck! Her observation skills are much, much better than I thought.

'Suppose so, Mrs Esterhuizen', I lamely smile at her.

'Come on, off to the lounge you lot, he's not got all day for you, and has a lot to teach you. Unless you want to fail? Do you want to fail? Not become doctors? You think Dr Burger will like it when he hears you've been lazy here in the unit? Yes? No?' she glares at them to add emphasis to her damning prediction of failure.

As one the students jump up. The boxer has spoken. I follow them to the lounge.

Even though at times it is difficult to keep a straight face, I teach the medical students the basics surrounding bedside cognitive testing of neurological patients. The stuff I only very recently learned myself, and am continuing to learn. After what had just happened to me and them thanks to Mrs Esterhuizen, I don't forget to emphasise the difference between perception and fact, in other words narrative versus objective, when testing patients. After the session, they go on their way, I return to where Mrs Esterhuizen and company are sitting in the office.

I open my mouth to say something, but don't even get that far. Mrs Esterhuizen and Sister Jantjies start laughing again, before Sister Jantjies tells me, '*Ek wens jy kon jou eie gevreet gesien het!*' ['I wish you could see your own face'].

Mrs Esterhuizen quickly trumps her.

'Ja, maar het jy die kinders gesien? Hulle het gelyk of hulle gesuip was!' ['Yes, but did you see the kids, looked like they were drunk!'].

I smile, before starting to laugh, of the variety that makes your muscles refuse to collaborate. Perhaps also because for the first time I realise how Mrs Esterhuizen and her colleagues have been looking out for me from the start. How they care about the people they work with, including newbies like me. They want us to be happy, and feel supported in this difficult environment. I hope that I will become good enough to never let them down, even one day when inevitably the heat is turned up much higher.

Fire

The light reflected off the highly polished vinyl floors of the unit today cannot make up its mind if it is shining back summer or winter. Mr Xihole Mkosi (case # 1) has arrived, and has been walked down to my office by Sister Jantjies. Mr Mkosi sits patiently on a chair outside the door by my office, Sister Jantjies still by his side. Her hand is placed protectively on his skinny shoulder. He is a 45-year-old male from a rural coastal area, about 1,000 kilometres north-east from the hospital. The story is that a few weeks ago he was taken by his family to see the nurse at his local, rudimentary clinic. Apparently there have been problems with Mr Mkosi, and for a quite while. But even the local clinic is not easy for people to reach. Making the journey was put off a few times. It is too far away to walk to from where Mr Mkosi and his family live. They are very poor, and live in a *rondavel* (a very basic, often brightly painted, thatched roof round hut). Mr Mkosi and his wife have five children, and the maternal grandmother also lives with them. They try to plant vegetables to help feed the family, and have a few animals. Water is a big problem. Sometimes it does not rain for many months. Then suddenly everything comes in one big black cloud storm. These storms leave the landscape badly scarred, with long lashes of brown soil erosion cutting through the green grass like angry claw marks from a giant animal, injuring their precious land. There is no piped clean water, only a little spring used by the Mkosis and a few other families who live nearby. They have no electricity, and with that of course no lighting, heating or refrigeration. Food is cooked over an open fire.

The story leading up to Mr Mkosi now being in our hospital, continues as follows. Mr Mkosi eventually makes the journey to the clinic with his family, on the back of an old beaten up Toyota pickup, through the kindness of a distant relative who lives in the small village approximately six miles from them. It is a bouncy trip along the dirt roads, leaving a long ribbon of red dust behind them as a marker of the slow progress being made to get some help for Mr Mkosi. At the clinic, they are seen by a nurse. Mr Mkosi's wife in a very distressed state reports that he is suffering from *uqhaba* (madness) and has been possessed by a *umoya ombi* (a bad spirit). He has also become lazy, 'taking much too long' to tend to their livestock as well as the small vegetable patch. Mr Mkosi does not really participate in the discussion. While he sits passively staring into space, his wife tells the nurse that when the spirit brings badness to him, he falls on the floor, shakes and wets himself. She wonders if it might be a snake's spirit writhing inside him. She tells the nurse he is not well the day or two after the spirit has attacked him. Mrs Mkosi assures the nurse her husband does not drink, they have no money for that sort of thing. Mrs Mkosi thinks the only possible explanation is that an evil spirit has entered him. Therefore he must have done something very bad. Maybe he cheated on her with that bad woman across the fields, but she cannot be sure. Because of her concerns, she has been considering taking him to a *sangoma* (a traditional healer) or if that did not work, the *n'anga* (a witch doctor) to expunge the bad spirit. But the clinic was nearer, so they came here first.

The heat inside the clinic building is oppressive, trapped under the silver corrugated iron roof. The noise from outside drifts in through the open windows, but the nurse listens patiently to everything Mrs Mkosi tells her. Based on the very detailed description of the 'badness attacks' the 'spirit' brings to Mrs Mkosi's husband, she correctly identifies the likely presence of suspected seizures. She goes to great lengths to reassure Mr Mkosi's wife that he is not possessed by demons, evil spirits or for that matter a snake spirit. She also says that she thinks it unlikely that he has been cheating on her. Mrs Mkosi seems to doubt this, and asks the nurse how she knows that. The nurse patiently asks Mrs Mkosi to have a look at her husband. Then points out that he seems to be so passive and lacking in drive, that he would never be able to visit other women. Mrs Mkosi's wife counters this by shouting that he is guilty, that's the reason why he is so quiet, because he is trying to hide his wrongdoings. But the nurse sticks to her guns, points out that he is incontinent, and therefore surely must have an illness? Mrs Mkosi finally comes round to the idea of her husband being unwell. The nurse says she is sending Mr Mkosi to the doctors in the big hospital in the city. They may be able to better help him than is possible locally. She eventually also convinces Mrs Mkosi that she should accompany her husband to the hospital down to the south of the country, and gives her a handwritten referral letter to take along. It will be a very long, hot journey on a crowded minibus, to be paid for with money they can barely scrape together. Meals might have to be sacrificed. But the nurse explains to her again that it is very important that he is seen at the 'big hospital' in the city.

Mr Mkosi and his wife make the long journey to the city in the far south of the country, on the tip of Africa, where the cold and warm oceans meet. After a 10-hour drive they arrive in a world completely alien to them. The hospital's sprawling buildings are all huge, and there are busses, ambulances, noise, different languages, a cacophony of perceptual overload and confusion. Mrs Mkosi is overwhelmed by panic. The taxi driver points them to the main entrance of the hospital, and tells them who to ask about where they need to go from there. After waiting three hours in a busy, overcrowded outpatient waiting room, Mr Mkosi is seen by the duty doctor, and duly admitted to hospital. Exhausted, he falls asleep on his bed almost straight away. While on the neurology ward, observation of a couple of his attacks, plus an EEG confirms a diagnosis of seizures. As part of his diagnostic work up, he is referred for neuropsychological testing. He is accompanied down to our floor in the hospital by a porter. Mr Mkosi is of slender build, but over and above that also appears underweight, to the point of his body looking wasted. This is how I first see him, with Sister Jantjies' hand on his shoulder. A nail shoots into my heart. Poverty and malnourishment like this is awful to see. I wish I could look away. I can see Sister Jantjies' eyes also seeing what I see. Defeated by her eyes, her hand limply slides off his shoulder, and she leaves without saying anything. Mr Mkosi, bringing with him his story from another world, follows me in silence.

Mr Mkosi and I enter my consultation room. He stops by the chair, looking lost, standing with his head bent. His hands are protectively placed over his groin. I can see the tendons and veins of his hands, a roadmap of little ropes looking for something lost. He is dressed in the standard-issue hospital pyjamas with its little imitation paisley pattern made up of the letters CPA and KPA crossing, to form little 'X's. His cheekbones are protruding so far, it makes his brown eyes seem sunken unnaturally deeply into their sockets. A black mole on his left cheek almost manages to keep itself hidden thanks to his dark skin.

'Please sit down, Mr Mkosi', I ask quietly.

I ask him why he is here. After a long delay, he looks up cautiously and very slowly replies.

'I have badness in me'.

'Tell me a little bit more about that, Mr Mkosi?'

Another long pause. English is not his first language.

'I fall down. My head feels not right, bad'.

The onset of his symptoms is difficult to determine, because of his slowness and difficulty expressing himself. Nevertheless putting together all the little bits of information he can provide to me it looks like there was an insidious evolution of his behaviour changing, followed by the onset of seizures.

'Would you like a bit of a break, Mr Mkosi?' I ask.

He does not make eye contact. Looking ashamed he eventually just shakes his head. Mr Mkosi won't have money to buy anything for himself in the hospital canteen. We continue with the assessment.

Mr Mkosi struggles to answer questions about his background history. It is as if his thoughts are being delayed, no, held back, by some sticky substance. The most striking feature of his clinical presentation is slowness of processing and responding. His inertia in responding, when he actually manages to, is of such magnitude that I actively have to remind myself to wait much longer before asking the next question. It must be torture for him, and those living with him. Nevertheless, with enough time we piece together some sort of very basic personal history. Mr Mkosi was born, and grew up in the region where he is from. He never went to school, and has no formal education. At times he managed to work on local farms looking after cattle or goats, or perform other manual jobs. Mr Mkosi also tried to grow some vegetables for his family to eat. They are unimaginably poor, and have almost no money. It is impossible to understand exactly how hard life must be for them under 'normal' circumstances, never mind now that catastrophe has decided it is time to make their lives even harder by paying an unexpected visit. I wish I could offer him something to eat. Instead, with guilt consuming my full belly, I explain that I will be doing some tests with him, to help me better understand his difficulties. It is unclear if he understands exactly what I am explaining to him, but when I ask if we may continue, he nods that he would like to proceed. Or perhaps that's simply my defence against the poor man just agreeing with whatever any authority figure asks of him.

The Western tests on the table collide with the world he is from. Mr Mkosi frowns, looks a little bit startled at the red and white blocks placed in front of him. I explain what he needs to do. He tries his best. I find myself wondering what exactly in his stomach, bones and blood is fuelling his effort, as there must be so little to draw upon. Mr Mkosi's slowness dictates that fewer tests are completed than one would normally do. I also don't have any reliable norms to consult. Nevertheless, his results indicate widely distributed, severe cognitive impairment. On a short Wechsler Adult Intelligence Scale with four out of the five subtests language-free, his prorated IQ score equals 49. There is no scatter between any of the subtests. On the Raven Progressive Matrices (at the time considered a little bit more culture fair for someone who has had no formal schooling) it is slightly higher, with a score of 60. The Rey Complex Figure Test copy trial takes him seven minutes, and he scores 8 out of 36, clearly severely impaired. One subtest of the Wechsler Memory Scale provides enough evidence of profound amnesia. He can only recall one element of the story (logical memory), the rest is a blank in his mind. Mr Mkosi is unable to do Trail Making Test A, after five minutes managing to get to only number 4 (out of 25). I check his ability to count. While it transpires he can count, his motor and processing speed is so impaired that it would be inhumane to wait until he completes connecting all of the numbers. Once something is clear it is unnecessary to continue testing, is a valuable lesson I have already learned. Mr Mkosi can list four words in a minute. Enough is enough, I decide. I thank him for his hard work, terminate the testing, and send him back to his ward. My hypothesis, considering his neuropsychological test results as well as clinical presentation, is that he must have a condition that has a more general as opposed to focally damaging effect on the brain, most likely one of the dementias. Although I do wonder about the dramatic onset of seizures.

In the meantime, unbeknown to me, a drama is unfolding on the roof of the hospital. I later hear the story from Dr Ana Sharkova, the new consultant in psychiatry. Dr Sharkova also provides input to our neuropsychiatry and neuropsychology clinic. In fact, her horrible dark little office is in our unit, at the top of the passage. During a coffee break Dr Sharkova tells me about the drama. One of their patients left the ward undetected and used a service door at the end of the staircase reserved for access for workmen, to get onto the roof, 11 floors above the ground. When discovered, she was sitting straddling the low wall on the edge of the roof, sobbing uncontrollably.

The clinical team including Dr Sharkova rushed to the roof, stopped in their tracks, then froze in a half moon. Watching, collectively holding their breaths. One of the clinical psychologists, Gito, tentatively asked if she was OK. Would she like to come and have a chat with him? This only made her sob even more uncontrollably and rock more vigorously. Left, she lives, right, she dies. Suddenly, in the distance from ground level the air is shot to pieces by the sound of a vehicle aggressively braking, skidding to a standstill. A quiet sigh of relief from the half moon, it must be the emergency medics arriving. But no, it is the type of converted white pickup truck used by the police. A sight loathed and feared by most. Dismissively parked right by the side entrance, on the ambulance parking bays. A few minutes later a police captain, bursting out of his safari suit, pistol casually swinging from his belt, stomps onto the roof. The captain gives the half moon a sour sideways glance, marches to the edge and in a loud voice commands: *Kom hier!* [come here]. She immediately complies, gets up, stumbles towards him and collapses into his arms. Dr Sharkova stares icily at me at this point in the story. Unless I am intent on having lunch on my own, I dare not say a word, and definitely nothing about the limits of psychiatry.

Later that afternoon, I go up to the ninth floor to discuss Mr Mkosi's results with Dr Carstens. He listens attentively, and then shows me what looks like a 'pock marked' CT scan, full of white dots. Like a brain full of neatly settled, evenly distributed birdshot, but no skull abnormality indicative of an entry wound, if that were possible. I ask Dr Carstens what the white dots are.

'Well, Mr Mkosi has neurocysticercosis. Basically, he ate something bad. Almost certainly infected pork, which was then probably inadequately cooked, I suspect over an open fire. The pork, or other meat for that matter, has been infected with tapeworm, tenia solium, which is then ingested. The tapeworm eggs hatch in the stomach, and the worms can grow to huge lengths. They are parasites, feeding off the human host, who then starts losing weight'.

That's shocking, I feel ill.

'Sadly it is one of the more common sources of brain infection in developing countries. Simple to treat, or prevent the later problems really, provided it is detected early. Unfortunately when untreated sometimes the eggs cross the blood brain barrier, and lodge in the tissue of the brain. Over time the eggs calcify. That's the white dots you see here'.

Has hunger and poverty destroyed his brain, I wonder.

'Remember what I told you about scans? Just glorified X-rays, high-density material shows up as white. These little white dots, or calcifications, then of course irritate the brain. The first neurological presentation is usually when a seizure occurs. But by then it is much, much too late, the damage is done', he says solemnly.

I feel faint hearing Dr Carstens' explanation. But decide to ask anyway.

'Will he die?'

A silence follows. Dr Carstens is looking intently at the scan still on the viewing box, while stroking his goatee. The white dots now look like huge full stops.

I learn from Dr Carstens that Mr Mkosi will not die. Or at least not immediately. I ask him what exactly that means.

'Not while he is here in hospital', comes his quiet answer.

I am not sure if that is a good thing, or a bad thing. Where will he go after this, and who will look after him? I ask if there is anything that could be done to help this poor man. Dr Carstens tells me he will give Mr Mkosi steroids. Once Mr Mkosi has completed the treatment, Dr Carstens wants me to retest him to see if there are any changes in his cognitive functions. A couple of weeks later, Mr Mkosi is back at our clinic. I start retesting him, and find myself hoping that he will be *better* today. That the medicine *worked*. He is still very slow. Now, on the same short form Wechsler Adult Intelligence Scale his performance equals an IQ score of 53. Once again, there is no sub-test scatter. The Raven Progressive Matrices this time yields a score of 65. He also scores a little bit better on the Rey Complex Figure Test copy trial, 14, as opposed to 8 prior to treatment. The Wechsler

Memory Scale score is identical to that obtained two weeks ago. He can now list six (rather than four) words in a minute. With the Trail Making Test for trail A he gets a bit further than 4 this time, making it to the number 9. The numbers do show very modest improvements in some areas of his cognitive function, which is from a purely clinical point of view a good thing. However, I am not sure how the lifeless numbers on the page in front of me will translate to everyday life in his faraway world though. There is, however, one certainty. Mr Mkosi will be going home tomorrow. Which I suspect is a bad thing. Unavoidable badness, because we can't keep him here forever. It is a hospital. Others need to take his place.

Sorrow

The heat is such that you can almost hear its silent weight pushing down, infusing everything with lethargy. It is early Wednesday afternoon, becoming hotter by the hour. Mr Dan Strong (case # 31), aged 36, has been sent down from neurology, for neuropsychological testing. He is a government official in a high-ranking position. He looks a bit drained to me, but then so do a lot of my patients. Maybe the heat today makes it even more noticeable. Mr Strong shuffles into my office. We start with the history. His early development and schooling was uneventful. After finishing school, Mr Strong went to university and obtained two degrees. He started working in a government department straight after university. He describes himself as a hard worker, conscientious. Over subsequent years he worked his way steadily up the corporate ladder. I ask him about his current difficulties. Mr Strong tells me that he enjoys nothing. Every day is an effort. Sometimes he feels so low, that he starts crying. To him it feels like life has no purpose, filled with sorrow. He hides his feelings from his family, puts up a brave face for them. He feels ashamed to tell me this, and looks out of the window while speaking. I am sorry to hear that things have not been great, and reassure him that it is OK to tell me.

Mr Strong is depressed. I ask him to tell me when things started to go downhill. It transpires that the onset of his low mood follows being seriously ill with encephalitis two years earlier.

'Before the illness came, everything was good. Now all the good has turned bad', he says barely able to hold back his sorrow.

Just speaking to him, there is no suggestion of any obvious cognitive impairment. Perhaps he made a full recovery, and is just depressed? The best way to explore this hypothesis will be to test him.

After a short break, I start testing Mr Strong. He first completes the Wechsler Adult Intelligence Scale, to obtain an indication of his general intellectual abilities. My initial impressions of there being no obvious, or at least global cognitive impairment looks as if it may indeed be correct. Another short break gives me time to score the test, and decide what to do next. His total IQ score is 118, verbal IQ 118, and performance IQ 116. But wait, looking more closely at the subtest scores something's not right. The difference between the highest and lowest subtest is 5.5, with picture completion the lowest at 8.5. Surely that could be due to a visual-spatial impairment? I'll check that out with further testing. Mr Strong returns from his break, tells me he managed to go to the canteen and have a cup of tea, as well as a piece of cake. I explain that I'd like to do a few more tests, but that so far things seemed OK, with nothing obvious to worry about. I now test the hypothesis of a possible visual-spatial dysfunction. However, I find no evidence to support the hypothesis. Mr Strong performs well into the normal range on the Rey Complex Figure (copy and recall), Trail Making Test, Rey Auditory Verbal Test, Word Naming Test, and the Wechsler Memory Scales. Reflecting on the results thus far, I carefully consider the convention in clinical neuropsychology that if only one test is outside the normal range, the result should be viewed as possibly being a chance finding. Back to the first hypothesis. Mr Strong is depressed.

As we continue the testing I observe that Mr Strong is a little bit lethargic. Nevertheless his endurance and effort is very good. He does not give up when he starts to fail items, nor does he display any signs of a catastrophic reaction when he is confronted by more difficult items on a task. When confronted with their own test failure, some patients show what is known as a catastrophic reaction, a sudden, intense display of emotion out of proportion to the situation. Returning to Mr Strong, on the whole, it looks like thus far he is doing just fine with the testing. However, then just as I was thinking everything is OK, to my surprise Mr Strong really struggles with the next test. He scores 17 out of 30 (below the 'cut score' of 24) on the Hooper Visual Organisation Test. That is a bit perplexing in an otherwise almost entirely normal protocol. Finally, finishing off the neuropsychological testing we complete a couple of tests of executive function, the Austin Maze and the Porteus Mazes. Mr Strong flies through these with ease. At this point Mr Strong goes out for another short break to stretch his legs, while I put together all the results so that I can give him feedback when he returns. I am very aware that the ward wants to discharge him, although it is not known exactly when. As I finish the scoring, there is a hesitant knock at the open door to my office. Ah, Mr Strong is back a bit early. I look up. One of the interns is standing in the doorway, and asks if he may borrow the Wechsler.

'Sure, I am done'.

While waiting, I reflect on my conclusion that despite the illness that has come Mr Strong's way, at least today there may be mostly good news for him. When Mr Strong returns, I explain to him that on the whole his cognitive profile suggests that in the majority of areas he has made a good recovery, with only one fairly specific area of relative difficulty. I tell him that unsurprisingly, given all that has happened to him, one of his main difficulties is that he is depressed. Mr Strong looks relieved when he hears this. I also tell him that depression is mostly treatable, and that specific cognitive impairments such as the one suggested by his test results, are with rehabilitation intervention generally much easier to compensate for than global problems. It has been a long afternoon, and the office is now in the shade. The heat does not feel that oppressive anymore. Or maybe Mr Strong and I just got more comfortable with it during the course of the afternoon. A confident knock at the door interrupts my thoughts. It is a porter who has been sent down from the ward. The porter asks if I am done with Mr Strong, as he needs to go back to the ward now. His discharge documentation needs to be signed off.

'Are we done, Mr Strong, or is there anything else you'd like to ask me?' I check to see if he is ready to go.

'Thank you very, very much, you have been a great help', Mr Strong replies, as he starts getting up.

When he leaves, he hesitates at the door, turns around, and smiles very briefly at me.

Mr Strong goes home without a cure, but possibly with a bit less sorrow and more hope than he had when he woke up this morning. Sometimes hope is all we can give our patients.

Whereas I need hope, she needs evidence of progress. Her office is quiet, and has to be filled with knowledge. She awaits a demonstration that learning is taking place at the required pace. In today's supervision we are covering the clinical neuropsychology of brain infections. I present what I have learned thus far, and try to integrate this knowledge with patients I have recently seen. Sometimes brain infections result in catastrophic damage, with neurological devastation associated with severe disability or even death. Most brain infections can have either a widespread or random area of affected tissue. Some, like herpes simplex encephalitis affect a specific brain area, in this case the medial temporal lobes. Neuropsychological impairment tends to broadly mirror the regions affected by the illness. At other times the impairments secondary to a brain infection are so subtle, casual observers will never pick anything up. Infections can also affect the coverings of the brain, the meninges, in which case it is meningitis. Generally the prognosis and outcome after meningitis is better than when the brain itself becomes infected, encephalitis, in which case the impairment and associated disability can be much more pronounced. Nevertheless, meningitis should not be underestimated as it can indirectly cause damage to the brain through oedema (swelling) and other factors. Brain infections are transmitted through viruses, bacteria or parasites (for example, as was the case with Mr Mkosi).

Some brain infections have a very slow course, and are perhaps rarer now, for example neurosyphilis. It can take decades for tertiary syphilis (neurosyphilis) to present. Some colleagues, including Dr Burger, say neurosyphilis is 'the great pretender' because of the wide variation in presentations, often psychiatric. In other types of brain infection the onset is much more rapid, evolving over hours or days, for example, herpes simplex encephalitis. Sometimes the exact mode of transmission is known, for example, HIV, or neurosyphilis. In others, it is assumed, or not much is known about the mode of transmission.

She finally gives her verdict.

'OK, that's not too bad, actually', she says, while looking at me intently.

To my relief today my clinical supervisor, Ms Carla De Bruin, looks as if she is reasonably satisfied with my progress.

Goodness

Located at the end of the passage, my office blocks out most of the daily sounds in the unit. Across the desk from me this morning sits a Mr Jannie Carrolisen (case # 65). He is 39 years old. According to the referrer, the main problem Mr Carrolisen presents with is memory difficulties. These started a couple of years ago. Mr Carrolisen's memory difficulties followed an episode of pulmonary tuberculosis. Unfortunately his tuberculosis was not treated promptly. Mr Carrolisen stoically tried to continue working while clearly very ill, until his family forced him to go to hospital when he took a turn for the worse. He developed secondary meningitis as a consequence of the tuberculosis. Now here in my office, it is proving rather difficult to make progress with the initial clinical assessment. Mr Carrolisen is powerfully built, the green veins on his upper arms contrasting with his brown skin, looking like taut little hosepipes straining over his biceps. There is very little expression to see in his face, and he looks at me blankly when I ask him what the matter is.

'How old are you, Mr Carrolisen?' I try another angle to try and find out the nature and extent of his difficulties.

'*Ek sal self nie kan se nie*' ['I don't know'], he replies.

'What year is it, Mr Carrolisen?'

'1954. 1954. 1954'.

Goodness me, that's way out, actually almost 20 years in fact! Does he even know what we are trying to do here today? I ask him what I asked a minute ago. He looks at me in surprise, almost as if to say 'did you ask me something?'

A very basic bedside assessment reveals that Mr Carrolisen does not have any gross perceptual difficulties. His language function as far as comprehension of simple commands, reading and repetition is preserved as well. In fact when talking to him, one does not pick up much other than that he does not initiate any conversation himself. It also becomes apparent that his concentration is quite poor.

Mr Carrolisen's apathy and slowness is palpable. Akin to refloating a heavy sunken ship bit by bit, we manage to piece together a history. Mr Carrolisen's early development was normal. He grew up in poverty, one of several siblings. Mr Carrolisen completed six years of formal schooling, before trying to find work to help feed the family. Ever since he has worked as a butcher.

'*Ek was goed*' ['I was good'], Mr Carrolisen takes me by surprise when for the first, and only time, he volunteers something spontaneously.

'I am sure you were', I reply not really knowing what else to say.

As regards his medical history, he has never sustained any head injuries of note, and has never abused any illicit substances or alcohol. In view of Mr Carrolisen's obvious cognitive impairment, his lack of formal schooling, and significant apathy, formal testing is kept to an absolute minimum. The harsh reality of the situation is that a number will be needed to evidence how the meningitis savaged his mind, and with that his ability to support his family. I need a number to apply for a *Ongskiktheids Toelaag* (disability allowance) for him. The Raven Progressive Matrices provides the 'evidence' I need to help

Mr Carrolisen in the only way I can. He scores 16, which equates to an IQ of approximately 60. The score is low enough to ensure that he receives a little bit of financial support from the government. Even though this will be a meagre amount of money, it is the only possible good I can do today. There is no realistic prospect of rehabilitation. The time for providing that will have to be saved for later, and given to those deemed to have a better prospect of benefiting from rehabilitation. It is an uncomfortable and difficult decision to make. Who gets what, and who does not. Most clinicians hate having to do it, but ultimately all have to. There simply isn't something for everybody.

I feel drained. Before writing his notes and filling in the form he needs, I stare blankly into the room, before my gaze drifts towards the chair where he sat a little bit earlier. The lingering image of Mr Carrolisen in my head takes me back to clinical training a few years earlier. The sheer volume of academic material covered perhaps made us miss the true meaning of the more philosophical and moral aspects of clinical practice surreptitiously weaved into our lectures. I now recall how in particular the principle of 'in the first instance do no harm' seemed so blatantly obvious. If only it were as simple as doing no harm. Mr Carrolisen reminds me why a lecturer at that time tried to get us to understand *something*, when he said, ideally the principle should be expanded to include 'and if possible, do some good'. I now wish that he also spoke a bit about how many times in our future careers we will find ourselves feeling deflated and disheartened by how infrequent and limited the good is we can realistically do. Nobody taught us how political systems, poverty, society and deprivation in all guises are intricately intertwined with causing and potentiating neurological disability. Nor did anyone ever mention how to fix society. A large part of the early stages of being a clinician is to get to know this strange hospital world filled with lots of badness, and occasionally, very modest doses of goodness. A succession of failures, interspersed with small miracles. Maybe academic training deliberately protected us from early exposure to reality, to prevent early disillusionment with our fate as clinicians.

5

Fate

Unpredictability in brain injury

Fate determines many things, no matter how we struggle.

(Otto Weininger)

Randomness

It is 7.30 a.m. and I am running late. The alarm clock must have lost a few minutes during the night, when Wednesday marched into Thursday. Now it is going to be a struggle to find parking at the hospital. Everything is conspiring to delay me. Even my dog is for some reason this morning slowing me down by getting in my way, and feels like a big iron ball chained to my ankles. The phone rings in a distant room while I try to find my car keys. While the 'please leave a message' soundtrack plays somewhere in the back of the house, I find my keys in the study, behind Kevin Walsh's *Understanding Brain Damage*. How annoying! But finally the show is on the road. As I look at the clock in the pickup, I realise that while it all felt very time consuming, I am only three minutes 'late' in leaving home. Just the anxiety of not wanting to be late for work. Three minutes really makes no difference, there should still be almost no traffic. The sun is not even properly up yet. But to my surprise after about four kilometres there is a short queue of cars, already starting to dam up. Looking ahead, the cars are cautiously threading their way around an obstacle in the road, in front of a stationary truck halfway into the intersection. The hospital is now in full view, just down the road. Suddenly it becomes clear that 'it' is not an obstacle, but a motor-cyclist, lying in an impossible position on the road. A person's legs simply cannot bend into that position. He (or she?) is lying very still. There is a dark pool around his yellow helmet, turning the grey tar-mac reflective black. Someone is kneeling by the body. In the distance there is the howling of a siren, and then the emergency ambulance appears from the direction of the hospital.

Or was it? I find myself struggling with my thoughts while com-pleting my journey to the hospital. Was it an accident? Or did the impersonal randomisation of daily events, or fate by another name, make this motorcyclist end up crashing into a truck, today? What if he left home 10 seconds later, or earlier? Who would then have had to take his place? Or did fate allocate, no, perhaps 'choose' him (or her) to be sacrificed today? Tomorrow it is someone else's turn. Many peo-ple, in fact. I block out any thoughts about my own 'lateness' today. To even briefly think about your own mortality or if (maybe when?) what you see every day in the building I am nearing, might visit you too, we would be too distracted by anxiety to look after those who need us to do just that. Look after *them*. Of course clinicians get sick, injured, maimed or aged and demented. However, to keep going our defence is that we are immune to these things, it happens to *other* people. Just remain on good terms with fate, lead a decent life helping your fellow humans and all will be fine. Anything other would be unfair, but I know it is not a very nice thought. However, not as disgraceful as the one that very, very briefly enters my mind as I turn off to the hospital site. I am not sure if it will be a good thing, or a bad thing, if the motorcyclist survives. It he does survive his life would have been dramatically altered by fate, bad luck or however you conceptualise it. And survivors of neurological illness and injury very often ask their clinicians why, *why* did this happen to them.

Even though we don't want to think about life-changing injury and illness too often, 'Why did this happen to me?' cannot be wished away when patients ask. I don't yet know the answer. After only a few months in this job, by now I already suspect I may never know. Does anybody? Sometimes patients ask me if they are being punished for their sins. To this I have even less of an answer. I wish I could say to them that logic then dictates that my own would earn the same payback, so that they can see their argument does not add up. But I cannot share my most personal thoughts with them. Furthermore, there are no textbooks to tell me what to do in these situations. I usually tell patients that I am first a clinician, then a scientist. Per definition then, there are more things I don't know, than know. I often get the feeling patients see this answer as a cop-out, or just plain avoiding the question. Sometimes I remind them I am not a priest. A better answer is stating the truth. What is the truth? It is that I don't know why this happened to them, but that it was not because they were 'bad'. Science certainly does not provide a *rational* answer, nor does philosophy or even religion. I may try to explain this to patients. But mostly though I say very little, delay or even defer the assessment, and instead feebly try to dry their tears, metaphorically speaking. Some things cannot be explained, least of all fate and all its many ramifications. To remain emotionally resilient, clinicians probably fairly soon in their careers have to make their peace with the limits of what can be known, explained and proven. Fate has many dresses. Who our mothers or fathers married. A bullet can ricochet off a pavement at an almost infinite number of angles, but today it's the wrong one, that one or two degrees that makes all the difference in the world. Forgetting to look left once more. Being ever so slightly late for work on a Thursday morning.

Denial

As I look at my Thursday schedule, the motorcycle accident and my ruminations about it swiftly drift away, to nowhere. Mr Danie Nel, 40 years old (case # 40), has been referred to see Dr Burger and I for a joint appointment. Or as we sometimes say, a 'two for the price of one'. Never mind the special deal. He does not look particularly keen to see us. Mr Nel is a busy man. He works full-time in financial services. Mr Nel is very neatly dressed in a grey business suit, pressed white shirt, complete with a conservative navy blue tie. His pale skin mottled red here and there with having been shaved too closely. You would feel confident with him managing your finances. No, maybe, I start to doubt my immediate impressions. He looks a bit uneasy, but perhaps I am just underestimating his unwillingness to come in for a hospital appointment in the middle of his busy day? We ask if he knew why he was referred. Mr Nel immediately denies that he has been troubled by anything and that he cannot see why his time has to be wasted in this way. I notice his sentences are a bit short, even terse, almost as if the words are ended a bit too abruptly. We probe a bit more, and he volunteers that perhaps it is for a 'routine check up or something'. His doctor did not give a full explanation. Or at least not that he can recall. Mr Nel looks almost impenetrable. There is a real sense that he wishes us to get on with the consultation as quickly as possible, so that he can go back to work. He is continually looking towards the window, almost as if every few seconds he is checking if his car is still parked in the same place. Maybe he just wants to escape.

86

The room is not peaceful. Something else is noticeable as well now. Mr Nel's movements do not exactly flow smoothly. Every few seconds Mr Nel gives a little shrug with his shoulders and neck, and then in the same movement pushes his spectacles back up the bridge of his nose. It is actually quite distracting, is he aware of it? The movement resembles an uncoordinated, slithery pre-pounce of a snake when sneaking up on an unsuspecting prey, but with the symmetry of movement completely lost. He is also quite slow generally. The more I look, the more I realise the 'adjustment of his spectacles', as well as the rest of the movement, is involuntary. It is completely random, left or right, which arm is involved in the 'adjustment'. Like something is misfiring. A twitch that has to be hidden. It is now more obvious that his speech is affected also. Listening carefully, Mr Nel sounds like someone who has just returned from a visit to the dentist. Sounding ever so slightly slurred while the effects of the injection is taking its time wearing off. And in all of this, he is clearly still keen for us to finish our assessment as soon as possible. But surely he must be aware that something is not quite right with his motor functions? It must drive him mad, and I find myself wondering if it affects his sleep. Obviously a person cannot sleep that well if they twitch and writhe all the time?

Dr Burger starts with doing a standard neuropsychiatry assessment. After striking a blank while enquiring about current complaints and problems, Dr Burger instead starts to go over Mr Nel's history. Mr Nel is still impenetrable and provides only the most basic of histories. A brief bedside cognitive assessment follows. Mr Nel is struggling a little bit but that may well be due to his motor problems. Although someone in finance should find calculations a piece of cake? He is definitely struggling I decide when I see a bead of sweat running down his forehead, detouring to his left eyebrow. The poor man, this is not easy for him. A feeling of futility and powerlessness washes over me. Do we have to do this? For a brief moment my eyes make contact with his, and I imagine that we might have momentarily felt exactly the same thing. But I cannot be sure. I do know the background to the referral and suspected diagnosis, but was unaware if he actually had any symptoms or signs as yet. Plus of course I had up to this point never actually seen in clinical practice a patient suspected of presenting with what is thought to be the diagnosis in Mr Nel's case. His clinical history is as follows. A year or two ago (they were apparently not quite sure) Mr Nel's family gradually started to notice Mr Nel displaying out of character behaviour, for example, struggling to plan his days as regards organising appointments with clients. This in a man who was normally so conscientious and meticulous, to the point of his relatives at times thinking he was almost being obsessional about his work. They also thought that he had become more 'clumsy'. In some respects almost exactly like his mother who died a few years earlier, which they thought was as a result of 'dementia'. Dr Burger though felt the comprehensive family tree pointed to a specific genetic disorder.

Mr Nel is now shifting around in his chair, looking even more uncomfortable with each creak the cheap imitation leather of the chair makes. We are trying to explain to Mr Nel that we are worried about his presentation, and that it may be the same thing his mother had. We do not yet give it a name, as we are still not 100 per cent sure. The next step would be for him to have a brain scan and neuropsychological testing. Depending on the results of these, possibly request some other medical tests too. I explain what the neuropsychological testing entails. Mr Nel does not hide his displeasure. The more I explain what my testing will involve, the more irate and hostile he becomes. He is making no secret that in his view there is nothing wrong with him.

'I have seen the doctor, with great respect, a *real* one, and there is no point in seeing a neuropsychologist. Little tests with blocks and puzzles are for children or people with mental problems, not a successful self-employed financial advisor', he fumes.

Mr Nel's face is now even more flushed, and he is sweating profusely. But in a strange way the primary emotion he expresses is not purely about being angry. On the contrary, hidden in his narrative I can almost taste the metallic smell of fear in the stuffy consultation room. Although I am not entirely sure if it is also ours, or just his. Please, I wish I can just briefly go outside, where the sun is shining on this mild early spring day. My thoughts are drawn back into the consultation room when Mr Nel suddenly at the top of his voice shatters the silence, and agrees to attend for the planned diagnostic tests, including neuropsychological assessment. I suspect that agreeing to what we are recommending is in his view the only honourable way of getting out of the room, fast, to get the consultation over and done with so that he can escape into the air outside. I don't blame him at all.

Mr Nel keeps his word and attends for neuropsychological testing a few weeks later. The results reveal a reasonably average verbal IQ score of 95, but with clear problems evidenced by a nonverbal IQ score of 65 on the Wechsler Adult Intelligence Scale. However even an average verbal IQ score is almost certainly below what would be expected of a person functioning pre-morbidly at such a high level as Mr Nel. Furthermore, he has obvious impairment of visual-spatial functions. On a test of a person's ability to integrate fragmented visual stimuli (the Hooper Visual Organisation Test) he is severely impaired, with a score of 12½ out of 30. His poor speed under structured test conditions is almost impossible not to notice. Memory performance on the Wechsler Memory Scale is poor for both auditory and visual material, with the exception of learning and recalling a short story, where Mr Nel's performance is about average. Problems on maze learning very quickly become apparent while he completes the Porteus Maze Test. And while despite his motor difficulties he can accurately copy the Rey Complex Figure, his strategy in going about the task is poor. As a consequence, after three minutes he has almost no recall of what he had drawn.

Viewed together, the test results indicate that Mr Nel's actual measured cognitive level of functioning is much more impaired than meets the eye when just speaking to him, and encompasses a fairly wide range of neuropsychological functions. This is in fact one of a few very big advantages of performing formal neuropsychological testing – its ability to identify serious cognitive impairment hidden under a misleading layer of verbal proficiency. After an abnormal CT scan of the brain, further medical tests are performed. When the results come back, we unequivocally know that the suspected diagnosis has been confirmed. Mr Nel is due to see us for feedback soon. We will have to tell him the terrible news. Fate so had it that a long time ago his dad fell in love with a beautiful, but 'wrong' woman. They soon had a baby, a little boy. In doing so, his father unknowingly signed his son's mid-life death sentence. Unfortunately, love does not know what our choice might bring in the future. Genetics on the other hand has a somewhat better idea of what our decisions might have left waiting for us around the corner.

Choices

Dr Burger likes to remind me that he is a medical doctor, even though after a brief spell in another speciality, he made his choice and settled on psychiatry. I like to tease him that psychiatry is the same as clinical psychology, but with 'bottled psychotherapy' thrown in. He sometimes reciprocates by concluding that therefore clinical psychology is the same as psychiatry, but with 'empty bottles and stopwatches' in the place of soulless reflex hammers and stethoscopes. Today we are not bantering. He is as always very generously helping me to learn the things I need to know if I want to become a clinical neuropsychologist. We recently saw Mr Nel and are now discussing genetic disorders. Genetic disorders manifest when genes transmit all, or a significant part of the information or 'code' involved in causing subsequent abnormalities or illness. In our conversation today in particular referring to neurological illness, although naturally any body system can be affected by genetics. Huntington's Disease is a genetic disorder affecting the brain. Mr Nel has Huntington's Disease. It is autosomal dominant, with half the offspring developing the illness, usually around the fourth decade of their lives. By which time it's too late for their young children already born. Fate has already intervened. Life expectancy is reduced, Dr Burger points out. The head of the caudate nucleus is affected by the illness. After an insidious onset, patients present with choreiform movements, cognitive impairment and personality change. Often subtle cognitive impairment and personality changes can precede the abnormal movements and more severe cognitive impairment. There is no treatment and the outlook is very bleak for patients and their families. Patients' children may themselves present with the illness when they are adults. This part of the bad news is especially difficult to communicate to patients, as witnessed during our follow-up with Mr Nel. Many other conditions, including some of the core psychiatric illnesses, while not necessarily exclusively hereditary, are still thought to have a genetic component necessary for their manifestation in actual or assumed brain pathology, in combination with other factors, for example, environmental or even psychological.

While the brain dominates much of neurology and the genetic disorders affecting it are of considerable interest to both neurology and neuropsychiatry, it does not have a total monopoly on who a hospital clinical neuropsychologist might be asked to see. Take Miss Fatima Januarie (case # 44), 24 years old. She has come down from neurology, with the help of a porter to push her rickety wheelchair and to make sure she does not get lost in the hospital. Miss Januarie can stand only with assistance, for a short period only, before having to precariously lower herself back into her wheelchair. Clinical bedside evaluation shows that she has poor fine motor coordination and reduced verbal fluency. Nevertheless she can still perform more automatic motor tasks such as writing. Something more novel, in this case copying a figure, throws her off course and she struggles because of her motor difficulties. Miss Januarie has been diagnosed as suffering from Friedreich's Ataxia. Friedreich's Ataxia does not affect the brain itself though, and cognitive impairment is usually not suspected as being part of the clinical picture. The manifestation of the illness is in the spine. Miss Januarie has been referred for cognitive testing. On this occasion though the purpose of psychometric testing is to determine her general intellectual ability in view of decisions potentially involving making choices regarding her future care needs, rather than a full neuropsychological testing.

As is often the case, there are additional complexities to manage today. Miss Januarie is from a very deprived socio-economic background. She has had almost no formal schooling. I start with administering a five subtest short Wechsler Adult Intelligence Scale. At least I am able to test her in her first language. There are more problems. The norms for the local version of the Wechsler Adult Intelligence Scale are very suspect, and for swathes of the population, non-existent. Bearing all this in mind, Miss Januarie's performance translates into a prorated IQ of 50, which just does not feel congruent with how she presents clinically. I decide to do a Raven Progressive Matrices as well. Miss Januarie scores 23, equating to an IQ of approximately 70. I decide to put my faith in the score produced by the Raven. Otherwise her ability to make her own decisions might be questioned, and as a consequence ignored. I think she deserves at least some say regarding the care options for her dreadful illness.

Faith

This morning a sermon is in full swing in the basement. Pastor Soloman Gabriels (case # 122) is fully charged, and speaks non-stop about the church and all its blessings. He is 44 years old, and known to me. I saw him four months ago. Here in our clinic he is on long-term review so that we can keep an eye on him for possible changes in his clinical presentation. He has epilepsy. His ictal presentation manifests with aphasia and visual hallucinations. Returning to the here and now, today there is a non-stop torrent of sin, good deeds and the power of belief bubbling from his mouth, and bouncing off the sinful walls of the consultation room. I have to stem this energetic flow before I can do a Mini Mental State Examination. The worst strategy is to try and interrupt patients. Much more productive is to just keep quiet, listen out the story or rant, and patiently wait. Sure enough, Pastor Gabriels finally spontaneously runs out of charge, and the pace changes. Sanity returns, the sounds of the dull questions and tasks from the Mini Mental now fill the room. He performs dismally, managing a score of only 17 out of 30. Pastor Gabriels's new learning and retention, or short-term memory, is particularly poor. I do a bit more testing, while intermittently, like spikes reducing in magnitude over time on an EEG, he surreptitiously tries to convince me to become a better man. Pastor Gabriels does not realise that this may require a divine miracle. A sense of guilt suddenly comes over me. What if I were him? I hope to be forgiven as I religiously pay my dues for everything bad out there, here, in this building of newly born, rescued, lost and dead souls. Looking down at the numbers in front of me, while there might be hope for some, in his case faith has failed. Pastor Gabriels's cognition cannot be saved anymore. His Wechsler Adult Intelligence Scale short form (five subtests) prorated IQ score is 65. And while he can copy the Rey Complex Figure to a good standard in anyone's currency (percentile 80), his memory scores show how brutally wasted his mind is, with performances equal to the first percentile on both associative learning and visual reproduction.

After the testing is completed, Pastor Gabriels leaves me with a few more pearls of wisdom on how to secure a good life, and returns to his ward on the eighth floor. But somehow although he has left the consultation room he also stays here with me in the basement, swirling around my mind. He is a very interesting patient. I know from Dr Burger that with temporal lobe epilepsy, there can sometimes, in addition to severe memory problems also be unusual personality phenomena. Including hyper-religiosity. What I cannot figure out though, is why his language functions have been affected. Why does he have an aphasia? Of course after several months in this job I completely get it that in a right-handed man such as Pastor Gabriels, who has a left temporal lobe epileptogenic focus, the presentation will almost certainly include memory and language problems. But why, in a *pastor*, why on earth did fate choose *language* to be impaired in this poor man? It feels a bit, well, cruel. Bizarrely, he does not appear to view it that way. Pastor Gabriels is very cheerful every time I see him, completely focused on 'being good', and joyfully encouraging others to be too. His memory and language might have failed him, but his faith has not. He blames nobody, and nothing, for his impairments which must be particularly disabling for a man of the cloth, religion. I wonder then, if in this respect he is a better person than most? Are we really just synapses? The next patient is already here, and I dispassionately remind myself that there are only so many lobes in the brain, hence the odds are against huge randomness of lesion sites. And his pre-morbid personality of course also explains why he is so sanguine about his fate. It is time to move on from the philosophical debate about the existence of a god, punishment, fate and belief, to the next patient. But still . . .

Timing

The tired looking clock on the wall of the office where the unit's appointments book is kept, solemnly reminds everyone they are late. My next patient is Mr Gatiep Conradson (case # 81). Mr Conradson is wearing bright trousers, but nothing compared to the contrasting, luminous Hawaiian shirt that stops you in your tracks. I am slightly bemused and ponder that if ever trousers violently clashed with a shirt, this is it. He looks a bit grumpy that I went over the appointment time with the previous patient, Pastor Gabriels. If only he knows how parched I am, just lusting after a coffee, anything with caffeine in it in fact! But I am wrong. I introduce myself, and quickly learn that Mr Conradson, totally incongruous to his attire is as apathetic and as lacking in spark as can be. Mr Conradson is 30 years old, and has been referred to our clinic by one of the psychiatrists in outpatients. Out of the corner of my eye I become aware of Mr Conradson's kaleidoscopic outfit again. Given his attire he probably has a diagnosis of something like mania or bipolar disorder. But I better have a look at what the referral is actually all about before jumping to such conclusions. Referrals for neuropsychological testing from psychiatry can be complex to figure out. A quick read over the short referral form and halfway down the page I instantaneously forget about my fatigue and thirst. Thank heavens I did not sneak away for a coffee and make him wait even longer. Simultaneously my bemusement with his outfit evaporates. I blink and look back at the referral. 'Mr Conradson has recently murdered his wife'. The sentence, black on white, cannot be shorter, or more unequivocal. What will his story bring, what are the details of the history lurking in there? Will he even be willing to tell?

Of course he does. That is why he is here, he knows that, I know it, and we both *expect* me to ask. That is why I am here. To ask, and I do. He does not flinch when the question comes, doesn't even bat an eyelid. In fact, he does not blink much at all, hardly ever breaks eye contact. I notice that where the bright shirt's sleeve ends, he has a short linear scar on his right upper arm, like something had scratched him. Mr Conradson tells me he stabbed her. In the chest and neck. About some minor domestic agreement, so mundane it makes it difficult to recall. He hides nothing from me. Talks in a monotone voice, sounding completely at odds with the content of what he is conveying. There is no life in his opaque eyes. Whatever gives us our animatedness, expression of our feelings, has been extinguished. He describes the killing like one would when mentioning having made porridge for breakfast this morning. He is well, *unconcerned*, and detached, whereas I would have expected someone to at least rationalise, deny, defend or explain their actions. Or maybe show remorse. Fortunately, I don't have to drill down on this aspect – it's probably for the lawyers, prosecution and ultimately the courts to deal with that side of things. Way above a clinician's pay grade. Although revulsed by what I hear Mr Conradson telling me, I have to disentangle myself from what he has done and provide a clinical neuropsychology opinion. Which seems to be a timely mental reminder that the assessment, including a full history, and most likely testing will all need to be completed. It's not going to be a quick assessment. We make a start with his early development, before going over his social and medical history.

Mr Conradson was born in the nearby sandy, windy, flatlands, known to be notorious ganglands. A huge sprawl of socio-economic deprivation and danger encircling the hospital. He tells me that he does not think there were problems with his birth and early development. At least, his mother never told him there were. Today no relative is attending to help me with obtaining a collateral history. He describes terrible schooling, compliments of the unconscionable symbiosis of apartheid, poverty and deprivation. Mr Conradson had a total of six years of poor quality schooling. He left school early, and has worked as a manual labourer on and off. Unfortunately his history mirrors those of millions of others in the land. Like many, to block out the terrible life they received as a result of an insane ideological system, he also drifted into 'street medicine' – cannabis, mandrax, alcohol, anything to give the mind a temporary passport out of hell. With an abundance of 'street-corner pharmacies' all too willing to do business, he had no problems with access. Despite his habit, he earned just enough money to survive. Survive, but nothing more. That was his life. Until fate determined that the speed of the *bakkie* (a small pickup truck) he was a passenger on at the back of, was exactly right when combined with the speed and trajectory of the brick hurled at them by some *skollies* (thugs) standing next to the road, to miss all his fellow labourers, and hit him against his left eye. Mr Conradson was critically injured. He remained unconscious for three months. No, it's not a typo, three months, still clearly visible in my own handwriting scribbled hastily in the notebook two and half decades ago. And yes, he eventually woke up, that's why he is here today, and why he needs to be tested also.

After completing his history, formal neuropsychological testing is completed. Mr Conradson is fully collaborative. With time ticking on, I notice that I have warmed a lot to him. Mr Conradson scores a prorated IQ of 91 on a shortened Wechsler Adult Intelligence Scale. On the Wechsler Memory Scale, he scores at percentile 10 for associative learning, percentile 12 for logical memory, and percentile 74 for visual reproduction. The Rey Auditory Verbal Learning Test shows percentiles 8, 3, 1, 1, 1, and 1 for learning and recall. The memory test results fits left hemisphere damage secondary to a severe traumatic brain injury, in a right-hander. He can only list 12 words on the Word Naming Test, whereas the norm would be 28 words per minute. He scores 27½ out of 30 on the Hooper Visual Organisation Test, a normal performance. The Rey Complex Figure Test gives him no problems, with a copy performance of percentile 99 and recall after 30 minutes, equalling percentile 75. The Porteus Maze Mr Conradson also completes with ease. But then on the next test he suddenly flounders. The Austin Maze is totally beyond him, reflected in his performance of: 23, 22, 25, 17, 22, 46, 34, 16, 20, 20, 13, 14, 9, 9, 15 – discontinued. Taken together, it is reasonably clear that Mr Conradson has the classic neuropsychological profile of severe traumatic brain injury, comprising executive impairments coupled with largely unilateral memory problems. I am thankful that I am not the judge. From a purely neuropsychological point of view anyone should be able to see his vulnerabilities. But he did take a life. I am very relieved I don't have to choose who I have compassion with, and who not, based on their behaviours. I am free to feel intensely sad for him and his dead wife. Silence fills the office while I think over all of this.

The silence also means that Mr Conradson will leave my office in a minute or so, we are done. However, there is still one mystery to be solved. Something I have not so far come across in my work. I thought Dr Burger said that in most forms of brain injury the length of period of unconsciousness was related to mortality, and that very few people regained consciousness after four weeks. And that those few who did, were almost always very severely and quite obviously physically and mentally disabled.

'When you were unconscious for so long, Mr Conradson . . .' I don't quite manage to formulate the question.

I am experiencing a mixture of sorrow and curiosity as regards what his phenomenological experience of what *happened* to him for these three months might be. Even though obviously from a scientific perspective he would not be able to physically remember anything. Still, three months is a hell of a long time to be unconscious, survive, be left with no physical impairments, and only a few specific cognitive problems.

For the first time Mr Conradson smiles at me, although very slightly, when he hears my question.

'I went to heaven', he immediately beams, showing a bit of emotion for the first time.

What, I think, but don't say.

'Tell me what it was like?' I hesitantly ask, not being sure exactly what I am supposed to ask. Clinical training did not prepare me for this.

'Heaven?'

'Whatever. Just try to tell me', I reply.

'The grass was very green. Lots of little white lambs hopping about. I can remember it vividly. Then one day I woke up, just like you would from a deep sleep', he says, looking tranquil.

After fate sent a brick on an uninterrupted path that put him to sleep, and then decided to wake him up again, life went from bad to much worse. Because fate ultimately did achieve a kill through that flying brick. But someone else.

Interrupted

One of the neurologists from Dr Carstens' unit, Dr Fourie, immediately recognised what he was looking at. What he saw earlier this week, was a lady, Mrs Dora Ismail (case # 3), 63 years old, who was presenting with severe slowness. But there was more to her slowness than just a reduction in the speed of her walking. She also had a broad-based gait, was incontinent of urine, cognitively impaired, and yes, slow not only walking but in most of her movements. Dr Fourie explained what causes her symptoms and signs. Mrs Ismail had been diagnosed with Normal Pressure Hydrocephalus. Essentially Normal Pressure Hydrocephalus is due to the build-up of pressure due to problems with the fluid circulating around the brain, and the caverns inside it. Problems might be caused by blockages, for example, third ventricle tumours, or overproduction of fluid by the choroid plexus. Some clinicians remember the condition by the acronym 'WWW' – weird, wet, and wide, Dr Fourie told me. Since he saw her, they have confirmed the diagnosis by measuring the pressure created by her cerebrospinal fluid. Seeing my obvious astonishment upon hearing this, he explained that it is done by inserting a needle into the base of a patient's spine, by the *cauda equina*, or horse's tail. Now the plan is to have her cognition tested for a baseline, and then drain some of her cerebrospinal fluid soon after, probably early the next day. Thereafter Dr Fourie would like to me to retest her cognition within hours after the drainage. This is why Mrs Ismail finds herself in my office at the moment, after our interminably slow walk down the passage. A really slow walk, running out of small talk about one-tenth of the total walking distance to my office.

The impression of profound slowness continues during the initial brief clinical assessment. Every movement of Mrs Ismail looks like an incongruous stage performance, like a live show's slow-motion playback of a complex script with very little dialogue. To add to the strangeness of what occurs in front of me, Mrs Ismail is wearing hospital pyjamas, during the midday heat on a blazingly sunny day. She tells me she is exhausted and has just gotten up from bed, sounding like she was woken at the crack of dawn for her neuropsychology appointment. Her processing speed is effortful and slow. I explain the nature of the tests, and also that I will retest her in a couple of days after the doctors have drained some fluid from her back. She looks at me with mournful, exhausted empty eyes and simply states:

'Yes'.

The way she says it suggests she doesn't know what it is all about, but is too tired or frightened to think about it. Mrs Ismail has resigned herself to her fate here in the hospital. I wish I could comfort her. Tell her everything will be fine. Even though I strongly suspect it won't be. Instead of trying to make her feel better, I start testing her to obtain a pre-drainage baseline. A shortened Wechsler Adult Intelligence Scale yields a prorated IQ score equal to 88. She takes ages with Trail Making Test trail A, 245 seconds. Her memory is impaired on the Wechsler Memory Scale for logical memory as well as visual reproduction. She scores a raw score of 15½ on the Rey Complex Figure (copying), and takes 676 seconds. Percentiles might hide subtle changes, and documenting the raw scores would be better here. I also decide that timing of the Rey would be an additional, easy to repeat, measure of her psychomotor speed. After a few other short tests, Mrs Ismail goes back to the ward.

Two days later Mrs Ismail is back. I ask her how she has been since I last saw her. She looks slightly surprised, and looks at me quizzically. Her eyes narrow with concentration as she scans my face up and down with her dark brown eyes, frowning with deep confused furrows etched on her forehead. She does not remember ever meeting me, nor even having been to this part of the hospital. Mrs Ismail also does not have any idea that she has had very recent surgery when I explain that I need to retest her after the 'operation' on her back. That swings it for me, and I decide not to worry too much about equivalent form tests to minimise practice effects. Nevertheless I double check when I take out the first subtests, by asking if she had ever seen something like these. She scratches her head as if there is an invisible itch, thinks deeply, and then slowly replies she has never seen them before. I ask if she is OK. Mrs Ismail says she just has a headache, which I recall from Dr Fourie's explanation is a common side effect 24 to 48 hours after having had cerebrospinal fluid drained. While I am testing her, I become aware of how tense my neck, shoulders and abdominal muscles feel. And

100

my heart is beating a bit too fast. It is because I so desperately want her to do better, I realise. I am anxious because if her cognition improves on testing, plus if there is clinical improvement, then she will receive a shunt. I feel intensely sorry for Mrs Ismail. Dr Fourie explained to me that fitting a shunt is basically an operation where a small pipe (like a 'little straw', in his words) is inserted into a ventricle of the brain to continuously drain excess cerebrospinal fluid into the abdominal cavity, thus reducing the pressure causing a patient's 'WWW' symptoms.

To my relief qualitative observation is suggesting the testing is going better than two days ago. I am so pleased with Mrs Ismail's performance, it feels like disaster is going to be averted. I hold my breath when she copies the Rey Complex Figure. I score the test as we go along. She takes only 402 seconds this time, and achieves 29 (out of 36). I smile at her, and feel like I can hug her. But I do nothing of the kind, and continue to encourage her to do her best on every test. On Trail Making Test trail A she takes only 89 seconds this time, which to my relief is a dramatic improvement. One of her Wechsler Adult Intelligence Scale subtests lifts one standard deviation. On the Wechsler Memory Scale, only her logical memory score improves, but at least very robustly so. The remainder of her tests and subtests depressingly remain the same or show small, modest or insignificant gains. I tell her she has done well, and send her back to the ward. As she leaves she manages to quietly thank me, and then says goodbye. I smile at her and tell her I hope that she gets well soon. Later that week it transpires her improvement post-draining was deemed dramatic enough to be offered shunting. This time fate's course was intercepted. It is after all possible! Or is it? When I ask a few weeks later what happened to her, when she was due for post-shunting neuropsychological testing and did not keep her appointment, I hear that she failed to attend for the operation. Lost to follow-up. This is bad news, really bad news. Hope has evaporated with her not attending. Perhaps fate was interrupted, but not intercepted.

Hope

While I wait for Dr Burger to meet me at my house after work so we can go for a run, the television is on in the background. In the distance I hear the important news. I look around the corner, into the room where the television is. Something amazing happened in a faraway country with terrible weather. I have never been there, not set eyes on the landscape. But the news is there for all to see, the unmistakable green upholstered wooden benches, the magnificent old building. Nelson Mandela is in London and has addressed the UK parliament. It is a message of hope, irrespective of the actual content. I go back to the front door and my thoughts start to mix with the background soundtrack of the television, merging into one narrative, indistinguishable as regards who is saying or thinking what. Maybe the supposedly inevitable fate of South Africa is gradually, step by step being intercepted? We all hope in our hearts that is doesn't turn out to be an interruption. Or is there no point in worrying and was fate predetermined hundreds of years ago? Some say we should pray for the country, for its people. Bishop Desmond Tutu reminds us that our humanity is through others, *ubuntu*. He is right about that, certainly here in the hospital. Despite the sea of violence surrounding and spilling into the hospital like letters being posted, requesting a repair of the impossible, his message still brings hope. It is not always clear what clinicians should believe in. On one hand we are scientists, but on the other we are practitioners working with patients who hardly ever neatly fit the pictures painted in textbooks and research papers. Maybe one way to look at it is that being a clinician requires thinking constituting a mix of science, philosophy, spirituality, compassion and intuition. Plus a hefty dose of hope, for when there is very little else to counter fate.

I lock the front door and go and sit outside in the sun while I wait for Dr Burger. My thoughts return, now a mix of the day, the news and patients I have seen over the past few weeks. Fate and ethics are not always comfortable bedfellows in the clinical professions.

Too much belief in fate, or determinism and too little hope remains. Being too deterministic can also close our eyes to seeing the exception, those patients who don't fit what is currently known. For example, Mr Conradson, who was unconscious for 'far too long' to have survived. On the other hand, too much belief, and . . . well, I am not so sure of that one. If we could explain everything, there would be no science. The daily reality of science here in this ugly building is becoming more brutal every day. Most things we cannot cure, or make significantly better, even if we had tons of resources and money. With the little we have there are nevertheless a few things we can give our patients. We know the cost of these consumables, and the time units required to administer patient contacts. On some of the things we give our patients though a price cannot be calculated. Hope has no price code, and appears in no government catalogue for ordering health equipment and products. It is a precious commodity. Hope should almost never be destroyed. Caring unconditionally for others, without judging them or how they got to where they are is part of humanity, *ubuntu*, and ultimately the creation of hope. To do otherwise will result in all warmth dissipating into the lifeless pores of the bricks and cement of the hospital.

'Hey, are you asleep or something?' I suddenly hear Dr Burger announce his arrival from the bottom of the driveway.

'No, just hoping to catch up on some daydreaming while waiting for the eternally lost and late! Come on Tomas, let's go another way tonight. We need a new route. Otherwise we will become shockingly set in our ways'.

6

Shock

Epilepsy and pseudo-seizures

It's too much like lightning, which flashes and then disappears
before you can say, it's lightning.

(William Shakespeare, *Romeo and Juliet*)

Discharge

On the way up to the neurology ward, just as I reach the ground
floor lifts, there is the distant sounds of a commotion outside. The air
is filled with the hysterical barking of dogs, dull coughs of gunshots
and high-pitched shouting drifting into the corridors of the hospital.

Amamandla! (power!). Not too long after, the crowd I could hear in the distance, chaotically spills into the hospital corridors. The political situation is still electric, tense and the feeling that something is about to change hangs thick in the air. Violence suddenly spikes and then slowly subsides, its chaotic graph difficult to follow. The violent spikes are followed by deep valleys of confusion, irritability, inertia and despair. As the wave of the crowd washes past me, I can smell their fear and anger. One of the crowd, a young man, is directly in front of me.

Our eyes meet, and I ask: '*Hei my bra, wat is aan die gang?*' ['Hey brother, what's happening?']

'*Ons was buite om te se wat ons pla, toe skielik kom die boere in hulle vans, met guns en honde! Toe hardloop ons almal weg*' ['We were airing our grievances outside, when suddenly the police arrived in their vehicles, with guns and dogs, and now we are all running away'], he shouts excitedly.

The crowd are fleeing from the police, into the hospital, after a peaceful protest in the car park outside unexpectedly discharged into chaos and confusion. Then suddenly they are gone, and it is quiet again. As if nothing ever happened. The unease does not go away though. A ping pierces the quiet to remind me I was on my way somewhere. Oh yes, neurology.

For what feels like the thousandth time already, I wearily push open the double doors and enter the neurology ward. I tell the ward sister that I have come to see Miss Helena Simpson (case # 35). Today it feels as if the excessive use of dull green (and in some places a dirty yellow coloured) vinyl on the floors and walls make the passages look even more depressing than usual. Maybe the unexpected commotion on the way up unsettled me. The sister gives me a disinterested look and with a morose wave of her left arm directs me to the bay where Miss Simpson's bed is. The bay is the third to my left, and her bed is in the right-hand corner, by the window. Miss Simpson is laying on her tummy. A child-like outline of a little figure under the white sheet, with her head turned towards the window, away from me. I cannot see her face. Maybe she is sleeping. I move quietly and close the curtains around her bed in a pathetic gesture to create some privacy. Then there is nothing else to do but introduce myself. Miss Simpson turns around slowly. I am momentarily caught completely off guard, and take an involuntary small step backwards. Miss Simpson is totally, unimaginably beautiful. She has an angelic face, with surfer's golden blonde hair against her pale skin, her mouth a perfect mirror of a wave. But somehow she looks much younger than her 22 years, appearing more like a child. Her eyes are a luminous deep blue colour, exquisite, but at the same time with something quite unsettling about them. Like looking into a beautiful turquoise lake taken from a postcard, the colour of the water unfathomable, or perhaps about to foam. It is impossible to imagine what lies at its depths.

While wishing the curtains were weaved from bricks, I start by asking Miss Simpson what the matter was, why she came to hospital. She does not say much. Her eyes are overflowing with frustration. I quickly pick up on the fact that she is dysphasic. Due to her difficulty speaking, she can manage no more than a few single words when trying to tell me something, and only with considerable effort. Her words are enough though to convey that she knows what is wrong with her, how her illness has destroyed her life. A very basic, short bedside cognitive testing plus a few selected, more portable formal neuropsychological tests confirms her profound difficulty with productive speech. Her attention is poor, but she bravely puts what looks like herculean effort into the memory testing requested by the neurosurgeons. And all the time her blue eyes checking with me if she had done OK, following every move I make, seeking reassurance. Every time she looks at me, it feels as if my heart is being shocked with an electrical probe. Despite her supreme effort it does not look good. Both visual and verbal memory on the Wechsler Memory Scale are below the second percentile. She can list 16 random words, but formulating a coherent sentence is almost beyond her. Miss Simpson takes 28 minutes to complete the Raven Progressive Matrices test, achieving a score of 33. Now I also almost cannot put a sentence together, because I simply don't know what to say to her. I thank her for her time, and for trying her best. Turning around, I notice for the first time she has a little dimple in one cheek. I think she is trying to say thank you for seeing her, but cannot be sure. I quickly leave the ward, but feel her hopeful gaze is following me. Today I give the lift down a miss and take the long and lonely route via the bare cement staircase, feeling drained. The image of her face remains in my head, the echo of my steps her faint voice.

Combining various sources of information, it transpires that Miss Simpson's history is as follows. Her birth and early development were unremarkable. She grew up in a pretty little town on the coast, a few hours away by road from the city where our hospital is located. According to her mother, Miss Simpson learned to crawl, walk and talk earlier than the majority of her peers. Both her parents work, and they are financially relatively well off. She was a healthy, active child, always on the go. Her motor development was good, and she was excellent at running and playing ball sports. Picked up the rules of new games very easily. Once Miss Simpson started primary school, it quickly became apparent that she was not only very sporty, but also an intellectually gifted child. She was exceptional in all academic areas, but in particular as regards maths, English and music. At a young age she could already play the piano to a very high standard. But then, aged 10, catastrophe strikes. Miss Simpson has a major seizure while at school. And several more over the following weeks. After medical investigations, a diagnosis of temporal lobe epilepsy is made. Her parents are beside themselves. The unthinkable has happened to their beautiful, special child. They put all their faith in the doctor who sees her at the local hospital. Anticonvulsant medication is started, and the seizures reduce in frequency and intensity. Miss Simpson manages to return to school. But then after a few months the seizures come back with a vengeance. An increase in the dosage of her medication has no real effect on the frequency, nor intensity of her seizures. It feels like an unbearably cruel fate that their world has collapsed again.

Things become desperate as Miss Simpson's seizures gradually spin out of control and one day she goes into status. It's an experience beyond terror. Prolonged violent seizures, appearing unstoppable. Her family doctor cannot manage her epilepsy anymore, and refers her to a specialist. The neurologist at a bigger hospital in the next large town tries changing her medication, but this does not improve matters at all. Miss Simpson is becoming increasingly vulnerable to anoxic brain damage during her prolonged seizures. Her neurologist reluctantly realises that her seizures are uncontrollable, and that all known pharmacological options have now been tried. As a neurologist, she knows there is now only one, not to be taken lightly, option left. Two years after the first seizure she decides Miss Simpson needs to be referred to a tertiary university hospital for another specialist opinion. After extensive assessment and monitoring at the specialist unit, she is identified as a potential candidate for epilepsy surgery. Miss Simpson and her family agonise over the decision, their terror consuming them every hour, before they finally make what is an unimaginably difficult decision. A left temporal lobectomy is to be performed in an attempt to remove the focus of her seizures. The surgeon explains to them that this operation entails opening their daughter's head in the area above her left ear, and then cutting away some of the surface (cortex) of the brain (temporal lobe) directly underneath. Her parents pray that she will not die. Most people fear brain surgery as the ultimate no man's land, from where not everybody returns alive, or the same. Precision-engineered metal entering the soul. Miss Simpson and her parents are no different in this regard.

After the surgery, they anxiously wait by her bed. Mr and Mrs Simpson drown in their own emotions when their daughter starts to wake up. A miracle has happened! But as the hours pass, the veil of post-surgery delirium is lifted to reveal what is really left. With each new day, it becomes clearer that Miss Simpson woke up different. Altered at her core as regards who she was and could have been had it not been for her horrible illness. Prior to the surgery Miss Simpson was right-handed. Surgery unfortunately left her language functions compromised. The focus of necrotic tissue was more extensive than thought from pre-surgery neuro-imaging. As a consequence more brain tissue than planned had to be removed. After discharge from hospital, Miss Simpson bravely tries to fight her illness. Through sheer determination she learns to write reasonably well with her left hand. Post-surgery the seizures appear to be much better controlled taking less medication, with fewer, less intense attacks occurring. Things are looking a bit more optimistic, and she is able to participate in some pleasurable activities again. Playing the piano becomes her escape. Her parents buy an old, beautiful piano for her. The sounds of her bringing back to life the old piano, playing joyfully, sometimes fluently, sometimes hesitantly, fills the house, and makes it a calmer place to be in again. Her parents return to work. Miss Simpson starts attending school again, in a special class. She cannot participate in sport anymore. Then a few years later, unexpectedly her seizures worsen again, and eventually the terrifying episodes of status return. Miss Simpson is admitted to our hospital. Tragedy looks set to stay. Miss Simpson is running out of all options, and it looks like nobody can make her better. Her fate is inevitable. Perhaps that is what I saw in her beautiful eyes. The only thing that remains is her story. I keep it secure from fading away, and carry it with me everywhere. Clinicians are allowed to cry only when they are alone.

Magic

Dr Carstens never carries a stethoscope. 'It's for new house doctors', he laughs when asked.

Dr Carstens has a special interest in epilepsy. You see, for him the head is the thing, not the heart. With his slightly wild, dark eyes and black goatee, he looks like he could perform magic if he had a wand, but he only has a reflex hammer. Even though he wears a white coat, miracles are beyond him. Over time he tells me a bit more about this terrifying neurological condition, epilepsy. It is all about electricity, really, he makes me believe. A seizure is a change in behaviour stemming directly from a sudden, increased and abnormal electrical discharge from within the brain's cells (neurons). Epilepsy is diagnosed where a patient has more than two recurring seizures. Many conditions can cause seizures, for example, toxins, alcohol and drug abuse or sudden withdrawal from drugs or alcohol, scarring of brain tissue, the presence of objects such as bone fragments or metal projectiles inside the brain tissue, high fever and brain infections among many others. Some forms of epilepsy are idiopathic, meaning of no known origin or aetiology, Dr Carstens explains. Epilepsy is broadly divided into constituting focal or generalised seizures, and according to their aetiology. There are two main types of seizures. Partial seizures result from a focal disturbance in the brain, whereas generalised seizures involve most of, or the entire brain. For example, complex partial seizure presenting with an altered level of consciousness may represent the start of an attack, and then progress into secondary generalised seizures producing tonic-clonic muscle contractions. On the other hand, *petit mal* attacks are absence spells, while primary generalised seizure commence in both hemispheres, or most of the brain right from the start of the attack. The fact that everything is *invisible*, magically inside the brain, further stimulates my curiosity.

I ask Dr Carstens how epilepsy is diagnosed, if there is a blood test or special brain scan or something that can be used to identify it. His face lights up. The choice among special investigations is still the Electro Encephalogram or 'EEG' for short, he says. This measures electrical activity at the surface of the head, indicative of brain functioning underneath. He dismisses blood tests, but says the physician can ask for prolactin levels if the seizure occurred very recently. But EEG is clearly his thing. Interestingly, later I learn even more about electricity and the brain when Dr Carstens invites me to be a participant in his research. Essentially what my participation entails is that he administers small shocks to the scalp directly above the motor cortex until he finds the area of the thumb within the homunculus. I am not sure of the exact details of what he is researching, but am astonished to see my thumb twitch when finally receiving the 'on target' shock. Moving, *against my will*. For the first time I can understand why ancient cultures might have postulated that demons or evil spirits had invaded the person who suffered from 'fits'. It sort of feels like that! Dr Carstens tells me a bit more about EEGs, their patterns, what these might mean, as well as other stuff, but most of it goes over my head. It's a relief when he emphasises that epilepsy is actually a clinical diagnosis, and that EEG is more of a confirmatory tool. A normal EEG does not rule out seizures. Well, in that case, how useful are they then, or are other things more important?

Dr Carstens continues and tells me that the most important thing is to observe a seizure, or alternatively, to have a reliable observer report from someone who has witnessed a recent seizure in a given patient. This is easy enough to remember. However, something else remains unclear.

'So tell me, Johan, what can a clinical neuropsychologist really contribute to the care of patients with epilepsy?'

'Ah, that's a good one. It is very important to the neurosurgeons to know about the exact lateralisation of cognitive functions in their patients, before they operate'.

'Sure, in theory I see where you are going. Visual memory in the right hemisphere, verbal in the left. Provided they are right-handed, of course. But it is not an exact science, you know Johan'.

'Well, you should go and read up about a famous case, HM he was. You are right though. Sort of. Hemispheral representation of memory can be very tricky. Nowadays a special test, the Wada test, using a drug called sodium amytal to knock out one hemisphere, is done pre-neurosurgery. Simultaneously, and very quickly, while in theatre and the drug still has its effect, cognitive testing is performed. We are talking two to three minutes'.

'Really?' I ask, trying to visualise what he has just said.

'Oh yes. Which reminds me, at some point in the future we need to train you up to do the cognitive testing which is part of the Wada test. Also, coming back to epilepsy care, the neuropsychologist helps with serial testing, looking for decline, medication side-effects, you know, all that stuff. And to help them understand the nature of their diagnoses. I could go on forever, but must go now', he says while starting to walk towards the double doors exiting the neurology ward.

Dr Carstens, while not a magician, is an excellent teacher.

Lessons

'I wanted to teach him a lesson', Mr Klaas Pretorius (case # 72) replies in a rather matter of fact fashion.

Somewhat naively I have just asked him why he assaulted his fellow worker. And why so badly, in response to what sounds like by all accounts was a minor provocation. Mr Pretorius is 35 years old, not a good looking man, unsmiling, the scars on his face a rough monument to a distant episode of bad chickenpox. There is something menacing about him. His pristine white shirt is uncomfortably neatly ironed. A mix of coffee, cigarettes and mouthwash hang faintly in the air. Mr Pretorius has been referred to us by the medical director of the institution where he is employed. It is also not the first time he has assaulted someone. For now, it's best to leave the probing about the assault. I can ask more about the event later, if there is any time left. Just in case he becomes irritated. Plus I am not the judge of his behaviour, no, I have been asked to judge his cognition, by performing objective, standardised neuropsychological tests. Right now, taking a history is likely to be less provocative than asking him why he punched so and so. A quick look at his medical summary reveals that Mr Pretorius is in fact well known to our hospital. He is being monitored here for his epilepsy. The summary makes clear that he has suffered from this since the age of 8 months old, after he sustained a bad head injury when he was only 3 months old. I look up from the papers in front of me. Oh, no, that's a dreadful thing to happen to a baby. He almost certainly has a learning difficulty. As a consequence formal neuropsychological testing is likely to add very little to his management, I think by myself as I break eye contact with him and pretend to continue reading the summary, which I already have finished reading. Twice.

'Did you go to school, Mr Pretorius?' I get straight to the point. Time is precious.

Mr Pretorius's head jerks up, looks at me with icy contempt in his green eyes. He folds his arms in a slow, deliberate fashion.

'I passed matric, and well, thank you very much for asking', Mr Pretorius sarcastically spits the words out at me, almost spelling out the individual letters of the word 'matric'.

I feel ashamed of myself. He has just taught me a valuable lesson (for the hundredth time, at least) about not making assumptions about patients. Every brain is the same, but at the same time different. And to remember the role of neuro-plasticity. Not the first time I've had this lesson either.

'I am really sorry Mr Pretorius. Honestly, I did not mean it like that. Let's please continue and see how I can help you? I offer.

He gives me a sideways glance, and nods quietly.

With a 'Please tell me a bit about yourself, Mr Pretorius', the neuropsychological assessment is back on track. I don't interrupt, and listen very carefully to everything he has to say, while also having the opportunity to observe him uninterruptedly. In this way I learn a lot about Mr Pretorius. His speech is ever so slightly slurred on occasion. He is right-handed. Mr Pretorius is a very serious man. He looks pleased that I am taking him seriously, *listening* to him. Which, believe me, I am. He is very religious. Tells me it forms a central part of his life. He also writes extensively. Mostly about religion, but other topics also. Never light-hearted, almost sticky, like the low black clouds on the humid east coast of beautiful Africa. He has no friends, no girlfriend, tells me he has no sex drive anyway, and is generally unhappy. Nothing gives him pleasure. Mr Pretorius is depressed.

I offer Mr Pretorius a break of 'about 15 minutes'. After exactly 15 minutes Mr Pretorius returns for formal neuropsychological testing.

I very carefully explained to him I need to test him to better understand his difficulties, and not to see how clever he is. We start with the Wechsler Adult Intelligence Scale. The scores are an acute reminder of my lesson an hour ago. His total IQ is 98, verbal IQ 90, and performance IQ 107. He does not have a learning difficulty. How embarrassing to have even thought that! At least maybe the clinical observation about his speech could possibly be correct. Mr Pretorius can list only 13 words in a minute on the Word Naming Test, too low for him. He then performs well on the Trail Making Test, trail A percentile 78, and trail B 64. His performance on the Wechsler Memory Scale is slightly patchy, 57th percentile for logical memory, visual memory 62, but associative learning is only equal to percentile 20. The hypothesis that he most likely has a pure language theme to his cognitive underperformance is supported. This finding is most likely compatible with left temporal lobe epilepsy. Especially when thinking about his clinical presentation of being hyper-religious, depressed and having traits of a 'sticky' personality?

Unfortunately Mr Pretorius' performance on the next test unceremoniously sinks the hypothesis, when he achieves only 22½ out of 30 on the Hooper Visual Organisation Test. Next up he copies the Rey Complex Figure in an obsessive fashion, with a percentile score of 99. His strategy is methodical and meticulous. Even though drawn freehand, his Rey is so neat it looks like he used a ruler. But then on recall, he manages to perform at merely the 18th percentile. The visual theme has returned, and expanded to include memory as well. Maybe it's medication side-effects. Just executive function remaining to be tested now. Mr Pretorius has no problems with completing the Austin Maze within the norms, but makes two gross errors on the Porteus Maze. Perhaps the test loads more than thought on visual perceptual skills than we think? And maybe the Austin Maze is more a test of learning? It won't be possible to localise based on his protocol. Which is not a major concern. The role of clinical neuropsychology, since the development of reliable brain imaging techniques, is anyway not primarily to localise lesions anymore. I am left reflecting on my own learning today, while packing up. Don't jump to conclusions before you've fully listened to someone's story. And continue to test neuropsychological hypotheses until you have the full picture.

Testing

We have been left a bit short-staffed in the unit since one of our clinical psychologists has gone on maternity leave, severely testing our capacity to provide cover. The 'us' is Gito next door to me, and I, plus however many interns we can secure. It is one of the things I want to mention when the head of psychology, Dr Tanya Maxwell, comes over from the medical school to pay us a rare visit this morning. She brings no good news about vacancies though. Only forms, for us to capture our 'monthly activity levels'. In 15-minute units, tiny little blocks on the form. Complete with a list of codes for activities that bear little resemblance to actual clinical work. I hate forms. Dr Maxwell remains very friendly and chatty despite my sour face. I hope she cannot possibly know what I am thinking. None of us are going to fill these in. It is boring just looking at them. As she drones on, my mind drifts away from the forms, from everything. It's easy to spot ineffective clinicians. They love meetings and filling in forms. And are always conspicuously absent during referral allocations. Tend to rapidly climb the hospital management ladder in their little world far away from our wards. Sound, or perhaps my reticular formation, extinguishes my stupid judgemental thought-stream, saving me from social embarrassment. Dr Maxwell is still rambling on, smiling falsely, now about the dean having recently visited the wards. Says that he was 'a bit alarmed' by some staff wearing jeans, that he noticed some of the males had very long hair and, heaven forbid, pierced ears.

'Who is the dean at the moment, I've never seen him or her down here, Tanya?' slips out as a completely honest question.

I am stunned by my social stupidity, and immediately regret my question. I've just let my colleagues down badly by reducing our chances of getting a locum. Maybe this incident was actually a very good reminder of how we need our frontal lobes to survive socially.

I am still thinking about the visit by Dr Maxwell and what I will say to Gito, as I walk slowly down to my office with the first patient for the day in tow. Oh well, it is too late to change anything now. Ms Klara Janssens (case #64) is now my priority. She is 42 years old, and has been diagnosed with Broca's dysphasia. She has had poorly controlled epilepsy for many years. Ms Janssens is underweight. Her clavicles are prominent like exposed tree roots under the flimsy light green hospital garment she is wearing. About two sizes too big. She is also really slow, and does not initiate much spontaneous conversation. I ask her why she came to hospital. She tells me she ran out of fags, and would I possibly have one for her. I smile, and don't default to 'explaining my role' to her. Instead I ask her how long she has been in hospital for, and she replies *''n geruime tydjie'* ['a while, of indeterminate length'], and laughs jovially. Ms Janssens then looks out of the window, whistles quietly and seems genuinely surprise by the cars. She asks why there are so many and who owns them. Comments that she likes the red ones. Seeing Ms Janssens has already improved my mood since meeting with Dr Tanya Maxwell.

The bedside cognitive assessment continues. As regards Ms Janssens' speech, besides being reduced in quantity, it is now also looking like there is poverty of content. I ask her the date, and it transpires she is orientated for time. Ms Janssens knows she is in hospital, but it is not clear if she has any idea why, or what she is actually seeing me for. A fleeting frivolous thought that to her defence, it may be difficult for anyone to explain that, evaporates as quickly as it arrived. We continue with what can best be described as a very informal bedside cognitive assessment and mental status evaluation as she intermittently vacillates between being serious, then emotionally inappropriate, followed by being disinhibited. Nevertheless I manage to patiently wait, then seize the brief periods where she is more attentive and connected to what we are doing, and bit by bit determine that she can write, read and perform mental arithmetic to a reasonable degree. Testing her is like a dance between laughter, sorrow and madness, but in all of this it becomes fairly obvious that her long-term memory as well as short-term memory, (new learning and retention) are grossly impaired on even the simplest of tests.

Together, but often out of synchronisation, we continue our haphazard waltz of trying to assess her cognition. What the referrer wants, is an indication of Ms Janssens' general intellectual ability. What Ms Janssen would like is unclear. The referrer's question is difficult, and at the same time simple to answer. Given her obvious problems with language and long-term memory, the Wechsler Adult Intelligence Scale is out of the question. Furthermore, she is from a frighteningly poor background and has had very little formal schooling. Cultural bias and the absence of any norms for her demographic profile leaves very little room for manoeuvre. Unfortunately she has long-term poorly controlled epilepsy, making it easy to understand the referrer's entirely appropriate request. They must want to longitudinally monitor her for cognitive decline as part of her follow-up in neurology. The only realistic option is to administer a Raven Coloured Progressive Matrices to obtain some sort of language-free, less culturally biased measure of her intellect. But I am of course aware that I may be grasping at straws, or too keen to help. Sadly there is no other psychometric alternative, and it would be worse to send her back to neurology with nothing from the clinical neuropsychologist. I am reminded of the meeting this morning. Maybe always doing the right thing, following the correct procedures is the wrong thing for some of our patients? I decide the Raven it will be. Ms Janssens appears to enjoy the colourful nature of the test, and happily names the colours, makes me laugh when I ask what exactly *sonde rooi* (as red as sin) means, but does not perform so well with a score of 23. Her score yields a converted IQ of approximately 80. I write down her test result and my other cognitive findings in her medical notes, and notice that her recent EEG has been reported to show 'left anterior temporal discharge'.

Art

Dr Ron Hays is from the other main university teaching hospital of the region, located closer to the mountain. It is also where my supervisor in clinical neuropsychology, Ms Carla De Bruin is based. Theirs is the top academic university in the country, ours the feeder ground of Springbok rugby. Dr Hays does not play rugby. He is in his late fifties, balding and of delicate build. His small gold-rimmed specs emphasise his pale-skinned high cheekbones and super-alert, dark, almost black, eyes. Dr Hays spent a few years abroad, studying and being involved in key developments in neuro-radiology and neuropathology. He comes across more like an artist than a neuro-radiologist, which to some degree is true. He loves the arts, in particular painting, and plays violin in a classical orchestra. Dr Hays is attending one of our special ward rounds, where complex patients are presented. It is similar to a 'grand round'. Despite the fact that it is the early to mid-1990s, being a university teaching hospital ensures access to the things that really matter. Our patients who need it, can each have full neuropsychological, neurological and neuropsychiatric examinations, plus CT, MRI, EEG, SPECT and a wide range of blood and other tests. It is long before the days of cutting-edge functional imaging such as fMRI. Dr Hays and colleagues have figured out the importance of superimposing (with an overhead projector) SPECT images on anatomical pictures (MRI in general), and compare this sandwiched image to the neuropsychological test profile or neuropsychiatric presentation of a given patient for example. Crude, but, it did make sense. More importantly, at the time it helped us to consider lesions, connections and mental functions not in isolation, but together.

This afternoon in the hot room there is an MRI image projected onto a screen. The light of the projector adds to the heat. Dr Hays is explaining how the lesion fits with this patient's presentation. I cannot see a thing. Like many symptoms, lesions or signs referred to in passing, I fail to see what is being talked about. The done thing is to keep on looking intently, but remain quiet at these rounds. And never frown. Reassuringly, the registrars also look like they are pretending that they know what they are looking at, but not quite convincingly. The medical students and clinical psychology interns are looking at the floor, intently studying the cheap uncreative patterns on the synthetic blue floor tiles. It is very quiet, just the whir of the projector fan. Dr Hays is a sensitive man. He turns around, and says that he is aware it is not always easy to see lesions on neuro-imaging. I feel my shoulders relax a bit. Dr Hays walks back, into the midst of the audience, and then turns around facing the image on the screen.

'You need to look at these as you would at a work of art, say a painting. Don't focus on the details, stand back, far back if you need to'.

He takes half a step backwards.

'Take in the whole without looking at the details. Look for patterns, shapes, light and dark, texture, symmetry between the left and right, look for beauty. What is on the left, should be on the right. Look for outlines or order, ask yourself if something is out of place? Now look at the screen again. Can you see the magnificent butterfly, if you defocus from the region of the basal ganglia?' Dr Hays is now sounding like someone reviewing a work of art.

He is right! The butterfly jumps out. To learn to see the essentials in neuroscience, go to art school.

But for now on this hot afternoon, epistemology has not yet changed. We are all still in a lecture room in the medical school, the domain of science. Art school will have to wait for now. Dr Hays shuffles through the stack of overheads on the table by the side of the projector, considers a few and then lays down his final choice for projection. The light shoots out the new image he chose. It creates a complex pattern of luminous black, white and all the shades of grey code to a patient's mind, dispassionately displayed on the screen against the wall. It is an axial cut of the brain. It is easy to immediately recognise that. But the rest might as well be invisible to me. I can identify most of the individual details by now, or at least the ones of particular relevance to clinical neuropsychology, like, for example, the thalamus, or say the corpus callosum. I peer intently, wondering what we are supposed to see when Dr Hays's quiet voice reminds me what to do. He has the voice of a classically educated man who knows much more than his own subject matter, like a modern-day Humboldt.

'Look at it as a whole, squint if you need to, but ignore the details. Stand back in your mind's eye. Let your eyes swim around the image a bit', Dr Hays instructs the audience, and then pauses for what feels like at least a minute, but in reality is only a few seconds.

'Can you all clearly see the lovely smile, posterior, near the brain-stem?' he asks looking almost ecstatic. He tells us what the smile is, and means.

Dr Hays is a super teacher. Part scientist, part artist. Is there is a similarity? To some extent both, although through different methodologies, communicate to the recipient, making visible what was invisible before.

Invisible

Her symptoms are crystal clear. Ms Janita Kahn (case #42) is 50 years old. Her history is a bit vague. She has not had any education, and has literally received no formal schooling. She has never worked, nor ever managed to live on her own. Ms Kahn is being looked after by her extended family, who are acting as informal carers. I ask her to perform a few basic tasks, and quickly discover she cannot read, write or perform even very simple mental arithmetic. Which of course fits in with not having had any formal education. Although this is not necessarily always the case. For example, some kids receive some basic informal education at home, or their work environments, which sometimes can help them to learn to read and write. Ms Kahn's fine motor coordination is not very good, and she is also a bit clumsy. Likewise her articulation is subtly compromised, and some words she says are difficult to make out. It is almost certainly going to be a slow and laborious trudge assessing Ms Kahn today. In fact, it feels as if even the clock on the wall is ticking much louder and slower, with each click emphasising her lack of pace. My chair is sinfully trying to seduce me into a catnap, making my head heavy as lead, peripheral vision steadily more blurry. Then suddenly there is an explosion of movement, and Ms Kahn has a seizure. Right there in front of me, in her wheelchair. Despite being caught by surprise, I remember what Dr Carstens said. Epilepsy, or seizures, despite technology remains a clinical diagnosis reliant upon a good observer report. Keep calm, look, look, look and describe.

Feeling slightly faint, I watch Ms Kahn very closely for the next two to three minutes. Her seizure starts with her excessively grinding her teeth, so loudly that I involuntarily flinch. Then both her arms extend, go completely rigid, and remains like this for approximately 120 seconds. Suddenly her arms, still rigid, start swinging from side to side, clearing the armrests of her wheelchair. At least she won't injure herself. Her arms then come to a rest, falls flaccidly by the side of the wheelchair and she starts to breathe very fast. And faster. I can feel my heart starting to beat faster. The attack is going on for much too long. Is she in status? I call her name, ask her to tell me if she can hear me. No response. Oh no, she is about to fold on me unless she is helped right now, I think, my heart racing madly. I lurch up from my chair. But just at that moment she collapses back into a more comfortable position in her wheelchair. Now she looks like a ragdoll, but is at least breathing evenly. So am I. Still standing, I ask her how she is feeling, and she says fine. That quick? I sit down, look at her and decide that's enough for today. I call the porters to come and collect Ms Kahn, and take her back to neurology. Well, now I know firsthand what a seizure looks like. Completely understandable why people find them so frightening when directly confronted by someone having an attack in front of them. I write up my cognitive findings, in essence that Ms Kahn has a learning difficulty, and give a very detailed description of the seizure. I am sure Dr Carstens will find the latter valuable. I'll see him tomorrow afternoon at the neurology training round.

It is Friday afternoon, and one of Dr Carstens' registrar is presenting at the round. It's an interesting case, but a lot of detail to absorb. One overhead after the other, relentless, depressing like an army marching past. Seeing the height of the pile of those still to come is as demoralising. Looking around I wonder if anybody else is also having to work very hard to keep up with what he is presenting. Then the patient is called in. Dr Carstens takes over. Mentions that the patient used to be a tyre fitter, and asks him to take the top of his hospital pyjamas off. Dr Carstens looks at us, and tells us that we should have a good look at the patient's torso. There is nothing to see but . . . a torso. A few faint tattoos, but surely that means nothing. Or did he do some time? No, not any of the numbers 26 or 28 inked into his dusky skin. Well built though, quite slender, not an ounce of fat. Superbly defined muscles, six-pack, biceps with good veins, forearms like ships' ropes.

'Think about the nature of the job, it requires strength', Dr Carstens tries to help.

I don't get it, and I am not sure if anybody else is seeing what they are supposed to see. Well, nobody is volunteering an opinion.

'Look carefully. He is a powerfully built man. Compare his right arm to his left though?' Dr Carstens provides the guidance a good teacher knows when to do, problem-based learning long before it was even invented.

And it is the moment the patient's subtle muscle waste to the left arm jumps out at me. Almost like he has this very second for the first time removed his shirt. For the first time I see what I need to see to understand this patient's pathology.

Dr Carstens continues to explain that the condition being presented involves peripheral nerve damage, with consequent muscle wastage of the affected limb. The name of the condition fails to stick.

The round has ended, and everybody starts to saunter out. It is the end of the working day. There is no rush. Rushing will only get you stuck in the huge volume of traffic leaving the hospital site on a Friday afternoon. Dr Carstens is having a brief chat with the registrar who presented. I need to catch him, and ask him about Ms Kahn.

'Ah, Rudi, did you enjoy the presentation? I know it was not central, but it can do no harm for a neuropsychologist to be aware of peripheral stuff. Helps develop observational skills. Anyway, how have you been keeping? Busy? Dr Carstens enthusiastically blasts away.

'I am fine, thanks Johan, going on leave for a few days in a week's time. I meant to ask you what you thought about Ms Kahn? The lady you referred down to us, you know, and what type of epilepsy you think she has?'

I can almost see the cogs in his head turn as he rummages through the many patients he must see every day. For a brief moment he looks a bit puzzled. Then he finds her in his vast library of synaptic connections.

'Oh yes, Ms Kahn, the middle-aged lady from the *platteland* [countryside] who came in with these weird attacks. Has a mild learning difficulty, thanks for confirming that for us. Good description of what you saw also. We found that helpful, also managed to perform EEGs while she had some of her attacks. You know what, she had a normal EEG every time. She does not have epilepsy, Ms Kahn suffers from pseudoseizures. Or a conversion disorder, as our friend Tomas might say. Not that uncommon for patients to have co-morbidity, you know', Dr Carstens explains.

It's still early. I think I will take tonight off, and go and see a movie. Make myself invisible in the dark cinema. As long as the film is not a rerun of *Drugstore Cowboy*.

7

Reality

Co-morbidity in clinical neuropsychology

It's coexistence or no existence.

(Bertrand Russell)

Symbiosis

The car park is chock-a-block full, creating a mad mosaic of metal mirroring back a bright, hot sun. All different models, colours, age and specification. It would be very difficult to collect from this mass a representative sample of reasonably similar ones, never mind identical. My immediate dilemma though has nothing to do with randomisation effects. No, it is simply that there is not even the smallest gap between these little similar, but different, shiny metal tiles. This is very annoying. A huge overflow car park exists, but it is far from the entrance of the hospital. The annoying thing is not the walk, it is that it is unnecessary. There is no public transport system to the hospital – people get there by car or taxi, or simply don't get there. Which is the cause of several ills coexisting in a biopsychosocial broth of misery. Lack of parking delaying clinics is of course the least of the ills. It is the fact that because there is no public transport system that there are way too many cars on the roads. Which increases the risk of traffic-related injuries, making it very expensive for the poor to get to hospital, and bad air pollution, to name a few. Realistically very few problems exist completely in isolation from others. Therein lays the limits of supposed mono-pathology diagnoses. The more common situation is that frequently a few factors conspire to accentuate whatever the index problem or illness might be, making it much worse in the process. Which is my secondary dilemma.

The classic neuropsychology books that have thus far been a great way to lay down the essential basic knowledge at night for survival during the day, have recently also come in for a bit less uncritical internal acceptance. Yes, it's true these books all contain much more knowledge than I will ever have. Who am I to doubt Lezak, Walsh, Luria and the like? Nevertheless there is an increasing niggle, a growing sense of *doubt*. Is it really true that all and everything fits so *neatly* into little clinical neuropsychology boxes? I'm not sure if I'm a believer. Not in this hospital anyway. Here it resembles a warehouse of the wounded, mad, almost dead, dead, lucky, unlucky and hangers on (us). This is where I am learning my trade. Many patients, possibly more often than not, have more than one thing wrong with them. Not separate things, but *related*. At night, the case studies in the books all seem, well, so clean-cut, tidy and neat. Almost preppy. But in the day, the ones growing in numbers inside my little notebook are not like that. Traumatic brain injury? Yes, and usually poverty, social deprivation, substance misuse, speaking a different mother tongue and very little in the line of schooling. All providing the individual dominoes ready to fall, and together cause *the big combined injury*. Sometimes even a history of another, earlier traumatic brain injury to add to the mix. We have morale-breaking numbers of such patients. The opposite doubt sometimes also sets in. Maybe I am just tired, being gradually defeated by it all.

The unrelenting numbers must have over time conspired to influence, shape me as a clinical neuropsychologist. I am surprised to hear myself now, several months properly into my new job, regularly say to interns, 'It's not quite as simple as that', after they have presented a patient to me during supervision. In contrast to a few months ago, where the mantra was 'Can you see that little white spot in the medial left temporal lobe, that's why the patient's memory is impaired. Is it not awe inspiring how we are really just blood, bone and muscle?' Life in applied neuroscience is not always as neat and ordered as portrayed in classification systems. All patients arrive in the consultation room, pre-packaged with a past life and all its scars and bruises. Yes, of course, at some point they have had a traumatic brain injury or stroke or brain infection, with a resulting lesion, or lesions, corresponding to the nice illustrations and photos in textbooks. Only they, *my* patients, don't. I learn that the volume of knowledge I so dreaded in the beginning is possibly the least difficult to master. It is the interpretation of findings in a world less than perfect where patients simply don't meet the norm, that's the problem. Figuring out their co-morbidity – biological, social, psychological and environmental – is not easy. It requires a paradigm shift, into a world of an alternative academia. Learning to think until your mind hurts so much that you start to doubt everything, your working memory is totally overloaded, facts coming and going before becoming mirages. There is no Bonferroni correction for life. Learning to untangle damaged brains not on the pages of a book, a screen or a research protocol, but today, every day, in this moment, unselected, randomised and allocated to groups only by fate, creating accumulated sample sizes of hundreds.

Accumulation

The day ahead already looks, or rather sounds busy. The admin office at the entry to the unit is busy and noisy. So is the nursing office inside the unit. I look inside the unit's diary, to see what is under my name for the day. Mr Albert Roberts (case # 79) is first on the list of outpatients to be seen by me today. At least my list is not as long as Dr Burger's. Ah, the healing power of relativity. It does not last long. While his appointments might be shorter in duration, the length of our days is the same . . . Back to Mr Roberts' referral. He is 67 years old. Sister Jantjies tells me he is ready, came in early, and has been waiting. She seems to suggest that I should get out from underneath her feet and start the clinic. I get the hint, and go and collect Mr Roberts at the top of the passage, where our patients normally wait. His hand is cold and sweaty when I introduce myself. Something's slightly odd, he hesitates when he puts out his hand to greet, almost as if he could not decide which one to use. Mr Roberts is moderately overweight and walks slowly. He walks slightly behind me, to my right, struggling to keep up even though I have slowed down my pace. I wish he would walk faster. His breathing is audible, and sounds like the dry whisper of an exhausted athlete after a marathon run at the height of summer. I now feel ashamed of my impatience a moment earlier, and focus my thoughts on what I think the clinical questions might be. It's going to be an easy first guess. Mr Roberts has all the risk factors for a stroke. The other patients waiting silently follow us with their eyes as we walk down the corridor. They know their time to be seen, and find out, will come before too long.

Mr Roberts sits down at the other side of the desk. There is a clearly audible sigh of relief when he rather heavily sinks down in the chair. He takes a crumpled, slightly dirty handkerchief from his green check shirt and wipes the sweat beads resembling a frosted glass bathroom window from his red forehead. Fair enough, it is hot today, but it has only just gone 8 a.m. The real heat is to come from mid-morning onwards. Why is he feeling so hot? I look back at the file in front of me. Mr Roberts has been diagnosed with a Generalised Anxiety Disorder according to the brief referral note. No neuropsychology question? Rubbish handwriting too.

'How may I help, Mr Roberts?' I ask, mildly irritated.

'I'm not quite sure. There are a few things worrying me. I guess the main thing is that I worry a lot about stuff. All the time, in fact', Mr Roberts confirms what is already known from the useless referral.

'Maybe then we could start with you trying to tell me the about the things that worry you, Mr Roberts?' I ask patiently.

'Well, I have always been a worrier. I think it started in school. I was a nervous child. Not sporty. The other kids bullied me. Laughed because I could not catch a ball, never mind play rugby. Always on my own at break time. I had no friends. Absolutely hated school, and tried to bunk many times. Did not do well in my exams. The teachers forced me to write with my right hand, which did not help either. I hope you don't mind me telling you all this stuff', he says, sounding a bit ashamed to have made this confession to me.

I feel awful that I was annoyed with the referral, and hope he did not notice that, or think that I am not interested in his story. I am.

Don't feel sorry for yourself, think, and focus on the clinical questions, I remind myself.

'Do you mean you used to be left-handed, Mr Roberts?'

'Yes, but they did not like that at school, said I was weird. So I had to learn to use my other hand', comes the reply.

Together we do a more systematic history. Mr Roberts was born in the city. There were no complications with his birth, and as far as he is aware, his mother was healthy during the pregnancy. He reached his developmental milestones early. Being an anxious child, he did not do well at school. Mr Roberts did not complete any tertiary education and went out to work straight after school. Leaving school was an escape from daily misery. He held various jobs, mostly in administrative types of roles. To try and control his anxiety, especially in social situations, he started smoking. Soon he also started to drink heavily, again to manage his anxiety. He had a serious car crash 15 years ago. He was unconscious for a few hours and had to be admitted to hospital. Drunk driving, he confides. Mr Roberts has a history of mental health problems. Over the years he has seen various doctors for his anxiety. As regards his medical history, he has emphysema and is also hypertensive. The family history is unremarkable, except that his brother is an alcoholic. Mr Roberts tells me that he himself stopped drinking 30 years ago. I have no reason to doubt his word, as he very candidly admits that he is now simply addicted to benzodiazepines instead. His honesty touches a hard to find place in my heart. A place that in its better moments does not harshly judge people for 'things they brought on themselves'. Mr Roberts had a stressful life by the sound of things. The absence of a specific neuropsychology question in the referral note does not matter anymore.

Next up is a quick bedside cognitive assessment. Mr Roberts flies through this. He is fully orientated for time, place and person, his attention is good, almost 'too good', all language functions are also fine. His short-term memory seems OK, and he does not have any obvious executive problems on bedside testing. Mr Roberts is right-handed. Well sort of, technically yes, perhaps 'maybe' is the most accurate answer. Mental status evaluation shows clear signs of anxiety. He has a tremor of the hands and describes 'worrying himself sick'. His eyes constantly make him look as if he has been startled by something awful. He is not depressed and retains a reasonable sense of future, but there is something else. Something almost definitely not listed in a textbook. He looks, well, humiliated by life. Mr Roberts is sleeping well, provided he takes his sleeping tablets. His appetite is good and he is moderately overweight. Mr Roberts' thought processes and perceptual functions are entirely normal. Then the time is up for Mr Roberts' appointment. I provide him with a brief summary of my thoughts thus far, based on his history and clinical presentation. I confess to him that I am not at all sure what might be the main cause of his problems. I explain that I would like to perform formal neuropsychological testing to get a better understanding of his cognition. Because of the car crash. The formulation starts drifting a bit, 'and the history of alcohol abuse', I think by myself. As well as benzo dependence. Not forgetting his hypertension . . . The almost naive oversimplification of complexity so commonly portrayed in my textbooks is proving to be a bit of a curse when it comes to learning clinical reasoning. It is most likely going to be an exceptional intellectual challenge to bring neuropsychological order to the mess that is Mr Roberts' history.

I meet Dr Burger for lunch. We decide to go across to the medical students' canteen, the food is much better there than in the hospital. We start chatting.

'Hey man, I saw a chap this morning who has everything in the book. Honestly, I have no idea what precisely is causing his problems. We've arranged that I will test him in a couple of weeks', I confess between bites from a sandwich.

Dr Burger has been munching something greasy and unhealthy while listening.

'Tomas, how can you eat that burger, double cheese, meat patty de lux, actually double everything!? And you call yourself a doctor? I am not coming to see you!'

He seems genuinely surprised. Looks down at the last remaining bits of his meal with the eye of a scientist. Then picks it apart with his knife, to have a better look.

'Well, it has protein (he points at the patty and cheese), veg (a solitary leaf he discarded to the side of the plate is identified as evidence) and carbs (a bit of the bun is left), and as a bonus, sugars (tomato sauce) and fat (butter on the bun). Totally balanced, you see? And it's probably good for me. Anyway, since when has a single factor explained the majority of patients' presentations? That's why there is hardly ever a single magic bullet to cure it. Have you not yet figured out comorbidity is the majority's problem?' he refutes all my allegations in one shot.

Dr Burger has me there. I thought he was a black and white thinker, a *scientist*. Given my recent doubts, for once I am rather chuffed to hear I am wrong. Must have forgotten he is a psychiatrist, the medical specialtiy along with neurology, which defeated dualism. I will after all be very happy to see Dr Burger if I ever needed a good doctor.

It's not a doctor I need after two weeks, but a faith healer. Post-lunch satisfaction and the ever present African heat make the numbers swim a little bit on the page. Mr Roberts' formal neuropsychological test results looks unremarkable. Nothing seems to jump out. His Wechsler Adult Intelligence Scale prorated IQ score is 122, with no subtest scatter. Furthermore, his Wechsler Memory Scale shows an average score for logical memory, slightly below average for visual memory and associative learning as well. The Hooper Visual Organisation Test performance is normal also, having scored 25 out of 30. Mr Roberts' Rey Complex Figure copy performance is on the 60th percentile. Everything seems OK, but therein lies the problem. It may well be an average, or normal performance, but perhaps slightly below what would be expected of a person with superior general intellectual ability? And also, there are no norms for his age group (Mr Roberts is 67 years old) for all of the tests administered today, and instead the norms for a younger normative cohort had to do. Or not test him at all, and do a lame reply to the referrer. So what does his protocol mean? Heaven knows. I cannot tie his profile to any one of his problems. The anxiety is a factor in his cognitive performance yes, but almost certainly just a 'front of shop' symptom. There are several biological factors that may account for his profile, including medication effects, head injury, hypertension and possibly little strokes, he has them all, everything and more. Sometimes we have to say we simply don't know the answer. Nothing to put our faith in. But if I had to venture a neuropsychological formulation? I guess it will have to be that Mr Roberts has been ravaged by life.

Everything

The blue book on the desk is suffering increasing damage to its spine. Would Houdini have been able to untangle all of this? Everything?

On the one hand it feels like there is just too much factual knowledge to learn. On the other hand, untangling all this knowledge to understand the individual patient, an intellectual demolition like no other. It feels similar to the individual limits of working memory of Digit Span – forwards, backward. With an infinite number of permutations to make your head spin, before the next day, making your heart ache. The cycle of learning before dismantling once again commences this evening. It would be good to have another look at what Kevin Walsh and Muriel Lezak have to say about stroke. Before leaving the unit this afternoon, I checked what I am doing tomorrow, to read up a bit in preparation. I am seeing a patient with a middle cerebral artery stroke in the morning. I've now seen a few of these, but like exercise, studying is not always about reading every new research paper. In the twentieth century we cannot possibly know everything in our own field. No, studying is about also mastering the simple stuff that works, in this case basic applied clinical knowledge. Revision and repetition is a good thing. Even though by now I now know pretty well what a middle cerebral artery stroke is, as well as the symptoms and signs associated with the condition. Tomorrow should be fine.

Mr Peter Craven (case # 46) looks a bit weather-worn, dishevelled in fact. The rough texture of his three-day stubble could make copper shine. He is sitting almost bunched up in his wheelchair, brakes on, across from my desk. The illumination of the early morning sun provides classic black and white photography side-lighting to his face. Maybe it's the contrast of light and dark, but his face comes across as apathetic and hostile at the same time. Lifeless small pale blue eyes try to bring a bit of colour to his sickly grey pallor. Mr Craven has suffered a left middle cerebral artery infarct. As a result he has lots of problems. He is incontinent, has cranial nerve VII involvement via the right upper motor neuron, right-sided weakness, mild dysphasia, and a homonymous hemianopia. We put together a history from Mr Craven's self-report, and his medical notes in front of me. Mr Craven passed the equivalent of GCSEs, and after finishing school went on to train successfully as a motor mechanic. The infarct is not his only problem. Other things precede it. A few years ago he was involved in a car crash, and was unconscious for a few hours. Also, from the notes I see Mr Craven is known to be an alcoholic. Furthermore, the notes indicate he has tested positive for neurosyphilis. He is also being treated for glaucoma. The CT report says that the left middle cerebral artery infarct involves his capsula interna, but that there is also evidence of a granuloma. Plus the scan also reveals generalised cerebral and cerebellar atrophy, most likely due to long-standing alcohol abuse. Mr Craven's brain has over time been savagely and repeatedly beaten up by various neuropathologies.

The referrer requested neuropsychological testing. A shortened testing will be the most humane thing to do. There are so many co-morbidities, the hypothesis is that will be impossible to disentangle everything, what accounts for what. And so it proves to be. Mr Craven scores a prorated IQ of 64 on a short Wechsler Adult Intelligence Scale. His Hooper Visual Organisation Test score is very low, 12½ out of 30, with perseveration clearly evident from item 24 onwards. He is grossly impaired on the Wechsler Memory Scale for associative learning, less than the second percentile. I decide to call it a day. Technically Mr Craven's diagnosis is that of dementia due to multiple aetiologies. I have not come across anything like it in any of my textbooks. Life is different in the real world, and only death the same, irrespective of the pathologies involved. But wait a moment. The chaos coexists, like the individual ingredients of witches' broths. Think about it. Like everyone, Mr Craven will have a life story. Perhaps he started drinking first. Had unprotected sex at some point, possibly in a moment of alcohol-clouded judgement. Or perhaps it was his great love for that brief moment, who knows everything about the heart, or indeed the past? Autobiographical memories are sometimes like the clouds over Africa. He's single now. What is definitely known now though, is that any hope of cognitive survival was destroyed at that moment, unless he had his first symptoms treated with penicillin. With the continued alcohol misuse came cigarettes and other lifestyle problems, eventually leading up to a cerebro-vascular accident? At that point hope left, leaving him alone on his final path to inevitable collapse.

Hope

Outside the hospital, and occasionally inside also, the country still seesaws between hope and collapse. Direct, raw, wounded individual evidence of societal collapse compliments of an abundance of bullets, *pangas* (a sword of sorts), knives, sharpened bicycle spokes and any other sharp or heavy objects capable to penetrate or crush the skull, still trickle in through the front door of the hospital. The cost of an AK-47 is almost nothing, but also immeasurably high. Sometimes hope sneaks in through the back door of television broadcasts, newspapers and radio, or rumour. Some news items are heavily managed by the unelected government. Hence it is not always even clear if we are being visited by hope or deception. One of the forced political co-morbidities of friend and foe, the Congress for a Democratic South Africa (CODESA) collapses. Mercifully hope returns when a new co-existence of concerned parties approves the Interim Constitution during November 1993. Now in theory at least, a new Transitional Executive Council can oversee the lead-in period to the country's first democratic election. Provided everybody is not killed before then, I cynically think to myself. But then funnily enough, I remember during clinical training a few years earlier a lecturer saying we should never destroy hope. I guess so, if you are a believer. But never at the cost of truth? Cynicism has briefly gotten the upper hand in the internal battle between doubt and belief.

It is the afternoon clinic. Things have started to slow down a bit. Mrs Lettie Van Schalkwyk (case # 94) is only three years older than me, 33. It's even closer to home and fertile ground for countertransference. She is, or rather used to be, a physiotherapist. If the dice of life fell differently, she might even have been a colleague. Mrs Van Schalkwyk has blonde hair, is now a bit overweight around her shoulders and neck area compared to last time, I note. There is no obvious impairment of mobility or indeed anything else that could be unusual. She does look incredibly sad though, like someone who has lost an awful lot. Which fits in with the referral. She has been suffering with a treatment resistant depression, according to the referrer. I know this already. Came across from the off-site psychiatric unit to our unit at the main hospital today, for neuropsychological testing. But I also saw her at the psychiatric unit some time ago, where I completed a full neuropsychological testing. The referral at that time was for testing only, in view of her treatment resistant depression. Other than testing, I did not get to know her well. I decide that today I have more time, and will do a thorough history first before re-testing her. Not so easy though. I fall at the first hurdle. Mrs Van Schalkwyk starts to sob when I ask what is troubling her, and how I might help. I want to obtain her own view on her current presentation. The only answer is her quiet sobbing. She does not look up at me. If she did, she may have detected in my face that I feel intensely sorry for her.

Mrs Van Schalkwyk finally looks up and asks if I have a tissue for her. I feel like a fool for not having offered one before she needed to ask. She takes the tissue from my hand. As she reaches, I notice she has some bruising on her forearm. She wipes her eyes, and blows her nose.

'Mrs Van Schalkwyk, what is making you so sad?' I try to ask, despite feeling quite apprehensive of what I might open up, and then be unable to close or make better.

'Things were OK until about five years ago', Mrs Van Schalkwyk replies, but then remains silent, staring out of the window.

'What happened five years ago?'

'Well, I noticed that I could not keep up with seeing patients, and found that the physical physiotherapy manoeuvres just drained me. I just felt more and more tired. We also went through a rough patch in our marriage at the time, and I thought that might explain it all. But we patched things up, and then had a baby . . .'

Mrs Van Schalkwyk stops talking. Tears mixed with makeup and mucus are streaming down her face again, but she does not make a sound. The room is much too quiet. My heart is racing. What do I say now?

'Even if it is difficult for you, try and tell me what happened', I ask quietly.

'There were complications during the birth, and my baby was badly damaged. He had hydrocephalus, and eventually had to be shunted. He has never been well since. Never learned to talk. My husband could not cope with it at all. We divorced. I am on my own. I feel such a failure!' she sobs.

It is quiet in the room again. I wait for her to continue. Nothing anyone can say will help. Finally Mrs Van Schalkwyk speaks again.

'I wish I knew what was wrong with me', she says.

'Maybe I can, or I hope I can, help you by trying to find out', I reply, not quite believing my own words.

Mrs Van Schalkwyk does not reply, simply looks through me with her red eyes framed haphazardly with brown smudges.

I feel terrible to probe, being a voyeur on a stranger's suffering. But more questions have to be asked. I have to. It's the only way of preserving someone's hope, by possibly being able to help explain why she is feeling so far beyond terrible. From a more technical viewpoint, there is the decision to be made if re-testing is indicated, or if her presentation is clearly purely a depression secondary to awful life events. It is a difficult call. Now knowing the history of repeated losses, the most plausible hypothesis is that she is indeed depressed. And depression does affect cognition, through the general effect of poor concentration. The most compassionate thing would be to not put her through a heap of testing again. But I am not entirely sure. Focus, *focus*. Feeling very sorry for someone is hardly ever a good reason not to test them. Somebody must suspect something else, to have taken the trouble to make a referral for a repeat neuropsychological testing? Plus, thinking about it more carefully now, the tiredness she describes has a slightly different qualitative feel to it than that normally described by patients with mood disorders. Almost as if her muscles, rather than her mind, has become exhausted. I go with my intuition and decide to at least do a few neuropsychological tests again, even though last time I found nothing much. Mrs Van Schalkwyk has a short break, and when she returns looking a little bit more composed, we start the testing. In a way, testing the water. Mrs Van Schalkwyk bravely completes the testing and is clearly doing her best. It cannot be easy for her. I wonder yet again what relevance identifying her cognitive abilities might have for having a disabled child, a failed marriage and the loss of her job?

It is indeed as predicted. Her neuropsychological test results are normal. Again. Or are they really? The Wechsler Adult Intelligence Scale is not repeated. Her pre-morbid educational status is enough to go on, and previously her performance on this test was fine. Mrs Van Schalkwyk's scores on the Wechsler Memory Scale reveal normal performances on associations, logical and visual memory functions. The Hooper Visual Organisation Test yields a score of 26 out of 30, which is normal. Her Porteus Maze performance is entirely normal, with no errors. Trail Making Test A and B are both above the 90th percentile. Mrs Van Schalkwyk's copy of the Rey Complex Figure is near perfect, following a normal strategy, with a 99th percentile score. But her delayed recall is only on the 17th percentile. Possibly just a function of her mood, but it does feel low for her, and incongruous with her Wechsler Memory Scale performance. Maybe something else *is* going on? A week later it transpires that her depression and exhaustion is not entirely accounted for by psychological factors. In retrospect, perhaps the problem with delayed recall did provide a clue, or maybe not. I'll never know for sure, as with many things in this job. But I do find out a few days later that in addition to the neuropsychological test results, all the other medical tests have now also been completed. Maybe there will after all be some solace for Mrs Van Schalkwyk. Co-morbidity has been identified by the other medical investigations, which may partially explain some of her difficulties – she has been diagnosed with Pituitary Cushing's Syndrome. Mrs Van Schalkwyk's wish to know what is wrong with her, has been granted. Without this, she may have been treated for 'resistant' depression for many years.

Resistance

Even though it is raining cats and dogs today, I've definitely hit the jackpot! Professor Emmerson, who is renowned to have his finger quietly on the pulse of the morale of his workforce, must have decided that I could do with being sponsored to attend an international conference hosted locally. Two days in a smart hotel near the sea, listening to overseas and local experts on neuropsychology, neuropsychiatry and the broader neurosciences present the latest research and developments in the field. Thinking back now, a couple of weeks ago I did have a brief conversation with Professor Emmerson when he came to one of our ward rounds. Perceptive man, our Rolf Emmerson. He certainly must have read my mood correctly. Much more of work and this place and I would have needed to take leave, or do something drastic to get my enthusiasm back. There is only so much relentless patient contact one can deliver while at the same time trying to learn, before becoming mentally exhausted beyond what is thought to be part of the job anyway. Test materials, tissues and compassion dry up after some time. So the conference is just what the doctor, sorry, professor, ordered. In just over a month, there will be a very welcome little bit of respite from just working as a jobbing clinical neuropsychologist day in, day out. A much needed change in the daily physical and mental environment. The conference is also well timed in view of recently becoming more interested in research.

The hotel lives up to the conference brochure, but oddly the speakers in real life all look older than their photos. Tables draped with starched white cloths, pure filter coffee and delicate biscuits welcome the delegates. None of the 'nylon' coffee (instant) we have at the hospital. They foyer is buzzing with small talk, almost everyone is smoking, the mirrors on the walls vaguely reflecting their backs. The programme is as glossy as the speakers' overheads. Some are from faraway countries, others from local university departments. Over the morning, a steady roll of interesting talks on . . . What exactly?

The neuro-imaging of (insert a diagnosis here), and the neuropsychology associated with lesions of (insert your research interest and brain area here). Yes, it all starts to merge into one after lunch time. The next day it's more of the same. It is difficult to put a finger on it, but something is a bit annoying. Every talk, without fail, makes clean, neat conclusions free of any co-morbidity. *Where* did they find these patient participants? The results all seem so disconnected from *life*, for a better word. But why annoyance, it's the nature of research. Annoyed possibly because few are clinicians, but almost all throw in sound bites such as 'when I see my patients'? Maybe it's about a distant memory. 'If you want to do the clinician talk, you've got to first do the training walk', Sam my blunt, sometimes rude classmate once cynically said to a research assistant trying to recruit patients from him when we were interns. He said he was just trying to be protective of his patients. What on earth has become of us? There must have been a time when we were not so cynical.

It feels very good to walk back into the unit on the Thursday morning. Even though Sister Jantjies gives me her filthy look, and asks where I have been, because nobody told her I had annual leave. I correct her, and tell her I had *study* leave to attend a conference in town. An *international* one. With Professor Emmerson's blessing too.

'You? And what did *you* learn?' she asks incredulously while histrionically rolling her dark brown eyes.

'Me? What we do, what we know, and what we don't know. And how what we know we don't know is very important. But the main thing I learned was what I want to know as much as possible about, and what I want to do', I confidently reply.

There is a short stunned silence.

'And be less cynical', I add.

She looks at me suspiciously, the frown on her forehead pushing up her wild frizzy black hair, and asks 'Conference? Are you sure you did not go to the Palace Hotel in Kenilworth last night?'

'Hey, Sis, you know very well I don't do the grape or the leaf', I smile at her.

'You must have sins, and your first patient is waiting. Welcome home, Mr clean-living conference boy!' she mocks me.

Sister Jantjies is right. And not only about the sins. I look down at the referral she has dismissively shoved into my hand a few seconds ago. A 29-year-old male has been referred for neuropsychological testing in view of his recently diagnosed Multiple Sclerosis (MS). Should be very interesting. One of the talks at the conference was in fact on the neuropsychology of MS in young adults. The beauty of continuing professional development and remaining up to date.

To briefly recap, according to the referral, Mr Leonard Akkerman (case # 120) has a diagnosis of MS. He has been referred to us for neuropsychological testing by neurology. They suspect that although only 29 years old with recently diagnosed MS, he may already have cognitive impairment. Mr Akkerman is of slender build. Green eyes, brown hair, no real standout features other than a slightly skew nose, a memento from a fight long ago while at high school. Cleanly shaved. Smiles at me when I call him, seems like a pleasant enough guy. We walk to my office at the end of the corridor and once inside I invite him to sit down in the green chair opposite my desk.

'OK, Mr Akkerman, thanks for coming down. Dr Carstens asked me to see you. I'll be asking you some questions, and then we might do some tests if necessary. You up for that? I check with him.

'You're the boss, fire away', he grins, flashing a near perfect set of white teeth.

'What seems to be the problem, Mr Akkerman, why did you have to come to hospital?'

'I needed a bit of a break from my wife, a little holiday, or else I'd lose my mind, you know . . . Just joking! My GP did some blood tests when I saw her a few months ago. Said she was referring me to the hospital'.

I have a quick look in his folder. It says he tested positive VDRL (venereal disease), and was sent to hospital. For reasons unclear from reading the notes, he ended up with neurology, and eventually, additional to his positive VDRL test, MS was diagnosed. The VDRL finding was probably a red herring.

Mr Akkerman was born in a leafy middle-class suburb of the city. His mother and father both work. He is their only child. He had normal milestones, and an entirely uneventful early childhood. Had lots of friends at school, Mr Akkerman tells me. Achieved the equivalent of six good GCSEs (standard eight). No trouble at school, besides the one fight with another lad. Left school, completed two years of compulsory military service with an infantry unit to the north of the country. Returned to civvy street, and went to technical college to train as a boiler maker. I ask about alcohol or drugs, and he tells me not to be ridiculous, he drinks only grape juice, and the only leaves he indulges in, is holiday leave. I spontaneously laugh out loudly. Heaven knows what Sister Jantjies will think if she could hear the laughter. Mr Akkerman follows up immediately with a joke about a monkey who hitched a ride with a crocodile across a flooded river, or something to that effect. It's a treat seeing him. We continue. I ask if he has ever had any serious head injuries.

'Only when I get home too late on Friday nights!' he fires off another one-liner.

Barely able to contain my urge to laugh again, I try to give him a serious look. We will never finish if it stays as jolly as this. To make it work, this assessment will have to be like the choreography of a circus show. Deadly serious performances, interspersed with breaks of frivolity thanks to the clowns.

'Well, OK, once when I came off my bike, I was out cold', he confesses.

'How long for?' I ask.

'One hour, or maybe a bit more, but I don't remember any of it to be honest', he replies.

And that was that, as far as the history was concerned.

I decide to check out the lie of the land first, and do a Mini Mental State Examination to get an idea of what, if anything, should formally be tested. How naive. Mr Akkerman scores 30 out of 30.

This provides no information other than the conclusion already known, which is that Mr Akkerman needs to be formally tested. That's what clinical neuropsychologists do, and why he was referred, for heaven's sake! Oh well, such is the nature of attempting short-cuts. At least the formal testing progresses fast, and smoothly. But wait a minute, does he have a slight lisp, or something about his speech which is not quite right? Can't be sure. What is sure, it that he has no problems with processing and concentration. From the look of things, neither with his general intellectual ability. Mr Akkerman achieves an IQ score of 129 on a four subtest prorated Wechsler Adult Intelligence Scale. Follows that up with a good performance on the Wechsler Memory Scales also, associative learning percentile 81, logical memory percentile 99, similar on delayed recall and percentile 90 on visual memory. The Rey Complex Figure looks fine as well, with a perfect copy (percentile 99), a normal strategy revealed by the colourful pattern of his approach to the task. Thirty minutes later his recall of the figure equates to percentile 80. The Hooper Visual Organisation Test shows intact visual perceptual integration with a score of 28½ out of 30. Mr Akkerman lists 26 words in one minute, which is fine for him. I notice his possible slight problem with articulation again. He is fine on the Trail Making Test, percentile 67 for A, and 70 for B. We finish off with the Austin Maze. He scores 14; 5; 7; 6; 6; 6; 8; 2; 2; 2; 0; 0; 0. Which is normal. But it is very noticeable how he finds his numerous errors on trials 1–10 totally hilarious.

'OK, I go left here, oops, I went right instead! Now why did I do that, I knew it was wrong! he laughs.

I think I know at least a couple of hypothetical reasons why. And therein lays the problem of co-morbidity.

Mr Akkerman's protocol does not fit the conference lecture on neuropsychological deficits in young adults with early onset MS. Research participants are of course highly selected, and, if it's decent research, free of major co-morbidity. Not in the hospital setting, though, here we have to see all comers. Cream off the 'good' ones, and you are soon toast with the rest of the clinical team. Furthermore, while in this case Mr Akkerman was tested in his mother tongue, it does not always happen that way in a clinic setting. We simply cannot say, sorry, you cannot be tested because there are no norms for the tests that need doing, or they have not been translated into your mother tongue. Let's send you back empty-handed. No, clinicians invariably have to make a plan of sorts to help their patients. In fact, '*kom aan, maak 'n plan*' ('come on, make a plan') is one of the colourful local sayings for when things get tough. Returning to Mr Akkerman, his schooling achievements were average, and he had completed a further qualification. He also scored very high as regards general intellectual ability. Which makes it all the more surprising that he displayed such a gross qualitative sign of executive, or 'frontal' problems on the Austin Maze. In one of the worn blue books (Kevin Walsh) on my desk, there is mention of exactly this – a verbal-praxis disconnection. Interpreting the protocol, it may be Mr Akkerman's MS, or who knows, that head injury, which explains his performance. How can this be useful for his rehab? I might choose to ignore the fact that MS and head injury have different trajectories, and instead focus on his presenting problem in the here and now. Maybe suggest when giving him feedback about his test results, that he pauses and weighs options before implementing solutions to everyday problems. We'll work on that to start off his rehabilitation. But I suspect he'll shrug off what is an obvious plan to me for helping him, as being madness.

8

Life

Psychiatric aspects of neurological injury

No excellent soul is exempt from a mixture of madness.

(Aristotle)

Trust

I don't like it when I can see the smoke of something burning in the distance, usually in the direction of the airport. But today there is no smoke, only a quiet fragility in the still, clear African air. Even though it is a fresh summer's morning today, oddly something seems a bit stale, like old smoke. Less friendly, not exactly as welcoming as can be? It is difficult to put a finger on what exactly it is, but, as a lot of my patients have said over the past 10 months or so, something is not quite right. Is it imagination, or have people been less friendly than usual over the past few days? Some of the porters in the passages inside the warehouse of souls, bodies and corpses where we work have recently not greeted me. Sometimes even failed to make eye contact. Suddenly very immersed in whatever they were doing, or intently studying a piece of paper in the hand, as if it is a holy scroll. Maybe I'm imagining this too, but I also hear less singing, for some of our patients a threnody. Normally, in the distance coming from the direction of the emergency department, there is sometimes the muted sound of singing by the nurses. On the wards, some of the nursing staff encountered on daily visits also seemed a bit off recently. Even Dr Burger has been less talkative – possibly, given that he has a significant floor effect at baseline in this department. He's not a man of many words, and to top it all has been distracted by the new house doctor who recently started a three-month rotation in the unit. Or maybe it is his plans to return to Canada.

The path I follow this morning is my usual. Through the imitation brass frame glass doors, and into the face (-less) brick cave. It is starting to feel like a well-trodden route, although leading off to something new almost every day. No two days are the same, no two patients identical. I decide to buy a paper from the small tuck shop immediately to the left on the inside after the entrance on 'our' side of the hospital. This side is truly the 'back door', where the busses and taxis stop, and is much more noisy than the 'front' side of the hospital. A cove of perceptual overload by sounds, smells and sights. Under apartheid the hospital used to be divided into two massive halves, connected by long passages. A mirror image of each other, a reflection of the minds of mad politicians. Our side used to be the 'non-white' part of the hospital. Mercifully, much of so called 'grand apartheid' has been dismantled, even though not in every insane mind as yet. The first real (democratic) election ever is due in three months. But things have been a bit more unstable than usual. People are anxiously anticipating this momentous event. Better get that paper to find out what's happening in the world. The shopkeeper seems distant. '*More, more, hoe gaan dit vandag? Kan ek asseblief 'n Times kry?*', I ask ['Good morning, how are you today, may I please have a *Cape Times*'].

The paper is very carefully placed on the counter, and I am asked for 50 cents. We make eye contact. The shopkeeper gives a barely audible greeting. That's odd. I am a 'regular customer'. My new intern (Irene) and I often buy cheap pies here. Irene is married to one of the doctors in the hospital. I find it quite incongruous that someone who looks like Irene with her short blonde hair, as if she should be having her lunch in a coffee shop in Paris, actually claims to like, no, *prefer* these . . . The man is usually friendliness and fun personified, and always asks after her: '*En waar is blondie vandag?*' ['Where is the blonde today?'], should I arrive without Irene. In fact, he usually provides a running commentary on anybody or anything that enters his little kingdom at the entrance to the castle of injury, illness and madness. The visitors' attire, choice of purchase (always fiercely praised of course – he is a businessman after all). With a shrill voice easily beating the noise of the informal and formal transport hustle and bustle outside the door. None of that today. Nor the week (s?) before. I decide to ask.

'*Wat is fout, hoekom is jy so suur, het ek iets verkeerd gedoen?*' ['What's wrong, why are you so sour, have I done something wrong?'], I broach the subject.

After a long silence, waiting for a couple of other customers to leave, he looks around and then leans forward.

'*Is jy mal? Jy het niks gedoen nie. Dis die verkiesing, man. Almal is bang. Niemand trust vir niemand nie*' ['Are you mad? You've done nothing, man. It's the election. Everybody's frightened. Nobody trusts nobody'], he confesses.

I almost tell him that he can trust me. That I am a clinician, not a politician. And that I come here to *work*, not for photo shoots with newborn babies.

Suspicion

It is the early morning clinical team meeting in the green lounge. The discussion is about who will take which of the new ward referrals before the rest of the day's outpatient work can be started. Fortunately there is a large pool of 'takers'. The overnight referrals of patients who took overdoses ('ODs'), are seen by the sixth-year medical students, or student interns (SI) as they are known, the house doctor and the intern clinical psychologists. After they have assessed the patients, they in turn present each case to the respective psychiatrists and psychologists. If they are not around, a registrar will do. Although the registrars are difficult to find as they are usually seeing patients for their consultants, or studying for exams. I remember being an intern, and how this job, especially on a Monday, can take up most of your morning. It always made me a bit apprehensive on Sundays, because of the unpredictability of the new week starting the following day. Sometimes there were many referrals, while at other times perhaps only two or three. Whatever the case, if you finished with seeing your referrals too long before your peers, their suspicions were raised. Well, how thorough was he actually. Or, she just got the 'easy' ones, meaning the very clearly impulsive, non-lethal ODs. And, he must have asked one of the other interns (different rotation), his buddy, to help out. Thankfully those days are over for me. But they have been replaced by much more responsibility, and in a specialism that I am still trying to find my feet in. In effect, I am an intern of sorts yet again, a learner clinical neuropsychologist.

The referral allocation meeting attended by a pecking order scrum of students, interns, registrars and their entourages is left behind, to start the work for the day. First in the schedule is Mr Jannie Prins (case # 34). He is 22 years old. The referral is from the psychiatric hospital affiliated with ours, located a few kilometres across town. The referral letter says the patient has a provisional diagnosis of suspected epilepsy. The referrer makes clear that this is at present only a preliminary working diagnosis, and would we be kind enough to provide a clinical neuropsychology opinion. More specifically, formal neuropsychological testing please. I collect Mr Prins from the waiting room. He looks really young, younger even than his 22 years would suggest. He is slender, and makes little eye contact when I introduce myself. Maybe he is anxious. Or shy. Maybe both. He walks with almost too quiet footsteps, careful not to make a noise, looking down at the floor the whole time. We'll soon find out what's up. We enter my room and it is striking just how polite he is. He patiently waits by the chair, until I ask him to be seated, rather than just do the obvious thing and sit down. Once seated, he leans forward a little bit, almost expectantly, or like someone attending an important meeting. His pupils are quite large, looking a bit stunned. Suddenly he realises he is still wearing his cap, and hastily takes it off, revealing the early growth stage of a pretty afro. Mr Prins mumbles an apology. I tell him not to worry, that it does not bother me if he wants to wear his cap.

'How can I help today, Mr Prins?'

He immediately leans back into his chair, almost flinching. He seems to be thinking, pensively considering things. Then Mr Prins slowly leans forward again, although a bit more tentatively this time. He appears to be a little bit reluctant. There is a slight twitch in the corner of his mouth. His dark brown eyes are scanning my faces, in jerky movements like the metal ball in a pinball machine.

'Can you really help me?' he finally manages to say something.

'I will try my best'.

There is a long pause. The clock on the wall makes itself heard in the now overly quiet room, saying in its usual monotone that time cannot be stopped. The inevitable is on its way.

'OK. I am a bit stuck. Things have not been right, you know', he volunteers while glancing sideways at me.

It is not clear at all what he is trying to say, and I ask, 'What things? Do you mind telling me a little bit more?'

But Mr Prins remains as vague as mist in front of an African full moon. Whatever angle I try, we get back to the same nebulous theme of something being wrong. Square one on the chessboard of whatever is causing the checkmate in his mind. I almost feel like shouting that I know that 'something is wrong', and in fact that's exactly why he is here today! But *what* is the question. Of course I do no such thing. In a converse twist, his *symptom* is vagueness. I have a lot of compassion with his struggle to string together a coherent narrative from the pallet of colours he needs to paint his dark or colourful problems. It must be terrible. Or maybe I am projecting some of my own frustrations here?

It is time to change strategy, not for the first time, nor the last time. Perhaps doing a history at this point will finally get the show on the road. Patients generally like to talk about themselves, where they come from and so forth. Or at least prefer it to the bedside testing and assessment. Testing is normally experienced by patients as a bit more anxiety provoking and tiring, being put under the spotlight to perform. But we also get nowhere with the history. Has he got long-term autobiographical memory problems? No, come on, he is 22, for heaven's sake – pull yourself together, focus, think! I intently look at Mr Prins who is now frowning like a man on the verge of a breakthrough, while trying to order my own thoughts. Once again, something does not feel quite right. He is somewhat, what's the word, defensive? No, I think I finally got it now, *guarded*. Time to change strategy. Again.

Looking him straight in the eye, I ask, 'Mr Prins, I would like to do some tests with you. These tests will help me to understand how good your memory is, how well you can solve problems, how fast you are, and so forth. They will all start easy, and then become gradually more difficult. That allows us to see how good you are compared to other people. Would you be willing to do these?'

The word 'good' makes his ears prick up. This time here is no hesitation before he answers.

'Yes, no problem!' comes the enthusiastic reply. Almost as if he is saying 'bring it on'.

We start with a shortened Wechsler Adult Intelligence Scale, administered in his mother tongue. He engages from the start, clearly wants to do well, who knows, maybe even impress me. Or perhaps prove something. After the first three subtests Mr Prins is more relaxed. He makes much better eye contact now. Then something interesting happens. He has a quick look around the room, scans everything left, right and behind himself. Almost as if he is checking if everything is OK. And then he leans forward, and confides in me. In a secretive whisper.

'There are red and black forces out there. The black ones are good, they look out for me. The red forces . . .' He pauses suddenly, frowns, then looks me up and down.

'The red ones are bad. It's all the blood that makes them bad'.

Thank heavens I'm wearing white, I think before asking, 'Where are they, Mr Prins?'

'You can't see them, they hide everywhere, then at night they drain your blood', Mr Prins now sounding quite anxious continues with his explanation.

A much more detailed explanation will definitely be needed.

'Sure, I understand what you are saying, but how do they operate? Tell me more about that?'

Another long, intent look at me, before the answer comes, 'They send me messages. There was one for me the other day, on the radio. Radio Good Hope. A request for a song, and in the song they mentioned blood'.

Mr Prins stops.

'Please carry on'.

'Blood. On the railway tracks. I am sure the song was for me. They are coming for me. I stopped taking the train, and took the taxi. The black forces saved me. They are everywhere, in the air. You cannot see them. Like the shop. You walk down the street, then suddenly there is a shop. Or the time has changed. Almost like the taste of *bobotie* [a local version of something similar to cottage pie, or haggis]. You think it's this, then it all changes, in flash'.

'Thank you very much, Mr Prins, I think I get it now. We'll look after you very well here in the hospital. Please don't you worry about a thing. As you can see, the hospital here is on *our* side of Black River Parkway' [a major road dividing the northern and southern suburbs in the city].

Reassurance as part of good bedside manners is all well and good, but what about the science of Mr Prins' psychometrics? Well, doing the tests probably distracted him, and by default helped him to engage. Maybe it gave him time to suss out the situation, develop trust. Neuropsychological testing also provides the structure some patients quite desperately need to organise, even if temporarily, their chaotic cerebral traffic. Neuropsychological testing is in fact often the beginning of rehabilitation. Or perhaps Mr Prins saw there was nothing red in my office . . . But for the record, his short Wechsler Adult Intelligence Scale prorated IQ score was 81. The highest subtest performance was on information, with a standard score of 10.0, indicating a likely average pre-morbid IQ. The lowest subtest score was on digit symbol, with a standard score of only 5.0, suggesting problems with processing. The block design subtest I felt would be unhelpful to administer. As we all know, even on the original Wechsler Adult Intelligence Scale standardised for use in South Africa at the time, the blocks are white and . . . well, red. And what about the rest of the formal neuropsychological testing? Well, as can probably be figured out, we had a lot of bad groups of people and forces, their plots, counterplots, double crossings, betrayals and other important business to work through and fend off, or shall we say temporarily banish from the consultation room. Yes, at some point even the windows had to be closed, despite the heat. We never completed a full neuropsychological testing as its limits as a useful diagnostic tool for this patient had been reached early during the assessment. There was no need to continue as the diagnosis was clear when ignoring the numerical values and paying much closer attention to the qualitative data, Mr Prins' narrative and its content. Or as clear as these things can be to a clinical neuropsychologist still learning the trade. Mr Prins was indeed subsequently, when presented at a psychiatry ward round, deemed to suffer from schizophrenia, of the paranoid type.

Limits

When reading up about it a bit later, reassuringly the textbooks confirmed that Mr Prins' neuropsychological management was most likely correct. Cognitive impairment and its anatomical correlates are reasonably well understood within clinical neuropsychology and neuroscience. The same (mostly) with physical impairments after brain injury. But when thinking about behavioural or personality changes secondary to brain injury or illness, things become a bit more tenuous, to say the least. It is here in this intellectual no man's land that art comes to visit science, while philosophy keeps a watchful eye on the exchange, empiricism expectantly remaining in the spectator stands. And as regards mental health, or frank psychiatric illness, the empirical plot is sometimes lost in the duel. It is here where the clinical neuropsychologist, and, for example, neuropsychiatry and behavioural neurology, are taxed to their limits. It is in these borderlands between the sciences and arts that clinicians and scientists are often powerless to do nothing more than stumble in a darkness devoid of any owls. Under Dr Burger's watchful eye as well as the apprenticeship of daily hospital demands for answers, I learn some of the inbuilt limitations of science, of *life*. Dr Carstens adds his short, sharp insight also: try not to fall into the seduction of 'neurologising'. I am too embarrassed to ask him what he means by that, but later found out from my *confidante*, Dr Burger, what exactly this means. Dr Burger smiles when he explains, as if he has lived many times what he is about to tell me.

'Things should add up. Don't fit symptoms onto scan findings. Especially when the symptoms largely constitute narrative. Which is what we rely on to a significant degree for eliciting signs and symptoms of mental illness. *Narrative*. The ultimate catch-22', Dr Burger concludes with a weary look in his eyes.

Dr Burger got a lift to work with the new house doctor. He looks sheepish when confessing that now at the end of the day, he realises he probably did not think it through very well this morning when getting into her car.

I thought things were going really well for them, so barely able to contain my surprise, ask, 'Why?'

'She's on call tonight and obviously needs her car. I forgot about it when she told me last night. May I ask a favour, can I catch a lift home with you?'

I don't tell him that my immediate incorrect interpretation about what he first said, without the slightest warning nailed its own story to the notice board that must partly be my frontal lobes. Just that he is very welcome to get a lift home.

While driving home our conversation returns to the day, Dr Carstens' warning against 'neurologising', and one of its more potent anti-venoms, the ability to wrestle objective facts from the hands of narratives. We put the world of science, clinical practice and survival to rights while seated in a Japanese pickup going up an African hill. One of the simplest, but also paradoxically most difficult shifts to make as a clinical neuropsychologist is achieving intellectual, no internal *emotional* ownership, of the difference between objective and subjective. What patients tell us is their narrative. Speaking a narrative out loud does not necessarily make what is being said fact. Most mental symptoms cannot be objectively measured by only listening to a person's narrative. Doing things differently can. For example, someone reporting the terminal insomnia (early morning awakening), which is thought to form part of the diagnostic features of major depressive illness, can be objectively measured if a patient is admitted and nocturnal nursing observations are performed. Until then it remains reported, not observed. The context of patients' narratives are also very important to know, and consider.

The second point arrives seamlessly after the first as we reach the brow of the hill where the hospital is finally left behind us, out of sight even if you were to turn your head around to check. The beginning of suburbia, and more trees. For a man of few words, Dr Burger is suddenly very talkative. His point, it is becoming clear, concerns the origin, or neural correlates of symptoms.

'Let's take the following narrative: I feel depressed, and that life is not worth living anymore, doctor', he starts.

Fair enough. I hear that a lot.

Dr Burger continues, 'And for the sake of the argument, let's assume in this case it is the *truth*, and coexists with other features of depression. Say loss of appetite, poor concentration, weight loss, feelings of guilt and social isolation. Now what if I tell you that the onset of this came out of the blue, with no environmental triggers. And that the patient has a strong family history of depression. Contrast that with a wealthy mother who three weeks ago lost her only child, a little girl, when she drowned in a swimming pool. Or, the onset of the clinical presentation is six months after a stroke in someone so poor they have nowhere to live. Each of these have a different aetiology, some biological, some environmental, some psychological and some biological, psychological and environmental. Therein lies a dilemma, one of a few'.

Dr Burger pauses, before almost sounding like he is confessing, saying, 'The aetiologies of the different mental illnesses are at the best of times not well understood, and in the context of brain injury even less so. We won't venture into the territory of the same medication for our three hypothetical cases of depression'.

'OK Tomas, I get it, the dilemma of what you have just said. Just contrast it with the cognitive impairment revealed by testing in clinical neuropsychology, or the altered reflexes in neurology. More often than not the neural correlates add up, and both these and the symptoms or signs are objectively measureable. Repeatedly'.

'Well said. Poverty does not always explain everything. Thanks for the lift. See you tomorrow', and with that Dr Burger hops out of the car, absentmindedly fumbling for the keys to his house.

I have absolutely no idea what he meant by that.

Favours

'Can you do me a big favour, Rudi?'

Oh dear, quick, think of an excuse a little inner voice cautions. But I say, 'yes of course, Fana'. Saying 'no' before having even seen a patient is viewed as professional suicide in a university teaching hospital like this. First see, then, and only then say yes or no. To 'bounce' referrals before you've actually seen them is done at your own peril. If the interns do it, they fail. If we do it, we have no friends. Well not quite that bad, but anyway. It's not the done thing.

'Can you please, please test Miss Uys for me? Listen, I know she been in the psychiatric system for a good few years, with a confirmed diagnosis of schizophrenia. But still, I'd like to know more about her cognitive functions. And I also have not forgotten that there have been a few unsuccessful attempts to test her. She used to be at university, you know, had a life', he appeals to both the heart, and reason.

And it is a fair point, or points, he is making for ensuring the best care for his patient. I thank the psychiatry registrar Dr Fana Hudike (he is a good friend of mine, in fact, and will become a very important mentor in the future), and say, 'I'll crack on with it as soon as I have an outpatient slot, Fana'.

The phrase 'had a life' worms its way into my heart. Fana's request reminds me of the relativity of testing someone additional in my already busy schedule, versus sitting on the other side of the table in the consultation room, *being* tested. The thought makes me chastise myself for having been a bit of a cold-hearted, work-shy, clinical neuropsychologist when Fana asked me to do him a favour. I regain a grip on my thoughts. God, Ruuds, as she now calls me, but you are hard on yourself today! Even more than usual. Lighten up. Of course I'll see Fana's patient. It's not a big deal.

A couple of weeks later I see Miss Jamie Uys (case # 59). She is 26 years old. Looks both older and younger than her 26 years. Frozen in a time gone past, a moment in youth, and already burnt out to an age beyond hers. Has Miss Uys got Han Solo syndrome? I realise with a shock I am just four years older than her. Miss Uys has lovely, green eyes, but they somehow are empty of *something*. Dirty blonde hair, shoulder length and of slender build, about five foot six tall. Her skin is in a slight mess with acne, looking a bit raw in places. Like an adult wrapped with an adolescent's coverings. Miss Uys is casually dressed, as a student a few years ago would have been. But she is not a student anymore, not intellectually free. On the contrary, her liberty has been taken away many times over the years during periods of sectioning and re-sectioning for involuntary admissions to various psychiatric wards. The brief history is that she almost finished her degree at a good university, which must undoubtedly have been difficult to get into. She cleared the gates to the exclusive pen of academia, and her first year was a wonderful kaleidoscope of intellectual stimulation and socialising. However, during her second year things gradually started to go wrong. By the beginning of the third year the dream imploded. Miss Uys started to display increasingly strange behaviours, unusual thoughts and her self-care markedly deteriorated. She never completed her degree. After student health intervened halfway through her third and final year, she was admitted to hospital. During her admission there, a psychiatric assessment revealed the nature of her illness. The rest is history. She has spent most of her life since that time in and out of the local psychiatric hospital, in different wards. Her relapses are mostly associated with the sudden onset of very unpredictable behaviours.

I am apprehensive. This is a futile enterprise. Or as Fana said, 'a big favour'. It is unnaturally quiet in the room. I look up from my neuropsychology tests packed out on the desk, and become aware of her green eyes still being impassively fixed on me.

'Dr Hudike asked if I would be kind enough to perform neuropsychological testing. I am aware that this has been requested in the past. Would you be up for it today? Honestly, please say no if you don't want to. It's OK. What do you think?' I ask, anxiously wishing she would decline, refuse to consent.

I look at her. My anxiety suddenly dissipates, and a sadness takes its place. She looks so, so young. And yet, so aged, some facial features hard as old concrete. The shape of her mouth carved by loss. I suspect the testing is actually a big deal for her.

She is still staring, unblinking, but scanning what feels like every inch of my face, up and down, left and right, before she answers, 'Yes'.

'Thank you. Please tell me if anything is not clear, and I'll repeat. You know what it entails, you've tried a few times in the past from what I've heard'.

The way she looks at me stabs towards me again. She is so young, and so worn out.

'Also please tell me if you are thirsty, or hungry, and we'll sort out someone to take you to the canteen. Are you sure you are OK to be tested, and ready to start?'

Silence. But somehow I know she has consented.

Miss Uys' neuropsychological testing commences. She collaborates well. Looks like she is trying very hard. She bites her nails incessantly. Will they bleed? There are furrows etched on her forehead, her eyes slits of intense concentration, the green now barely visible. The room is charged with effort, suspense and hope, some mine, some hers, but none visible. Then suddenly there is a brief moment where the impenetrable veil of her green eyes drops and she looks at me with expectation. No, actually a desperately sad plea for approval, reassurance from me that she, her mind is OK. The first time today she has showed any emotion. In doing so, she catches me off guard. Oh no, how very powerless we are in this job! I pray she cannot see my impotence to make her 'better', or that in a moment of weakness I might be tempted to say, 'don't worry, everything is fine'. But would it be right to reassure her? Up to this moment it had not occurred to me – maybe she also *wants* to know? To know what's happened to her mind, the essence of who she was, and now is no more. Maybe I am projecting my own fears onto her, should life have worked out differently. I briefly look outside the window, searching for the sun, and then crack on with the testing. We finish after lunch. Miss Uys does not ask how she had done. I don't offer to tell. Maybe it would be better to first score all the tests. Or am I just buying time? She does not look at me when I say goodbye as she leaves with the orderly. The ambulance will take her back to her hospital. I leave to go and see an inpatient upstairs in ours. The last job before the weekend.

By Monday afternoon her test results are ready. However, Miss Uys is too unwell to travel from her hospital to ours to receive feedback. She has had another relapse over the weekend. Became obsessed with the devil and black wolves roaming the gardens, although there are no wolves in this part of the world. Not in the animal world anyway. Only leopards in the mountains in the distance, but they are way too shy to ever let themselves be seen by humans. Miss Uys was detained and moved to a long-stay secure ward in her hospital. Meanwhile back in an office in another hospital building about eight kilometres away from hers, Miss Uys' cognitive profile dispassionately etches out in a puzzle of numbers and percentiles, the tragedy of her altered life. On a shortened Wechsler Adult Intelligence Scale her prorated IQ score was 108. Well into the 'normal', or average range, but lower than one would expect of a star student. Her decline from pre-morbid levels is starkly illustrated by comparing her highest Wechsler Adult Intelligence Scale subtest score with the lowest: 12.5 vs. 8.5, which gives a much better indication of the sheer steepness of the fall in ability. On the other hand, her performance on the Wechsler Memory Scales, associative learning, logical memory and visual reproduction were all normal. Her Hooper Visual Organisation Test performance equals 26/30, again a normal performance. The Word Naming Test yielded a score of 23, within reasonable normal limits, although probably slightly low for her in view of her academic history. With the Trail Making Test, she scored at the 90th percentile for trail A, and on B, the 71st percentile. Both very clearly normal performances. But *applying* her preserved cognition in the world out there, is likely to be another story. The Austin Maze, a test of executive function, was her nemesis. She performed as follows on successive trials: 18, 11, 7, 5, 10, 8, 7, 5, 7, 5, 2, 0, 3, 2, 2, 1, 1, 2. Her inability to learn from, and eliminate the last remaining errors, graphically displayed by the shape of the curve these numbers form.

I really wish I could have seen Miss Uys again. Maybe I could at least then have told her that some, actually quite a lot, of the neuropsychological functions I tested were fine. But on reflection, even if she were well enough to attend a session for feedback, it may well simply have hurt her more. You see, she has insight into her condition. They may think otherwise on the ward, but I *saw* it. When? On which measure? Ward staff might rightly ask this question. The answer is not simple. It was just that brief moment when she looked me in the eyes while I was testing her, and her eyes made clear that during lucid intervals she knew, *something*. Later that day I bump into Dr Hudike, the registrar who referred Miss Uys to me.

He seems genuinely pleased to see me, and says, 'Thank you so much for testing Miss Uys, I really appreciate it. Now we finally have a baseline for future reference. By the way, did I tell you, her EEG came back abnormal, bilateral temporal'.

'What do you think will happen to her, Fana?'

I know Dr Hudike cares about her very much, feels deeply sorry for her. I also know that as her psychiatrist he realises the futility of trying to make her better. How there is no realistic treatment in the sense of providing a cure for the pollution of her genes, neurotransmitters, no, who knows, maybe her soul. Believe me, he has asked plenty a favours, tried everything from occupational therapy, psychotherapy, to drugs. I suspect he knows my question was a rhetorical one. Just a primitive mechanism to make sounds, words, to hide my ineptness in declaring my own sadness and frustration. I also suspect we both know she is now a citizen of the province of perdition. Without a passport to return to the country of free will, where she emigrated from against her will a few years ago.

'Honestly, I don't know, Rudi', he quietly replies.

Pollution

For today's schedule, a follow-up clinic has been booked for me. I see Miss Elsie Jakobs (case # 54) first, and ask how she got on with the tests I administered a couple of weeks ago. To my surprise, she does not answer me. Instead of being curious, Miss Jakobs, 25, looks paralysed with fear, stunned to silence. Her pupils are huge, her eyes wide open, as if desperately straining to let every ounce of information in. She looks like she is literally holding her breath.

I smile at her, 'I have good news for you, Miss Jakobs'.

Miss Jakobs has been through the psychiatric site's alcohol detox and rehab programme. She was already dry for four weeks when I tested her. She is young, pretty, educated to degree level, and a fellow health professional. Unfortunately Miss Jakobs had been drinking very excessively for several years, due to personal and work stressors. Hers is not that much of an unusual story. It's not easy being a full-time clinician. The emotional demands can break strong spirits. Things gradually spiralled out of control for her. Eventually she started to neglect her diet, went from drinking wine, to spirits. Soon her work started suffering and financial difficulties followed shortly after. Then after a weekend of very heavy drinking, she became acutely ill. A neighbour called an ambulance, and Miss Jakobs, after protesting that she was fine, ended up in the emergency room of our hospital for an assessment. She was very ill, apparently nearly died. After detox Miss Jakobs was referred to the off-site psychiatric hospital for inpatient alcohol rehab.

It is still deathly quiet in the room.

'All your neuropsychological test results were normal, Miss Jakobs. And they were normal for *you*, which is important. What that means is that we expect people who are better educated, or more able, to do better on these tests, than say someone who was less able before their illness or injury, or might, for example, be much older than you'.

The room is still apprehensively quiet, bar the new air conditioning unit humming it's reassuring tune. Despite waiting for her to speak, not a single question to break the silence. I look away from Miss Jakobs, and down at the list of numbers and percentiles in front of me, to double check I have not missed something. Clinician OCD, Dr Burger calls it. No mistakes this time though, there are indeed no impaired or even modestly low scores. From her medical file it is known how much alcohol she consumed, and just how unwell she was during the withdrawal phase. It's almost a miracle, like a second chance being given to a very troubled soul. Obviously lecturing her will be unhelpful. Miss Jakobs has been punished enough by life. My job is not to preach, lecture, condemn, tell her she's had a 'close shave', or punish by default. At its core our job is to reduce suffering. Plus science is on her side – the recently published neuropsychology research shows that abstinence from alcohol misuse can in fact result in some improvement in cognition.

'Before I go over the details with you, is there anything you'd like to ask me first, Miss Jakobs?'

She still says nothing.

'Miss Jakobs?'

She does not answer. But that does not mean she is refusing to communicate with me. I look up from the numbers in front of me. Miss Jakobs cannot answer me at the moment. Her neck is a nettle garden of mottling, her carotid overenthusiastically beating the rhythm of life and despair. She is sobbing very quietly. For once I am relieved to see a patient cry. Offloading pent-up emotions after pain and worry can sometimes, just sometimes be the beginning of the road back for even the most lost of souls. I suspect this might apply to Miss Jakobs. I will see her for support and psychotherapy post-discharge to help her on her way back to the past and hopefully a better future.

Shortly after four, I go upstairs to try and find Dr Burger before he leaves. We are supposed to go for a run after work, and I need to find him early enough to check if it is still on. No point phoning him at home after work, he's not a phone person. Abrupt, terse, believes telephones are only useful for work purposes. Like when he is 'op spoed' – literally translated as 'on speed', but actually meaning 'on call'. We meet as he exits the neurology ward. The lift down has nothing to say other than its usual groaning and protesting, begging the government to put more money into health care, and less into the armed forces.

'A busy day?' Dr Burger asks.

'Sort of, but quite varied', I reply.

'Hmm, should keep you on your toes', he says, his eyes suggesting his mind has already started the journey home.

I decide to prevent him from going home before me.

'Tomas, what will make me a good clinical neuropsychologist?'

'Umm, lots of things. Knowledge. The ability to apply your knowledge, think and reason within the limits of said knowledge. And so forth'.

He is not going to get away.

'Like what, Tomas?'

'Come on, you already know the stuff. Neuro-anatomy, diagnostics, testing, neuropathology, taking a history, not a good one, an excellent one. I could go on until Monday. But before it slips my mind, don't ever forget that all of these, however fantastic your knowledge might be, can be fatally poisoned by arrogance. Never stop imagining what life is like on the other side of the desk. Right, see you later, and don't be late', Dr Burger says as the doors open to let us exit the lift.

The tuck shop is full, and business must be brisk. A mad mix of Xhosa, English and Afrikaans spills out of the entrance, the shop acting as a boom box to amplify the plethora of sounds and languages. Diesel and petrol fumes gamely compete with the noise. The noise and fumes enter the building every time the swing doors to the hospital opens. The doors emotionlessly squeaking a hoarse metallic welcome to another planned, but unplanned arrival, thank you, thank you very much. To an alien world. The buses and informal taxis have delivered the visitors who will be coming to see their relatives in hospital. I suspect some might be scraping together their last few coins to buy a little present, or maybe just a paper for a loved one. Possibly as a feeble antidote to the poison that has brought their relative, friend or lover to this place. Now too frightened to know what to say when they see them incongruously in bed during broad daylight, they offer their pathetic gifts, like the widow's two coins. In the car park the heat is huge, crushing all in its way from above, simultaneously radiating back out of the black tarmac and breaking up the remaining light of the day. The scanning and searching of row upon row of illuminated car roofs for where I parked this morning makes me squint. Then, for the first time today, as I focus my eyes I notice the magnificent African sky. The moon rising over the mountains in the distance. It is divinely beautiful, unnaturally huge. Conspicuously standing out against a contrasting deep golden brown sky created by air pollution from the sprawling townships and informal settlements stretching for miles around the hospital. People are at home making fires, cooking, to keep on living for another day. Today it is not the smoke of violence and death. Sometimes there is, if not sorrow, at least the transient beauty of sadness in toxic pollution. Provided you know how and where to look. It is impossible not to irrevocably fall in love with this job that life so kindly let me inherit.

9

Inheritance

Genetic disorders

The stream of time sweeps away errors, and leaves the truth for the inheritance of humanity.

(Georg Brandes)

Wills

There is the sound of a slightly odd, but by now familiar gait approaching my door. Dr Sharkova saunters into my office, carrying her collection of bags. Such a small frame, how does she carry them all? I am pleased to see her. Ana has not been in the unit for a couple of days. She puts all her bags on the desk, and unceremoniously plonks herself down in one of the chairs. Her long-range pager clatters onto the floor. While the pager is picked up from the floor, she looks me straight in the eyes and drops the bombshell.

'Prof Emmerson said I could have your office', she says in a matter of fact voice.

I am not pleased to hear that. It's a great office, huge, one whole wall consisting mostly of a giant window letting in an abundance of light. It is almost never necessary to turn on the lights. Plus recently the hospital maintenance team came to install air conditioning, an unheard of luxury. But naturally entirely appropriate after a passionate, prolonged argument (plea?) making the case that it would be totally, indisputably essential for the office of someone who test patients for hours at a time. At which point I sensed the bureaucrat considering my request may have thought that I was precariously close to overplaying my hand. Something in the way he looked up from his clipboard holding a mindless form. Plus I had to wait a long time before I inherited this office after the retirement of a senior colleague. So while two seconds ago I was mesmerised by Dr Sharkova's face, I now let out a silent, inner expletive and quickly prepare a strategy to get rid of her.

Her head is slightly tilted to the right, face framed by a thick, glossy brown mane. She has really nice green eyes, I notice as if seeing them for the first time. Something slightly disconcerting though, maybe the colour of sadness or bitterness?

'Listen, I am sorry to disappoint you, but the professor is head of the department of psychiatry. P-s-y-c-h-i-a-t-r-y. Yes? He has no say over me. But I promise you I will put my office in my will. You can inherit it when I am gone'.

I only get a gentle I-am-trying-to-be-patient-with-you smile in return, fingers of her left hand drumming on the desk where so many patients have struggled with little red and white blocks. Her hands are small. Let's see who can outstare who. This is my office.

'Well, he said as a new consultant, and from abroad, I deserve an office befitting of my status. And I told him your office was the best in the unit, I'd like to have that one. Anyway, psychology is part of psychiatry, we are after all in the same department, aren't we', Dr Sharkova says with a confusing glint in her eye.

She is starting to annoy me. Time to play my ace and end the conversation.

'I know the professor much better that you realise, sister. I will walk over to the medical school later today and have a chat with Rolf myself. He will never give this office to you. Mark my words. Never in a million years'.

Am I imagining it, or is she looking bemused? Stuff this.

'Thanks for coming over, is there anything else I can do for you today, Ana? I am busy'.

Get out of *my* office.

Suddenly Dr Sharkova bursts out laughing, flashing the ever so tiny central gap between her perfect white teeth, her badge of honour, a protest against the convention of perfection.

'Got you, Ruuds!' she shouts like a little child.

'Such a serious, serious man, about his precious office, his profession and his patients, would I ever go and plead with the professor behind your back for your office? The clinical *neuro*psychologist of the department! And a loner like you, we all anyway know you *need* your own office. But please do put me in your will, I'd really love that . . .' her final victory cry.

She is right. It's a mortal sin for clinicians working in the same team to backstab each other, and definitely not about something as petty as office space. We rely on each other. Loyalty is an important currency for survival in the hospital. Individualism doesn't really work here, the group's well-being as a whole is deemed more important. I cannot believe I fell for her! I concede defeat, joke that I was not ready, never will be, well *maybe*, and only for her, depends on what the reward for my sacrifice might be, to inherit her 'crap office'. We laugh at how well and truly I've been had. Probably because of having been distracted – but that is a more complicated story.

Walking down the long passage, on my way to the opposite side of the hospital, I again smile by myself while thinking about Dr Sharkova. I pass a porter, one I know, and he must have noticed me smiling, looking pleased with myself.

'*En vir wat lyk jy soos 'n kat wat room gesteel het?*' ['And for what do you look like a cat who has stolen cream?'], he greets me with a wink.

'*Nee man, iemand het nou net 'n lekker grap van my gemaak. Waar is jy op pad heen met daai klein bedjie?*' ['No my friend, some-one just played a joke on me. Where are you going with that little bed?'], I return his greeting.

'*Na die babas, daar's 'n paar plaas vars nuwe aankomste*' ['To maternity, a few new farm fresh arrivals'], he laughs back at me before disappearing around the corner.

Hospitals are strange places, complex microcosms of extreme con-trasts. There can be intense joy upon the arrival of a new life, or the survival of those who were not meant to. But there can also be intense sorrow for those who don't make it and who in their loved ones' minds were supposed to. Or quiet wailing for those for whom there is only very bad news, even if expected, or suspected but not yet confirmed. Hospitals are also the ultimate equalisers. When the time comes to us all, no matter how rich or poor, strong or weak, deformed or beautiful, only life as it was, death now or soon, something unimaginable, can be the outcome of a visit to this world. Those are the only inheritances available on the menu of failed cures, partial cures and non-curable. Randomised by science and fate in unequal measures. Sometimes the patient's will for this life was drawn up recently, or continually updated and modified over time. At other times inheritances arrive in a split second, as if by special delivery. Others are already in posses-sion of their will at birth, their inheritance in life already unmistakably cast for the future. For those of us who work here, day after day, year after year, humour is one of the small mercies to preserve our sanity. Humour prevents us from falling over backwards.

Forward

Drama fell straight off the stage, and into the waiting lap of our unit this morning. Mrs Blanche Kruger (case # 33) has been referred to us from our off-site psychiatric hospital. She is slightly overweight, with a mane of curly dyed blonde hair, her lips way too red. Mrs Kruger leans just that much more than is socially comfortable towards me in her chair. She looks as if she has stepped straight out of a painting depicting a stage play from the previous century. It is proving a bit of a roller coaster to do a clinical assessment and explain the nature of neuropsychological testing to her. Mrs Kruger is inappropriate, forward, and gives me a cross-examination before I can even get a word in.

'You are much too young to be a, what did you say it was young man, oh yes, a neuropsychologist. You are just a boy, still wet behind those ears!' she emphasises her concern with an index finger wagging to point out every aspect of my assumed ineptitude.

Fair point Mrs Kruger, I catch myself thinking for a moment. But rest assured, I will do my best for you.

Mrs Kruger does not mince her words. She is blunt, speaks her mind as thoughts enter her consciousness. No censorship whatsoever. The border guard we in science call the frontal lobe, has been fired a long time ago, no passports are required anymore. Up and down, left and right the ride on the roller coaster of her disorganised mind goes. She only comes up for air every now and then, and just very briefly. Literally just to inhale before the next salvo.

Sometimes when a patient has processing problems, we use their distractibility to try and steer the interview towards the work and tasks that need completing. Today this strategy is not working with Mrs Kruger. Her distractions are to internal stimuli, not external. Suddenly Mrs Kruger tells me she'd very much like to marry me, once her divorce comes through. Emphasises the point by drumming on the desk with her fingers, her nails painted a vivid turquoise. I have no clue how to respond to *that*, we never had a class preparing us for this type of scenario. It is a struggle to contain my desire to laugh. Hardly a day passes where I am yet again totally surprised by what I hear or see. I wish I had a book to help me with the large swathes of life in this world here, which is never covered in academic clinical neuropsychology textbooks. The *missing chapters*, so to speak. But here in this room now, I must win a bit of time, and ask her how she is feeling today. No response. Or at least not one related to my question. I also enquire if she was up for the neuropsychological testing she has been referred to me for. Again, it is almost as if she did not hear, even though she looks me straight in the eye basically all of the time. The technicalities of testing, how long it should take us, breaks she will get, and so forth? Mrs Kruger instead starts to give me a detailed breakdown of the problems (as she sees it) leading up to her divorce. Some of the content makes me blush. Hopefully she thinks it's just a bit warm here in the office. Which with the new air-conditioning unit it isn't.

We continue with the assessment. Most of the effort goes into trying to keep track of the whirlwind of topics Mrs Kruger is covering.

'Do you think Johannes (her husband) will write a good will for me when we divorce?' she unexpectedly asks.

'I think you are confusing death with divorce, Mrs Kruger?' I say feeling even more confused.

Mrs Kruger thinks about it for a second, and then continues to describe her difficulties in a very disconnected, unemotional fashion. Next moment she takes another detour, and asks if I have got a cigarette for her. Before an answer is possible she has already moved on to the next topic. She never comments on her inner emotional world. Her locus is almost exclusively about thoughts, events and memories, as they come to consciousness, rather than any of her feelings. Mrs Kruger has Pick's disease. That is known from the referral and discussion with the doctor who referred her. The illness started 2½ years earlier. Mrs Kruger is only 41 years old. I feel bereft for her. Imagine hearing in your late thirties that you have an incurable, progressive neurological illness, which will gradually steal your soul, crush your cognition, before eventually killing you. And don't worry, you should not have to wait too long if it runs its 'normal' course. I would not even dream of telling Mrs Kruger I know how she feels. So I don't. What I by now do know is that Pick's disease is one of the fronto-temporal dementias. It is thought to probably be hereditary, although the exact mechanism(s) is not entirely clear. Mrs Kruger's narrative provides a colourful, at times humorous and at others tragic perspective of what is most likely a problem of aspects of executive control function, or the so-called 'frontal' functions. By the very nature of her pathology and how it affects the brain, this is a sensible interpretation of things thus far. But it would be important to test her anyway, as a baseline for future reference. For when the trajectory of her illness, or her ability to live independently, make her own decisions or instruct a lawyer might need to be re-considered.

Surprisingly, testing proves much easier to do than just talking to her. Somehow the testing situation perhaps provides the structure that she so desperately needs, but cannot initiate herself because of her executive problems. Her neuropsychological test results provide further evidence of how badly her illness has compromised her executive functions, in a person with exceptional pre-morbid general ability. As an indication of the latter, her Wechsler Adult Intelligence Scale Performance IQ is 141. However, in contrast her verbal IQ on the same scale is 108. Mrs Kruger achieves a normal (only just) score of 24 out of 30 on the Hooper Visual Organisation Test. There are a couple of very interesting qualitative signs though, for example, naming the fragmented flower stimulus on the test as 'an island, with a palm tree'. Her Wechsler Memory Scale scores are well within the normal range, but on the Rey Auditory Verbal Learning Test, she does display a ceiling, or 'frontal plateau' as it is sometimes referred to. Her performance is 9; 11; 11; 12; 11/7, showing rapid acquisition of knowledge but then no further significant gains. Looking more closely at signs for strategies she used on this test, the sequencing (numbered) of her recall indicates that there was most likely none.

Copying the Rey Complex Figure, Mrs Kruger achieves percentile 80, but the random sequence of the colour pens' lines, curves and curls we use to track our patients' strategy reflects the chaotic nature of her thoughts and actions. Her recall performance is equal to the 25th percentile, probably affected at least in part by her poor strategy when initially copying the design.

The Trail Making Test delivers another surprise. Mrs Kruger performs at the 39th percentile on trail A, but then unexpectedly improves to percentile 90 on trail B. It is usually the other way around in patients with frontal lobe pathology. It's not clear what exactly to make of this pattern, but it might have something to do with her fluctuating attention and distractibility. I make a mental note to ask my supervisor, Ms Carla De Bruin, when I see her next time. Next we do the Word Naming Test. Mrs Kruger manages 19 words, a performance that is too low for her, in view of her pre-morbid abilities and educational achievements. The main hypothesis is that she would have executive impairment. A couple of tests intended to assess executive functions follows. She struggles with the Porteus Maze, and makes four errors, an impaired performance for someone of her predicted pre-morbid intellectual ability. But it is the Austin Maze that really highlights her profound problems. Mrs Kruger just cannot learn the correct path, nor learn from her errors and use this knowledge to her advantage to eliminate mistakes. Her errors are as follows: 14; 12; 12; 5; 7; 9; 1; 2; 8; 5; 6; 4; 1; 4; 5; 4; 4; 5; 2; 3; 3. After the testing is finished, I have a closer look at her medical notes. A CT of her brain is reported as revealing evidence of frontal pathology. Reflecting on the case it is striking how for once there is no co-morbidity. Mrs Kruger did well at school, passing matric with university exemption. Meaning she achieved the required marks to secure a university place. Mrs Kruger also never had any head injuries of note, nor any past psychiatric problems. I wonder what will happen to her, and if I will ever see her again. What will she be like if she were to be retested in say two years? Will she even be alive?

Vacant

Several of the clinical posts continue to remain vacant, and a couple of these are in our unit. There is very little money going around. The currency has weakened on the international markets. The economy is just about limping along, political uncertainty dominating everything. The lack of maintenance of the hospital is becoming more and more obvious. In some of the hospital passages several of the ceiling tiles are missing. The arteries of pipes and wires keeping the place's inhabitants warm or cool, fed, lit, hydrated, transported, operated on, alive, just hanging on or stored for burial, are clearly visible here and there. There is a rumour that there are cats living in the ceiling because of the rats, but I find that hard to believe. What I do know for a fact is that it is becoming more difficult each day for everyone here than ever before to stem wave after wave of lost, and found, damaged human property. Even though not that important in the greater scheme of things in keeping the hospital able to provide the life-saving essentials, I can only hope that our psychology vacancies will soon be filled and that those arteries in the ceiling won't burst for a long time. I'll have to find time to plead yet again with the head of psychology, Dr Tanya Maxwell about our situation down here in the basement. Just the thought of walking over to the medical school to do this fills me with dread. First get through today though I decide. The unit's waiting space in the passage is already steadily filling up. Mr Chris Osler (case # 29) is the patient waiting to see me. He is 51 years old, and has recently been referred to us by neurology.

Mr Osler is sitting on a grey plastic chair with its impossibly thin black steel legs. When he stands up, I see he is of medium height and build, spindly legs, wavy brown hair and green-brown eyes. Mr Osler looks at me slightly disinterested I think, when I introduce myself. I ask him to come with me. It takes ages for him to walk with me down to my room. He walks like a much older man, short, shuffling steps. When we sit down, I ask Mr Osler what's been troubling him and why he thinks he is in hospital. He has freckles on his face, a mix of freckles and liver spots on his hands.

He hesitates briefly before answering the question, 'My memory is terrible. I used to be a plumber, with my own little business, you know. Did very well, it did, but now I cannot work. I forget too many appointments, where everything is, my tools get lost all the time, that sort of thing'.

'Anything else?'

'It's just chaos', Mr Osler says expressionless.

'Do you do any work now, Mr Osler?' I probe a bit further.

'Nothing, I am too slow'.

He struggles with his speech, and his sentences are short and effortful.

'Hmm. How long have you had these problems, Mr Osler?'

'I don't know, a few years I think?' Mr Osler quietly replies, sounding uncertain.

Mr Osler looks so unconcerned, no, that's not the right word, so unanimated about his problems that I ask him about his emotional experience of not being well.

'I guess I am a bit worried, but I am not sure', he replies with almost no feeling expressed.

He looks totally vacant.

A closer look at the file in front of me and the previous correspondence contained therein reveals that Mr Osler has had Parkinson's disease for the past three years. He indeed had to stop work, and now lives with his wife at home. He did OK at school, passing standard nine (one year before matric) and has no pre-morbid medical history of note. No head injuries, substance misuse, major surgery or psychiatric problems. Mr Osler functioned especially well in his job, and was respected as a competent and reliable plumber in his local area. I explain that I will be doing some tests with him, and what these are. For a moment he looks anxious.

'Are you a little bit worried about taking the tests, Mr Osler? It's not that bad, really. But you can say no if you don't want to do them', I enquire and try to reassure him at the same time.

'No. Not really', he replies with basically no emotion.

He comes across almost as superficial, his face completely expressionless.

It's puzzling. His affect is a bit odd, and he is really slow. Plus he struggles to talk, and by the sound of it, has quite significant memory problems. Mr Osler is the only patient for today, so I will have the time to do some neuropsychological testing while he is here. Plus then score and interpret it. The testing is the right thing clinically, and the subsequent scoring and interpretation also provides a watertight passport out of a boring meeting over at the medical school, anticipated to go on forever this afternoon. For once everyone's a winner.

During the formal testing, there are brief moments where Mr Osler looks a bit anxious, but when asked, dismisses the suggestion as being absurd. Without batting an eye. The main qualitative observation is that he is slow. So slow that I catch myself staring out of the window for periods, and also so slow that I can easily score his tests as we go along. We first complete a six subtest Wechsler Adult Intelligence Scale. Mr Osler achieves a prorated total IQ of 79. This summed score hides the fact that he scores 9.5 on both comprehension and similarities, but only 5.0 on digit span. It does look like he may have processing or working memory problems, so the decision is to test this hypothesis. Which is confirmed when he completes the Wechsler Memory Scales, performing on the first to second percentile for visual, associative and logical memory. While Mr Osler manages a reasonable copy of the Rey Complex Figure, he has no recall whatsoever of having even seen it before when I ask him to draw it again after about 30 minutes. Literally nothing, a score of zero. He tells me it's just not there anymore. But it is difficult to interpret his visual memory when he next scores 10 out of 30 on the Hooper Visual Organisation Test. Maybe his visual memory is affected by visual-spatial problems as well. Mr Osler manages a normal performance on the Porteus Maze. Or at least numerically, that is – his time taken to complete the test is way beyond what would normally be expected. I would never have completed Mr Osler's neuropsychological testing to make it in time for the meeting. The reality of testing patients who hardly ever perform as described in the test manufacturer's nicely bound manuals, today slowly turned a white lie into a fact.

Facts

The truth is that I don't know that much about Parkinson's disease, some of the dementias and genetic disorders. In our hospital we see a lot of head trauma, cerebro-vascular accidents, epilepsy and brain infections. These to a large extent mirror the broader psychosocial problems wearing the country down. A good opportunity then to spend some time with my supervisor in clinical neuropsychology to present Mr Osler, and also brush up on my knowledge about these other conditions. I, like my most of my peers, am in awe of Ms Carla De Bruin. She is probably one of the top clinical neuropsychologists in the country. She recently returned to the country after spending some time abroad with a highly regarded neuro-rehabilitation unit in the US. I tread carefully when I present Mr Osler. I depend on my supervisor for moral support, my own professional development and keeping up to date with new developments in the field, but ultimately also for a favourable formal assessment of my clinical skills and knowledge one day. I provide (I think) a good, structured but focused summary of my patient's history, main clinical features and psychometric findings to Ms De Bruin.

There is nothing more to add. Ms De Bruin looks at me with her piercing grey, almost silver eyes, remaining quiet. The light accentuates her high cheekbones and shiny light brown hair. She looks like someone inspecting something.

'I would have given him one look and know that he had Parkinson's disease'.

Oh no, I must come across as a total beginner. Her hair is very straight. Ms De Bruin has still not broken eye contact.

'Really nice presentation, Rudi, in particular the description of his slowness, and being so expressionless, one look at that, and I would have gotten it. By the way, how did you find this morning's neurology ward round with Bernard?'

I instantaneously relax, and say that it was very interesting and that I am very grateful for her organising that I can attend some of their rounds to help me learn more about some of the conditions more likely to be seen at their hospital. I omit to say that I almost fainted having to be on my feet for almost three hours standing around patients' beds, while Bernard talked almost non-stop, only pausing to histrionically act out some of the common neurological signs he was trying to illustrate to us.

Ms De Bruin is a super-fast talker, continually flitting between topics and concepts. My working memory is doing overtime all the time, just to try and keep up with her, never mind absorb anything. It is not always clear if she is disseminating facts, or testing the knowledge thereof. She goes through the core features of the dementias, emphasising that these disorders always entail a progressive decline in cognition. The pattern of decline may differ, for example, stepwise in vascular dementias, and more gradual with say Alzheimer's disease, she emphasises. The onset of a dementia can be at any time in life, but occurs mostly after the sixth decade. Dementia is not to be confused with a learning difficulty, which manifests before general cognitive ability has settled down, through pre- or peri-natal problems such as injury, toxins and other disasters. Some learning difficulties are genetically determined, before birth, she tells me, while others, about a fifth she reckons, through cultural deprivation. The latter sounds totally plausible, given the many patients we see who have through social ills such as lack of schooling been deprived of a healthy environment for learning. But at the same time I also guess that it depends on your tests, what they measure, norms, language and other factors such as a different (for example, to Western) conceptualisation of what exactly intelligence is. Ms De Bruin's voice demands my attention to her tutorial.

'Remind me to show you a couple of new tests I brought back with me from the States, a little bit later, if we have time left', she says.

She must have noticed that my thoughts drifted off.

We continue with the tutorial.

'Be careful not to confuse delirium with dementia', she warns with an ever so slightly raised eyebrow. Her grey eyes are boring through what feels like me radiating a lack of in-depth knowledge in this area of clinical neuropsychology.

She explains that delirium also presents with cognitive impairment, but that in contrast to dementia, a patient with delirium will usually noticeably fluctuate in their presentation.

'It's a disorder of attention, which fluctuates and affects other cognitive functions, including working memory. Not everyone with a memory impairment has dementia. Here are a few tricks. See the patients more than once to determine if they fluctuate, check the trajectory of their memory functions over time, ask a relative to tell you what *they* think is wrong and look for explanations, including a urinary tract infection, recent 'minor' head injury, suddenly stopping to drink', Ms De Bruin tries to cover the whole curriculum in one breath.

Speaking of working memory, how must I process all of that, I wonder? Undeterred, or maybe oblivious, she continues.

'Look for brain lesions, and if what is being reported on scan is compatible with the clinical presentation. If things don't add up, they don't add up. For example, in Pick's disease, you should look for evidence of frontal lobe problems and the psychometric profile should reflect this. And don't get caught out by the fact that many patients with dementia, may of course also sometimes present with a co-morbid delirium, or become depressed, to make it really difficult. Always consider the hierarchical nature of cognition. Basic functions such as processing influence higher-order functions such as memory and executive control. With testing, try to work more systematically. Test basic functions first, to make sure it is not impairments at this level, which may account for problems of say executive functions. Let's take a five-minute break now'.

Phew. Thank god for that.

The five minutes feels like five seconds, just enough to go to the bathroom, before we are back in her office. She is already waiting.

'I brought this with me from the States. See if you can do it. It's the Grooved Pegboard Test', is Ms De Bruin's opening line. Her energy is breathtaking. It is difficult to keep up with her.

The test on the other hand proves to be very easy.

'That was fast. Now I want you to try and solve this problem for me', Ms De Bruin says while taking from a grey metal filing cabinet drawer, what looks like a wooden base with three pegs, and some colourful rings.

'It is the Tower of Hanoi. A new test of so-called executive functions. You need to move the rings in the number of moves I tell you each time, to this position', she tells me while pointing at a photograph of the end goal.

Fair enough, seems straightforward. Indeed everything goes well up to the 4-ring, 11-move item. At which point suddenly things derail. Ms De Bruin's grey eyes are dispassionately carving into my hands and head, which are refusing to collaborate to solve the problem in front of me. The traffic and human bustle outside the hospital is sounding noticeably louder through the window. In a flash my heart starts to race and even faster, my mind runs away from me. The noise outside is now unbearably distracting. Why can't I do this simple test? Oh no, the ultimate nightmare, I have a frontal brain tumour! Suddenly I remember that I had a really bad headache after going for a run in the heat the other evening.

'Have a go in your own time while I go and make myself a cup of tea. There is no time limit on this test', she interrupts the internal noise of my super-aroused state of anxiety.

On my own in her office, in what suddenly feels like a peaceful and quiet environment, I complete the last two items without any further problems. After a few minutes Ms De Bruin comes back with her cup of tea. I casually show her that I can do the final items of the test. She smiles knowingly, takes a sip of her tea and tells me it is what is known as a 'single solution' test of problem solving. Once patients have seen the strategy they need to use to solve the problem, they can generally always do all the items. Warns me to be careful, especially when retesting the same patient. Advises me to not do this test only, but also other tests of executive functions. And to always remember the principle of double dissociation widely used in classic clinical neuropsychology. All useful stuff I already know. But does she actually know the most valuable lesson from today's supervision though? The role of anxiety on test performance. I felt it in my own body today. It is awful being tested when you are frightened of failing. It is easy to significantly underperform under such circumstances. Ms De Bruin is not very emotionally expressive. While in awe regarding her technical knowledge of clinical neuropsychology, I have always wondered about her bedside manner. How wrong I was. The fact of the matter is that today I saw for the first time that she is much, much more perceptive about emotions than I ever imagined. She just manages those in her care differently compared to how other colleagues might. Otherwise she would not have smiled when I said I could now do the test.

Ms De Bruin is looking at me again, but her expression is slightly softer than usual, before speaking. 'You are doing well. I have organised something that will be good for you. There is a weekend course on neuropsychological rehabilitation here on our campus, run by Dr Whitmore who recently returned from the States'.

Sounds like everybody either has been, or is going abroad.

'Remember her, or would that have been before you finished your clinical training a few years ago? Anyway, she went to work in a holistic rehab unit there for a year. You'll love her course on holistic rehabilitation, honestly. I think rehab is a large part of the future of clinical neuropsychology, and how we care for our patients', she says knowingly.

'Thank you very much for that, Carla. I do appreciate everything you do for me. See you next month, same time'.

Cycles

The past and future, birth, life and death. It's been around for hundreds of thousands of years. From a phenomenological perspective, as humans we know only the middle phase of this tri-modal cycle. The clinical neuropsychologist, given the nature of their work, gets a very special and privileged view on where aspects of life, the who we are, is suddenly altered or worse, dies, during life. Death, but not as you know it. What is all of this about death and dying? Clinical neuropsychologists do not cut open bodies, cast crushed bones, stitch wounds or give tablets to patients to prevent or delay death. No, but we are exposed every day to the invisible broken bits. Clinical neuropsychologists get to intimately know a person's cognitive functions, emotional experiences and behavioural changes secondary to suddenly acquired brain injury and illness. We try our best to make things a little better with what our patients have left, through support, rehabilitation and psychological therapy. But inevitably one day there will be nothing, the next time the sun rises, there it is, impossible to hold. However, the genetic conditions, and dementias, provide an altogether different perspective on how we all suspect death is. In contrast to acquired brain injury or neurological illness where patients mostly make some gains, if they survive, with the progressive conditions the clinical neuropsychologist becomes part of the relentless downhill march towards their inevitable physical death. Our role is different here. Baseline cognitive testing, mapping the cognitive trajectory, psychologically supporting the patient and even more so the family. It is a fierce finality for a person to lose his or her mind, while sometimes initially knowing that this is the beginning of the end. Some struggle, some fight, others suppress or deny their knowledge, a few commit suicide. Many don't have the cognitive capacity anymore to figure out what is happening. It is death while still alive. Mourning while passing away. *This* is what we are exposed to.

Work is finished for the day. I am out walking in the mountain above the city, climbing the head of the lion. The little sibling of the illusionary flat mountain overlooking the city. It is mid-summer, and the pale blue sky is fighting the brown smog of pollution hanging over the city. There should be enough light to make it to the top and back down before dark. The view over the cold blue Atlantic and the white beaches below is magnificent. You can almost touch life from here. I know the path, and the chains attached to the rocks to help you go up the last bit, very well from memory. Climbing upwards fast, Mr Osler drifts back into my mind. Does he feel alive or dead? I check my footing, then look left over the vast sea again. In the distance there is the notorious island from where nobody allegedly ever has escaped. My thoughts return to Mr Osler. If he cannot remember new occurrences from one minute to the next, has his life not to some extent ceased, lost its mental continuity? He will not ever remember spending the best part of a day with me, talking, telling me about himself and being tested. Nor did he appear to have any emotional experience of what was happening to him. If he cannot remember or feel things, is he not limited in his freedom to engage mentally with daily life? Does he simply live in the moment, merely exist, with all emotive and cognitive contextual continuity already dead? How does he process time, where is he anchored in this life, or is he incarcerated in a place truly impossible to escape from? The quietness is suddenly disturbed when an olive brown-green helicopter appears from nowhere over a ridge to my right, it's rotors desperately screaming as if in some panic. Very briefly there is a glimpse of the pilot and navigator. It is not a civilian helicopter. I wonder where it is destined to go, if it will make it in time and what human catastrophe might be awaiting its crew.

With the small units of time, the months also pass by, one after the other. I come to work, I do my thing, I go home. Everything feels familiar. My knowledge of clinical neuropsychology is now much better than at the start of the job. Anatomy, neuropathology, neuropsychological testing, rehabilitation, all now in a much better state of health than a year or so ago, even though there is still a very long way to go. Medical and other clinical colleagues seem to genuinely value having access to a clinical neuropsychologist in the hospital.

I am not apprehensive about seeing patients anymore, and in fact love the privilege of making some contribution to their lives, however insignificant it may be. That fear had to die during the first few weeks. Its cousin, doubt, still comes to visit often though, but that is a good thing. Gradually, clinical patterns within patients' stories have started to reveal themselves. I keep their stories alive for them, and in this way learn much more than science on its own can offer. Underneath our skins we all have the same fears, desires, sorrows, loves, ambitions and joys. In this very settled cycle I even start to like the building I found so imposing in the beginning. It is just like many of us, not perfect, but at least trying very hard to do a good job of containing some very broken people. On a spring morning, with an ice-blue sky as background, the sun over the mountains as side-lighting, the brown bricks even look beautifully luminous and alive contrasted with the sky. I love every moment of being here and what I do. This is my place forever. But I must somehow unconsciously know, or have some awareness, that this special part of the cycle will inevitably come to an end. Even the simple mathematics of my age and life expectancy, if any of the daily nightmares I see but deny exist do not come my way, whisper that this part of the cycle will die one day. Just a question of when the end will come.

10

Death

Dementia and neurological devastation

The boundaries which divide life from death are at best shadowy and vague.

(Edgar Allan Poe)

Travels

The medical school is a prettier building than its Siamese twin, the main hospital. Their relationship is an essential symbiosis. A long corridor forms the umbilical cord between academia and practice, and practice and academia. Somehow, and as is the case between all siblings, the relationship is not an equal one. The hospital can exist without the medical school, but the medical school will most likely struggle to survive long without the hospital. From most places in the hospital, after about five minutes of walking along various corridors there is a turnstile, which can, but not necessarily will, open when a staff card is swiped. If the electronic gatekeeper deems the holder of the card *persona non grata*, the road ends here. If not halted by the tense arms of the turnstile, the person is electronically judged to have *something* to do with the university, upon which the arms relax to let him or her enter through the back door of the university medical school. After the clunk of the metal, the huge, sombre face-brick building is immediately left behind. In its place suddenly there is the inner workings of a much lighter and brighter building. Everything freshly painted, white. Maybe it has something to do with teaching the skills required to preserve or improve lives, or prevent death. The corridors are white, there is a lot of light, and it is much cooler than in the hospital. The hospital on the other hand is an altogether different world. The heat can be almost unbearable in summer, and there is much more noise. The walls look as if they have been infused with the sweat and emotions of thousands upon thousands of strangers' suffering. It smells of pain, disease and trauma. The floors always shine, but the air is dirty. The medical school is . . . well, simply *sterile*.

At the front entrance to the medical school, there is a stone, a monument of sorts, complete with an incongruous inscription about a chisel breaking rock. Upon entering the building, it is not only a change in sensory experiences that is striking, there is something else evident in the air. Hope? An innocence not yet replaced by cynicism? The learning of the craft required for the world at the end of the other side of the umbilical cord, life as we see it, takes place here. But the juxtaposition of life is always death. No amount of white paint can hide that. It is logical that we die, *have* to die. Question is when. No, *how*. We know we should die, that we will, and won't even know at the moment of death that we are dying. Or have died. The exact moment of making the transition, is it really captured by our senses, to enter our awareness? Perhaps then there is no need really to worry or ruminate about it. As long as there is no painful and lengthy lead-in period, even the timing does not matter. But sometimes, just sometimes, after a long day in the clinic, the healers' bogeyman, who's been around since the beginning of time, returns to quietly whisper, to those brave enough to listen, 'What if you die, but don't, son?' sending shivers down the back of even the most cavalier white coat. Death is one thing, partly dead but alive incomprehensible. Not very long into time done on the other side, this Gordian Knot starts to suffocate the unprepared. The elders on that side, the hospital that is, tell us it is best to be prepared. They tell us not directly, but by mentorship to make sure we acquire the only realistic defence, knowledge. Sensible to learn about life, death, and what death looks like. And by extension, telling us gently to bury the past and figure out what makes us do, think, feel and be, *now*, before the end.

Funerals

Already during that very first chaotic ward round on day one, it became clear that neuro-anatomy is one of the core skills required to learn the foreign language of the neurology, neuropsychiatry, neurosurgery and neuropsychology clan. Which is precisely why today several months since starting my new job, I find myself at the left front entrance of the medical school. Professor Emmerson organised it. It is stiflingly hot outside, almost like the heat is trying to suck the air of life out of your lungs. I am here to learn the finer details of the complex language of clinical neuroscience. Or more accurately, to 'see' the language, to live it. I am at the entrance to the hall and a short passageway off the hall, leading to the dissection room. Will I faint? Everybody warns you not to. The advice passed down by previous cohorts is to have a fag, even if you don't actually smoke, immediately before entering. Will inhaling the African air be enough? I open the doors, follow the passage and enter through an imposing tall wooden door to my left a huge room that looks like a dormitory. It is really big, and there are rows and rows of tables, with a body on each. Each one covered by a standard issue hospital bed sheet. If they were not dead, one would possibly at first glance think it is a huge general ward, with a patient on each bed. Only it is much too quiet, and none of them move. The patients are cadavers. This is the final stop on the pathway, an exequy like no other you are ever likely to encounter. The room is unnaturally cool, and there is a strong smell of formalin. The ceiling is very high, almost like it was supposed to be a triple storey – and the rest of the building in fact is. High up, near the ceiling there is something else, invisible, hanging in the air, not moving. Perhaps it is Thanatos himself, to keep an eye on us below.

There are three students to a table. Young, enthusiastic, attractive, clever, animated, tomorrow's doctors. Very much alive. Our cadaver is a man, in life and in death. His face stares expressionless, never opening his eyes, at the ceiling high above him, lying flat on his back. I guess he is, but now *was*, in his late fifties. I wonder if he had a good life, and what he did with it. Did he make something of it? How did he die? Did he know his time was up, or did time just suddenly freeze in his synapses one day? I look away from his face. The sheet that is pulled over his body to cover him after each dissection session has been completed, is now hanging casually at the bottom of the table that is his final bed. The top of his skull has been removed by the tutor. There are dissecting sets for everyone, so that you can take apart the anatomical structures being studied at that point in the curriculum. I join the medical students for the central nervous system only. After a few weeks of lectures and practical tutorials like today, I will leave. To come back again in about a year with the postgrads. I look at the man's body again, and notice that they must have covered some part of the abdomen already during the curriculum. It is wide open, with the abdominal cavity impassively staring back at us. The tutor, Professor Allan Marlow, professor of anatomy, arrives and tells us to explore first the cortex, then generally work towards the midline and inner structures such as the basal ganglia and surrounding regions. Professor Marlow is also the lecturer who teaches us neuro-anatomy during the week. He is about mid-sixties and partially retired. He paces while smoking almost non-stop. The professor is rumoured to be a world expert in anatomy. Although some might want to make the point that surely not much could have changed in the field of anatomy over recent centuries. True of structure, but not function, anyone will tell you. With function we are still in the Dark Ages.

Professor Marlow, as quiet as a ghost returns to our little group. He gives us a list of specific brain structures to try and identify. He then briefly refers back to his lectures, what we most recently covered there. Then, as inconspicuously as he arrived, Professor Marlow leaves from where he was standing next to our table, and starts walking around the room. Disappearing and reappearing as if on a predetermined invisible timetable, visiting the other tables. Not even his white coat makes a sound as he moves, almost as if he was not walking, but floating. I look at the man on the table again. The calmness of death makes it easier to now look at his face for a bit longer than at first. It is difficult to get used to him not moving. No, it is not that which is disconcerting. It is the fact that his chest is not moving, with the rhythm of breathing, the ebb and flow of life itself. If there were such a thing as sleeping like a log, this is it. His complete stillness makes me start to wonder if the frantic part of life is not trying to stay alive? In the quiet of the room, my mind drifts off to Mr Van Vuuren (case # 5, Chapter 2), who I saw a few months ago. Where did Mr Van Vuuren *go* after he shot himself? Is there a station, a holding place, where we go while it is determined if we will die or live and possibly (for now) avoid the final stop? Maybe it was a brief pause in purgatory. Does Mr Van Vuuren remember the helicopter ride, the frantic battle to save his life? Did he have any sensation of his life, and parts of his history physically pouring out of his head as his vitals tried to cling on for dear life? Maybe parts of his personality evaporated when the key frontal lobe structures essential to his being in the world, ceased to function as they should. I am simultaneously in awe and horrified at how what just looks like a mix of white and grey building matter, cells organised by evolution and expressed in the moment by genetics and the environment, can be so central to who we are. Or were.

A surprise break in the silence sends a sense of panic and guilt suddenly rushing through my body. One of the medical students is speaking. I should really focus on the body in front of me, pay attention, learn what I have to.

'I am sorry to bother you, professor, but could you please show us the corona radiata?' the medical student asks tentatively.

Everybody is a bit afraid of Professor Marlow.

The professor paces three steps towards us, hands behind his back, as he always does, even when teaching in class. His thinning hair is greased back. He stops by the side of the table and looks up impassively at the student. His irises are a dull green, with a little bit of bloodshot contrast provided by the sclera. What have they witnessed in their time?

'A knife, please', Professor Marlow asks sounding remote and detached.

The student fumbles in one of the dissection kits, trying to pull out a scalpel. Professor Marlow sighs, turns around and from the laboratory sink behind him takes a huge knife, what actually looks like a bread knife. He moves back towards the head of the table. With utterly steady white hands that look as if they don't ever see the light of day, in one confident flowing movement he gently positions the knife to the left temporal area of our man. Professor Marlow makes a half-moon shaped cut inwards towards the midline, pulls the knife out, reinserts it to the left of the longitudinal fissure, and cuts again. Professor Marlow now gently lifts out the rounded wedge, and shows us the most beautiful white matter pathways radiating up towards the vertex of the brain. How many thoughts, perceptions, feelings and other neural exchanges passed here during the man on the table's life? I wonder yet again if he had a good life, sufficient to write a book about. But he cannot say. He's left what once was daily life, home. We can see, feel and smell that. Immediately after arriving back at home that night, my clothes go straight into the wash.

Back

Dr Burger and I are in the medical school canteen. He is becoming increasingly resistant to having meals in the hospital canteen. Says it's worth the extra walk to the medical school canteen, because it is a 'brighter' environment. And speaking of light, his eyes certainly seem brighter, perhaps recently even a glint in them? Nothing to do with the hospital food, he swears, breaking eye contact. After finishing lunch, we go through the turnstile, and back into *our* home, the hospital. He goes back to our unit in the basement of the hospital, I go up to the department of neurology on the ninth floor. Dr Carstens said I should come up this afternoon. I have known Dr Carstens for about a year now, and like him very much. He is funny, very clever and unbeknown to me now, one of the best teachers I will ever meet during my career. He regularly invites me to come to their neurology grand round on a Friday, where patients are presented and registrars wish they never chose to specialise in neurology. It is like a university academic programme keynote presentation, but for every patient discussed. The anxiety and personal stakes are so high it makes us forever after bemused with 'important' presentations in the white building next to us. After a year, Dr Carstens now has a couple of standing jokes every time I attend his grand round. Maybe it is his little ritual to reduce my anxiety, but much more importantly for me, to convey that I am part of 'the team' now. He does not joke with everybody. To introduce me, he says the following at these rounds when my turn to speak arrives, without fail, 'OK, next Rudi will tell us about Mr So and So's memory loss'.

Irrespective of what neuropsychological findings there actually were after assessing Mr or Mrs Whoever, all neuropsychology functions are 'memory loss' in Dr Carstens' mind.

And at the end of my short feedback of results, or presentation, he beams and announces to the audience, irrespective of if they want to listen or not, 'One day I will write a book: *How to make the best use of your three minutes*'.

Who knows what will happen, Johan Carstens. We'll just have to wait and see what becomes of us, and our thoughts.

Today Dr Carstens is taking me along with his entourage of medical students and registrars to see Mr Julio Adriato (case # 103). Mr Adriato is 65 years old, and he has been diagnosed with progressive supranuclear palsy a few years ago. Three days ago Dr Carstens asked me to read up about the condition before I come to the ward. Mr Adriato attends hospital for reviews, and has kindly agreed to be a teaching case. Dr Carstens introduces us to Mr Adriato, asks if it is OK if he examines him so that the students can see what his problems are. Mr Adriato is sitting on the edge of his bed, and speaks in a friendly, but very quiet voice. He says it's absolutely fine, and gives us a shy smile. He is quite short, of slender build, and balding. His cheekbones are high, and I wonder if he is from these shores. His illness hides a once beautiful face. Dr Carstens does a neurological examination. Stands to the side, so we can see what he is doing. He is gentle, but at the same time very fast. He shows us one of the classic signs of progressive supranuclear palsy, the inability of a person to move their eyes in the vertical plane. I didn't see it, so have to stand closer, and guiltily ask Dr Carstens to please elicit the sign again. Then I see it, and know instantaneously that I will never forget it. It must be so horrible for Mr Adriato, he would always have to move his whole head to look up or down. Exhausting, and I suspect humiliating when he is with other people. I also wonder about how it must feel for him to repeatedly show others his symptoms, be reminded of them, so that they can learn. Do they, no us, ever pause to consider and appreciate that it is something very personal of himself that he is giving, expecting nothing in return? Mr Adriato is allowing others to learn from his misfortune, but in an unexpected way.

The entourage leaves, and I am left on my own to perform a bedside cognitive assessment with Mr Adriato. Dr Carstens asked if I would do this for him, just to have some sense of his patient's cognitive abilities. He told me that they've not yet had a neuropsychologist present when Mr Adriato last attended. For this reason there is no documented baseline of his cognition. I start, and ask Mr Adriato the date, day, place and the other usual markers of orientation. He is fully orientated. His barely audible voice, and also the fact that he actually hardly speaks at all, are now much more noticeable. Unless he is asked questions, Mr Adriato does not speak. He clearly finds it effortful. Next I test his verbal fluency. Mr Adriato can only produce five words in a minute. His short-term as well as long-term (autobiographical) memory is patchy. He must know his memory is not what it was. For a split second I am distracted by the sadness and expression of desperation in his eyes, framed by his beautiful high cheekbones. I proceed to testing executive function, knowing I have to perform this paying particular attention, given the nature of his diagnosis and brain areas affected. Dr Carstens spent some time explaining the historical context of the disorder. According to Dr Carstens progressive supranuclear palsy historically is considered one of the very first neurological disorders where the brain pathology is at a sub-cortical level, and unlike many other sub-cortical pathologies, clinicians became aware that in addition to motor and other neurological signs, there was also cognitive impairment present in many patients. Patients who present with this disorder, originally termed Steele-Richardson-Olszewski syndrome, can have significant cognitive problems, in particular impairment of executive control functions. It is considered to have been one of the first neurological disorders, if not the very first, where a cortical basal ganglia disconnection syndrome was identified and described. Disconnection syndromes have enormous implications for modern clinical neuropsychology.

We continue with the assessment, now looking at Mr Adriato's executive functions. I use very simple bedside tests. These are possible to administer in environments like wards, by the 'bedside'. In this case, the patient is actually still sitting on his bed. Privacy is provided by the thin curtain around the bed, hanging like the emperor's clothes from the chrome rails near the ceiling. Everyone else in the ward can hear what is being said, even though they cannot see what is being done behind the curtains. Or at least, nothing more than the ghost-like outlines of the felled, and those still standing. Mr Adriato sits motionless. Walking is more difficult now, and he has also more generally slowed down a lot. During the assessment of executive functions he displays signs of perseveration and also poor set-shifting on, for example, the red-green test of mental shifting. Furthermore, Mr Adriato is also stimulus bound, and finds it difficult to disengage from tasks. It is as if a magnet mentally holds him to the previous test, before needing to be cognitively pulled towards the next already placed in front of him. The assessment takes a bit longer than anticipated. When he starts to show obvious signs of mental exhaustion, we stop. I thank Mr Adriato for his time, and his generosity to allow me to test him. I want to say something else, but cannot possibly find the right words. He looks at me, moving his head. I am not sure if he wants to ask me something, or if he is simply positioning his head so that he can better see me. In his unmoving and faded opaque eyes the desperation is now plainly visible, even though as a result of his motor problems, his face is less animated. His eyes can still communicate emotion. Without a single word being spoken between us, he is pleading. I pause, look at him, and wait. He slowly turns his head, and looks away. I suspect that we both know the same thing. Yes, he has cognitive problems, and yes, we are both very aware of his disabling physical symptoms. But my intuition in that brief moment when he looked away was that we both know that he has not long to live. We will never see each other again.

It is a very sobering experience when our patients physically die, or are about to die. Physical death is not very frequently encountered by the clinical neuropsychologist, but it still happens occasionally. You go back to the ward, and the bed is empty. Sometimes in your outpatient clinic the waiting room remains empty of that one person you want to be there, now. As the hours pass, you wish, pray, curse, worry, sweat, withdraw, pace and check, check, drink more coffee, take an oath, double check incessantly and pray more. Please let it be a DNA. Sometimes during the next appointment, unbeknown to you organised by admin after the previous DNA, they reappear as if rising from the dead. But sometimes they don't. Or as happened to me, someone else is in the bed where my patient was the day before. I check the ward number – yes, I'm in the right ward. Then ask the nurse where Mr or Ms Whoever is today. Only to be told in a 'I thought you knew' voice that my patient, who I was due to see again today, has died. I look around to see if perhaps they are not just lost and in another bed, as can happen when patients are disoriented, and in fact has happened to me. But of course I don't find them in another bed. The only person who is lost, is me. Patient deaths put into perspective the irrelevance of the minutiae of our daily sources of irritation. That could be me, or you, with a dementia or severe head injury, if fate randomised events slightly differently. Dead, or dead but still alive. Who cares about lack of parking, mindless forms to fill in, waves of corporate letters, that important presentation or lecture, a research paper rejected again, not having had something to eat because the clinic ran over, or who has been promoted and who not? There are other things to care about, before it is too late.

In the world of unrelenting one after the other, day in day out seeing brain-damaged patients, it's only human that we try to guard ourselves against thinking about the possibility that we ourselves may become disabled through neurological illness or injury, or those of us who may still fear it, our own end. Think about it. Where our patients sit now, one day we will sit, where they lie down tomorrow, we will one day lie down too. But we can't dwell on that. The only outcome would be burnout. And as a result even less to give our patients. There are different ways to rationalise the contrast between what we experience in this building, and away from it. Shutting off, 'throwing the mains' when we leave. Living very hard. Taking risks.

Distraction. Mental statistical modelling – the game of 'the odds are such that it won't happen to me'. Denial, 'these things happen to other people, not me, I'm the clinician'. Or ideally we become so fully focused on our patients that we forget about 'me'. But at some point for many clinicians an insight arrives. It's surviving when Mother Nature wanted you to die, which is excruciatingly hard, not actually dying. The pain of death is reserved for those left behind, if there were any who loved the deceased in life. *Not* dying is the shadow following us. Test the statement by asking a few random hospital-based clinical neuropsychologists if they would want to at all costs survive a severe brain injury. Please don't judge them too harshly if the answer is no. Instead ask them if they would like to do any other job than looking after neurological patients then. The answer will again be no. It is doing something for our fellow human beings that so powerfully draws us to these jobs.

One day I go up to the ward where I know I will find Dr Burger. He has not yet made an appearance back in our unit since earlier the afternoon. It's a Friday, and time for us to go home. I find Dr Burger in one of the medical wards (I think it was, anyway). Dr Burger looks at me blankly, as if studying something behind me, where there is nothing much to see other than a hospital wall.

'It's been very busy the whole afternoon. Sorry I did not make it down for coffee. I have one more patient to see', he says sounding a little bit vague.

'Sure, Tomas. What's it about?' I ask without thinking.

Dr Burger pauses before replying, I have to tell her about her scan finding'.

'Who are you talking about? Do I know her?' I ask trying to remember all the places I've been to see patients the past week.

'It's a malignant, inoperable tumour. Um, can you come with me?' Dr Burger asks while looking straight down the corridor, all the way to its end.

Did I hear that correctly? Slow growing, or aggressive? He didn't say. He looks exhausted, but says nothing more. We walk in silence to the patient's side room. Having a side room of one's own here in this hospital is a precious privilege, or ominous curse.

For the life of me I cannot remember the patient. Only that she was female, about early forties. I did not ever see her for neuropsychology input, the first time I set eyes on her was with Dr Burger. Her identifying features are gone, no trace, completely left my mind. No, never processed to be committed to memory. Or maybe pushed down, to an inaccessible place somewhere Freud knew. I cannot recall her face at all. I cannot describe what she looked like. Which is unusual for me. Patients, through their stories and faces tend to etch themselves surreptitiously in exquisite little patterns somewhere in the grey landscape of long-term memory. I think I remember more about her room. On this occasion it was a curse. Small details like the colour of the pathetic standard-issue blanket on her narrow metal frame bed, I can remember. It was light green, washed many times, to cover some who lived, some who did not. Most of all I can remember Dr Burger's facial expression. In the room, he proceeds to tell her about her scan, and with that, the truth. She is going to die. She is too shocked to cry, I think. He talks to her in the most compassionate way I think is possible, gently, with kind eyes, while remaining truthful. He does not even disturb the air in the room.

Rebooted

Even though it is only the start of January, I now have to fear that the end must surely be near. My two brand new interns, Chris and Willem, are having a heated argument. Not a good start for a specialist placement? The one took one more referrals than the other this morning, five versus four. The other now feels that having been 'forced' to take one less referral puts him in a bad light with his supervisor! It's a good start to the new placement . . .

'Hey, Chris, Willem, relax, chaps, everything will be fine. Honestly, every one of our problems in this old world always gets solved with time, one way or the other. Including this one. Mark my words. You'll agree. Maybe not yet. But by the end of the year . . .', I try to tell them what I have learned over time in this place.

I've been on leave, it is my first day back. A road trip through the semi-desert *platteland* (countryside) to the north-west of the city, and thereafter into Namibia itself. The vast open space, achingly faraway horizons where earth meets heaven, sparse vegetation, dry, fluid-sucking heat and the unpredictability of the next stop was totally reinvigorating. A mental reboot. This morning I still feel refreshed, lighter, as if anything is possible in the future. Life is good. But the reality of the daily routines of work soon bites through these thoughts, fragmenting them into a puzzle that will need reassembling. An out-patient clinic waits for me.

The first patient of this morning is attending for a new assessment. The patient is Mrs Sarie Theunisen (case # 75), and she is 59 years old. The background history is that she worked full-time for 28 years in the same firm. Never missed a beat in her post. Not a senior position, but nevertheless very serious about her job, and from all accounts had a super work ethic. That was just the person who Mrs Theunisen always was. As a result of her reliability, she was soon given lots of different responsibilities. You could rely on her. In later years her fellow workers noticed that she gradually started slowing down. Now she took a little bit more time to complete her daily work. Around this time Mrs Theunisen also became troubled by headaches, but only when she bent forward to file stuff, or pick up boxes. She says she thought that it was due to her increasing age, becoming a bit less physically fit than in her twenties. Then one day her headache was particularly bad, 'the worst one ever'. Or, she tells me, she thinks it must have been, her memory of the day is a bit patchy. Thinks she may have vomited, or maybe she was shaking, because she has some memory of not feeling very well. She says she thought she must have eaten something that was off, but again can-not remember what she actually had for lunch. Or, come to think of it, breakfast for that matter. Possibly *mieliepap* (maize porridge), she laughs. But she cannot really say, or be 100 per cent sure of every-thing. Mrs Theunisen was found on the floor near a cabinet, fitting. Work immediately called for an ambulance.

I wonder how Mrs Theunisen is now, only three months after becoming unwell, and ask, 'How are you feeling today, Mrs Theunisen? Any headaches?'

Mrs Theunisen leans forward, and tells me, 'The doctors operated on my head, and removed all the problems I had'.

Just like that, I wonder quietly by myself.

'What problems?'

'I had the shaking attacks in hospital, before they fixed me. I still have a few, but most have been cut away, so I'm not worried. By the way, have you heard the one about the doctor who called the nurse appendix?' she asks with a glint in her eyes.

I am not concentrating fully after my holiday, and reflexively ask, 'Why?'

'Coz he wanted to take her out!' Mrs Theunisen giggles.

'No, I meant why you were not worried anymore, Mrs Theunisen'.

'Well, I don't have to work in that boring job, with all those dull people around me anymore! So now I have a lot of spare time. Want to go on a holiday with me, doc?' she fires away again.

'I've just been on a great holiday, Mrs Theunisen', I manage to stutter, before realising the absurdity of my reply.

'No. no, what I meant is that I am your neuropsychologist, and we have a lot of work to do this afternoon', I manage to dig the hole even deeper.

'So? I love a man in a white coat . . .', her voice and eyebrows conspire to help me see the obvious error of my ways.

'Actually, I am just your neuropsychologist, nothing else', is my last attempt to turn things around towards the task of testing her.

Mrs Theunisen starts crying.

'You don't like me', she manages to say between her sobs.

I stop myself just in time from saying 'I like you very much, Mrs Theunisen, but not in that sort of way'.

'Why don't you tell me what is bothering you, Mrs Theunisen, and I'll see how I may be able to help you?' I ask after what I hope looked like a thoughtful pause.

Mrs Theunisen is distracted enough by my question to refocus on the purpose of our meeting. She tells me she sleeps way more than in the past, at least 2 hours in the day, and 10 to 12 at night. She also tells me she very easily feels cold (in this climate, I wonder), like a cold wind blowing down her back, and also her whole body feeling, just, well, cold. Suddenly she looks out of the window and asks me if I like the lovely hot weather we are having at the moment, ideal for the beach. Then winks, and says we should get a taxi to the beach, go for a walk and a swim.

'Hey Mrs Theunisen, what do you say, before it gets too hot, how about we test you?' I try to redirect things back to the consultation again. She briefly looks stunned, then smiles.

'Will you help me, I'm rubbish with tests, doing crosswords and that sort of stuff. I am stupid', she says with a note of alarm detectable in her voice.

'Since when, Mrs Theunisen, we have it on good authority that you were excellent with these sort of things in your work?'

There is the by now familiar but fleeting awareness, this time through the story of Mrs Theunisen, of how enormous a privilege and responsibility it is to have the opportunity to do this fantastic job.

As I walk past our unit's lounge late afternoon, it looks like the interns must have found a solution to their problem. They are best of chums again, drinking coffee together. I join them. Afterwards I go back to my office to look over the formal neuropsychological test results for Mrs Theunisen. Her Wechsler Adult Intelligence Scale four subtest prorated IQ is 93, about average, and about right for her premorbid academic and occupational achievements. On the Wechsler Memory Scales, for associations her performance is fine, as is logical memory. But her performance on the visual memory component of the test is impaired. Her performance on the Trail Making Test is OK, percentile 63 on trail A, and 35 on B. I wonder if trail B was a bit low for her, but then decide that the 35th percentile is in the normal range, and not two standard deviations away from her own projected average. The convention in clinical neuropsychology is that an impairment is a score two standard deviations below the person's own projected baseline of general cognitive ability. However, her Rey Complex Figure Test performance is poor, as a result of impaired planning and strategy. The theme of executive impairment continues with a sub-par performance on the Porteus Maze Test. The overall profile shows what looks like impaired executive control function, and possibly some visual memory problems also. I reflect on the history in Mrs Theunisen's medical notes. Three months ago a slow growing frontal tumour was removed from her brain. Between the scribbled lines, there is evidence of a massive operation being performed, but she survived. And as she herself said to me, she still has some residual fits, although much less. Thanks to brain surgery Mrs Theunisen was rebooted, to live a bit more, and longer. In the process, some cognitive ability had to be sacrificed, and her previous personality as it used to be, died in her place. It's not necessarily a bad death of what was, though? Nevertheless, only the future can truthfully answer that question.

Death

'*Tot siens dokter, kom kuier gerus weer, enige tyd, hoor*' ['Goodbye doctor, feel free to come and visit again, anytime you'd like to'], Mrs Kotze says in a cheery voice as she leaves my room. Her faded pink gown hangs loosely over her scrawny shoulders, like a cape still demanding respect for long forgotten victories.

Today I have absolutely no idea if I will pay a visit again at some point in the distant future. But somehow I doubt I will come back. Mrs Hettie Kotze, (case # 87) aged 61, has been diagnosed with dementia, and is very clearly confusing me with the doctor who referred her for a neuropsychological assessment. She is also mixing up social and professional (hospital) visits. But she is happy enough in herself. It is unknown why she has developed dementia at such a young age. There is no contributory medical history. She functioned well prior to an insidious onset of cognitive problems a few years ago. Mrs Kotze was educated to the equivalent of GCSE levels (standard 8), and left school at age 16 with six subjects passed. Mrs Kotze is neat, friendly but a bit perseverative while we complete the baseline neuropsychological testing requested. On a three subtest short Wechsler Adult Intelligence Scale Mrs Kotze scores a prorated IQ of 85, with her highest subtest score 10.0, on picture completion. Her memory is patchy, with a percentile of 21 on the visual memory part of the Wechsler Memory Scale, 19 on associative learning and on logical memory she scores at the first percentile. Mrs Kotze has already passed the very early stages of dementia, where awareness can make many patients anxious, agitated or depressed. She is now at the middle stages during the journey of intellectual death. It is here where cognition is likely to be impaired enough to protect the person from being able to explicitly dwell upon, and ruminate over what is happening. For Mrs Kotze the present is short, the past shrinking and the future already dead.

Meanwhile somewhere else there is another death of the past. This death, like many, follows after a protracted and painful period of intense suffering. And for once, on this occasion it is an unequivocal and indescribably excellent death. Yes, finally after too much blood to physically measure has been haemorrhaged into the African soil to make it even redder, pathetic little graveyards overflowing with humble wooden crosses, the first democratic election in South Africa takes place in 1994. With each and every little pencil cross, the rainbow nation is gradually born. The queues for casting a vote are long, snaking along to the moment of releasing a little personal cross. How strange it feels to vote for the very first time aged 32, I think to myself as the queue edges slowly forward, metre by metre. There are helicopters overhead, coming and going. As an incentive to vote, at the station where I cast mine, you are given a double movie ticket.

Two movies, back to back. To see after making your decision and go to another world. The world of the silver screen, where everything is possible, but hardly anything true. Inside the future is full of artificial light. Outside in the real world, light comes, is replaced by darkness, only to rise again. This ancient rhythm of existence still giving hope. Reminding everybody that there is still tomorrow, a future to come.

Later, much later, not weeks, not months, but years into what was then the future, Dr Burger and I are out walking. Dr Burger is not party to my thoughts. Yet. I am reflecting on the profound influence Dr Burger had on the direction life took when he asked me to cast a vote for his master plan. And since voting for a change that night at the bins, how my thinking, and feeling, about caring for patients completely changed. Dr Burger reaffirmed that loyalty, compassion and truth without harm should underpin all of what we do with people, patients, colleagues, all those who cross our paths. He hardly speaks, Dr Burger, a cool head he has, but often surprises me. The biggest surprise? That the stories our patients bring to us, and our gut instinct, is always better that the latest cutting edge diagnostic imaging or other technologies to tell us more about the human condition, and who we all are, or will become. Anyway, there is no life in pixels, they are dead light. Life itself we find in the hospital. Sometimes. But not always. My footsteps relentlessly tell me I have to stop ruminating and tell him about what happened a few hours ago. About a death. Of what was, and a life of what might still be.

'Tomas, I have to tell you something'.

'Go on, what is it, Rudi?'

'I have had confirmation that I have an interview for a job next month, Tomas'.

Under the sun, the cicadas screech that it is the truth, he need not see the letter.

'Where?' Dr Burger asks calmly.

'Britain', I hear someone, no, *me*, say.

My heart starts to race, briefly dies and then splutters back to life. We walk on in silence. For now.

Epilogue

The journey of a thousand miles begins with one step.

(Lao Tzu)

'Relax, everything is going to be fine, Flo'.

'Have you gone mad or something? The cognitive colloquia are high level *research* talks', Flo says with alarm in her voice.

'So? I love research'.

'Why did they ask you? *Who* asked you to do a Friday talk?' the alarm in her voice changing to irritation.

'Two doors down. He organises the programme. You don't know him. He's a really, really nice guy', I answer, motioning to the left with my head.

It is almost a year now since our 'extensively reviewed and re-reviewed paper' was finally accepted for publication. Flo takes her glasses off, and puts the tip of one arm in her mouth. She looks at me intently with her blue eyes.

'Listen Flo, relax. It's a rite of passage. Everybody here has to do a talk. I am delighted that I have been asked to contribute to the colloquia. It is great being here. I love the people I work with, they make me think, help me, even make me laugh. Everything will be fine. Anyway, it is December. Everybody's away'.

I wish the American professor could attend. I miss him.

'Sure, but you are not an academic. You've been to many of these talks by now. You should know . . .', she reminds me.

'You are trying to be my mother, aren't you? Calm down, the talk is only next week. Come on, have a block of dark chocolate. It's good for you. Compliments of your eldest son'.

'What. Are. You. Going. To. Talk. About?'

Flo briefly hesitates, and then breaks off a block of the chocolate.

'I will talk about history', I tell her after a long pause.

'*What*?' she almost chokes on the block.

'Remember my notebook? My talk will be about what came before, and determined now', I try to make a start.

'I don't know what you are talking about. Show me the first slide'.

The PowerPoint slowly loads. The first slide of the talk is an aerial photograph of beautiful but not so flat Table Mountain. Eighteen years ago I had exactly that view. As seen out of a window of an aeroplane. Like mental superfast broadband, the images, thoughts and emotions come rushing back.

'Please keep your seatbelts fastened until the seatbelt lights go out. Please note, smoking is not allowed on this flight', the metallic voice announces.

Into an impossibly blue sky, the plane steadily cuts a path to the unknown. What have I done? Looking down, below there is under the blinding sky now a better South Africa, even if not even nearly fixed. The long snakes of people queuing to vote in the first democratic elections four years ago, finally gave birth to the rainbow nation. It's mad to leave now! But an opportunity too good to not embrace arrived, creating turmoil, confusion, and at times, huge excitement, a sense of impending adventure. Associative memory is powerful, that's why as clinical neuropsychologists we test it. The land below hosts my few friends, and remaining family. The red soil of Africa now with each minute further away, permanently associated with them. The noise of the plane does its best to etch into memory the finality and sadness of leaving behind what is dear, before banking steeply. It then casually turns its back on Cape Town.

The sadness makes it difficult to talk to a forlorn Ana sitting next to me. Next to her sits Sylvester, Sasha's seat not yet taken. My thoughts, battling the din created by the plane, feel like they belong in someone else's head. It is 1998, and I am leaving Africa behind, not forgotten. It is 11 years since I finished my clinical training, and 6 since that first year of an unpredictable journey of pursuing a career in hospital-based clinical neuropsychology. The 6 years taught me many things. I now speak the clinician-scientist language I heard during that first frightening ward round. Nevertheless, after literally hundreds upon hundreds of stories entrusted to me by now, the patient's narrative remains the most important language I learned there. Their stories still the most important language, requiring considerable skill to decipher.

'So, what is your talk about then?' Flo returns my inner world to the pixels from the past now illuminated on the computer screen in front of us.

'Well, I'm new in the academic department, nobody knows much about me. I will tell them a little bit about where I worked before, all the speakers do that. I will then start with presenting very briefly one of my patients from the time in Africa. His is a phenomenally interesting story, about a very focal lesion of the right frontal lobe. A stab not to the heart as was often the case in those breathtakingly dangerous sandy flatlands, but the head. Delivered under cover of dim light in a pub, the knife as quick as the muzzle flash from a gun. The blade breaking off inside his brain, something he was totally unaware of. For 18 months. Which is the part of the story that to this day intrigues me. It is about self-awareness after brain injury, what makes us human, how the brain is involved in our most complex phenomenological experiences', I start off, as I move on to the next slides, outlining the clinical details of my patient from many years ago.

The office has gone quiet. Flo is leaning towards the screen, peering intently at the on-screen images conveying a story from another world very far away. The phenomenology of suffering a brain injury.

'His story, and history, made a very big impression on me during my early days as a clinical neuropsychologist. It had, and I think still has, profound implications for clinical practice, but much more so, research. My research themes, which to reassure you will be presented during the talk, were almost certainly very significantly shaped by his case, and the hundreds that came since. And that is my point Flo, clinical practice and academia are two sides of the same coin'.

Flo smiles, and helps herself to another block of dark chocolate, before saying, 'Well, I think I will come to the talk'.

After Flo leaves, I continue my preparation, and go back to the first slide. Clinical neuropsychology has significantly developed since those days, although a fair amount of the basics probably remain the same. Some of the landmark texts of the time at the hospital in Africa have endured, and stood the test of time. Lezak's classic book lives on, in 2012 entering its fifth edition, co-written with the next generation of clinical neuropsychologists. It still contains all the wisdom from the past, but the world of neuroscience has since raced ahead. For example, in recent times we have learned about chronic traumatic encephalopathy. In fact, I almost certainly once saw this condition as an intern, 30 years ago. Testing a retired boxer revealed a very abnormal cognitive profile, but without a history of being knocked unconscious. I just did not at the time know what it was, nor which questions to ask. Neuro-imaging has exponentially developed, and pushed the boundaries of science. Or has it? In 2017 we still need to *talk* to patients. More is also now made of the patient's phenomenological experience, to help us understand how their personal thoughts and feelings travelling with them everywhere are coloured by damage to the very apparatus used to create these experiences for them in the first place.

My trainee sounds a bit tangled in the barbed wire of her thoughts, and very nervous about her upcoming viva.

'Listen, everything is going to be cool with your viva. It's just the first of many steps on your way to becoming a clinician, and whatever else you might do after qualifying. We have *all* been there'.

My trainee's apprehension has me thinking about the past. One of the main lessons of that formative first year, and the ones that followed, was about how to best help our fellow humans who have sustained an injury to the most precious of organs. 'Wanting to save the world', may propel many of us into some sort of clinical profession in the first place. Unfortunately the 'world' within which hospitals everywhere function is never perfect. It is often itself socio-politically broken or damaged. Hence health care is hardly ever changed significantly for the better through an obsession to change everything that's not quite perfect, while the world outside the hospital burns. Indeed, the philosophy of care, compassion and cure is ancient, going back to Hippocrates and before. Health care happens . . . still mostly in the *hospital*, on the frontline caring for patients. Amazing how much you can do with very little, and some-times, how little with so much. It's not important to be important, to be successful at looking after patients. It is about something else. *Primum non nocere.* In the first instance do no harm.

My trainee is staring at me.

'Please don't worry about your viva. Everything becomes his-tory. One day soon when this stressor is just a memory, remember to always put your whole heart into caring for your patients, all the time. Then everything will be fine'.

Late Sunday afternoon, sleet is falling from a beautiful dark metal-lic grey sky outside. I am at home. A last look at Table Mountain under the African sun, and I decide that it's finally done. Ready to be saved to a memory stick. Still not nearly as research heavy as is normally the case with talks at the cognitive colloquia, but a first step towards being part of yet another 'home', a new family. Where *is* home? After so many years of living here occasionally people still ask when I will go 'home'. I now always reply, 'Later today, straight after work'. Here in a new home, my patients' stories live on in my memory. Their histories and clinical details, but also their sorrow, resilience, stoicism, loss, forgiveness of themselves and sometimes embracing how life is for them now. Maybe then learning from patients, 'home' is probably simply where we are, where we find ourselves now. Perhaps it really is possible to have a 'taxi heart' as we sometimes said in Africa. There a taxi has many seats, and is often overloaded to make sure nobody is left behind. We can love more than one thing, more than one person, and more than one country if we are open enough to embrace opportunity. And North Wales is an exceptionally easy place to love, despite the cold. The Welsh weather reminds me of Dr Burger's words shortly after he returned home from Northern Canada. The distress, symptoms, pathology, suffering, fears and hope of patients are the same, wherever in the world you go. The individual stories connecting all of these though are never quite the same. This is exactly what makes them *arbennig* (precious). There is no going back. It is already Sunday evening, in a new, and old, country. Sometimes even the most ordinary things are also not that different at all. The bins need putting out in time for Monday morning's collection. Like most memorable stories it's the truth – the local council's annual roster of refuse collections says it is a Monday collection. I wonder if anyone else will be outside when the bins are put out?

Bibliography

Baddeley, A. D., Wilson, B. A. and Watts, F. N. (1995). *Handbook of memory disorders*. Chichester: John Wiley & Sons.

Folstein, M. F., Folstein, S. E. and McHugh, P. R. (1975). Mini-mental state. *Journal of Psychiatric Research*, 12: 189–198.

Hodges, J. R. (1994). *Cognitive assessment for clinicians*. Oxford: Oxford University Press.

Hooper, H. E. (1958). *Hooper Visual Organisation Test (VOT)*. Los Angeles, CA: Western Psychological Services.

La Cock, C., Hugo, F. J., Coetzer, R., Van Greunen, G., Kotze, C. and Emsley, R. A. (1999). Establishing a neuropsychiatry clinic at Tygerberg Hospital. *South African Medical Journal*, 89(6): 655–660.

Lezak, M. D. (1995). *Neuropsychological assessment* (3rd edn). New York: Oxford University Press.

Lezak, M. D., Howieson, D. B., Bigler, E. D. and Tranel, D. (2012). *Neuropsychological assessment* (5th edn). New York: Oxford University Press.

Luria, A. R. (1972). *The man with a shattered world*. Cambridge, MA: Harvard University Press.

Luria, A. R. (1973). *The working brain*. London: Penguin.

Milner, B. (1965). Visually guided maze learning in man: Effects of bilateral hippocampal, bilateral frontal, and unilateral cerebral lesions. *Neuropsychologia*, 3: 317–338.

Nell, V. (1994). Interpretation and misinterpretation of the South African Wechsler-Bellevue Adult Intelligence Scale: A history and prospectus. *South African Journal of Psychology*, 24(2): 100–109.

Osterrieth, P. A. (1944). Le test de copie d'une figure complexe. *Archives de Psychologie*, 30: 206–356. Translated by J. Corwin and F. W. Bylsma (1993). *The Clinical Neuropsychologist*, 7: 9–15.

Porteus, S. D. (1959). *The maze test and clinical psychology*. Palo Alto, CA: Pacific Books.

Reitan, R. M. (1958). Validity of the Trail Making Test as an indicator of organic brain damage. *Perceptual and Motor Skills*, 8(30): 271–276.

Rose, F. D. and Johnson, D. A. (1996). *Brain injury and after: Towards improved outcome*. Chichester: John Wiley & Sons.

Sacks, O. (1985). *The man who mistook his wife for a hat*. New York: Summit Books.

South African Wechsler Adult Intelligence Scale (SAWAIS) Manual (1969). Johannesburg, South Africa: National Institute for Personnel Research, Human Sciences Research Council.

Strub, R. L. and Black, F. W. (1993). *The mental status examination in neurology* (3rd edn). Philadelphia, PA: F. A. Davis Company.

Walsh, K. (1987). *Neuropsychology: A clinical approach* (2nd edn). Edinburgh: Churchill Livingstone.

Walsh, K. (1987). *Understanding brain damage*. Edinburgh: Churchill Livingstone.

Wechsler, D. (1939). *The measurement of adult intelligence*. Baltimore, MD: Williams & Wilkins.

Wechsler, D. (1974). *Wechsler Memory Scale manual*. San Antonio, TX: The Psychological Corporation.

Wechsler, D. (1987). *Wechsler Memory Scale revised manual*. San Antonio, TX: The Psychological Corporation.

Appendix

A short note on tests

A wide range of neuropsychological tests were not available at the time in South Africa. More troubling though were the significant problems with lack of standardisation, translation and adequate norms for those tests that were available. An example would be the (South African) Wechsler Adult Intelligence Scale, not only still based on the original Wechsler-Bellevue Scale, but also only translated into 2 of the 11 official languages, with associated very serious deficiencies as regards norms. Furthermore, almost all the tests would have been originally developed for Western cultures, with no cognisance or recognition of the multicultural nature of South Africa's population. Political factors created huge problems also, for example, inferior schooling for certain groups of people, poverty, violence and many other serious issues affecting people's performance on psychological tests, including neurological patients with brain injury or illness. The reality was that clinical neuropsychological services still had to be delivered to the uncountable numbers of patients affected by injury and illness.

Perhaps then it is to some extent understandable that the clinical neuropsychology tradition of bedside cognitive testing to consider hypotheses in a deductive manner (for example, in the tradition of Luria) to complement the imperfect data provided by formal neuropsychological testing, gained popularity in many of the South African hospital settings where clinical neuropsychologists worked at the time.

Index

neurosyphilis 80

new learning/short-term memory
15, 30, 37, 57, 93, 117, 129, 191

Normal Pressure Hydrocephalus
(Dora Ismail, case # 3) 98–101

notebook xii, xii–xvi, xvii, 11, 14, 23,
203; see also individual cases

nursing staff 13, 53, 54, 64, 65, 145

observation: assessment process
overview 14; importance of
facts and scores 35, 56; mental
status examination 15–16; Mrs
Esterhuizen 67; Red Cross lady
63; seizures 71, 111, 121, 123;
signs and symptoms 16, 153;
skill development 122, 123

Ongskiktheids Toelaag (disability
allowance) 81–82

Osler, Chris (case # 29, genetic
disorder) 172–175, 181

overdose, drug 147

oxygen starvation 47; see also
anoxia/hypoxia

paranoid schizophrenia (Jannie
Prins, case # 34) 147–151

parasite-induced brain infections
74–75

Parkinson's disease (Chris Osler,
case # 29) 172–175, 181

patient files 13–14

patient histories 14–15, 162; see
also individual cases

patient stickers 11, 14, 25

penetrating brain injury 31

personality and behaviour:
following removal of a tumour
(Sarie Theunisen, case # 75)
197–198, 199; frontal lobe
mediation 29, 30, 116, 168, 187,
199; Huntington's Disease 91;
limits of science 152; medical
files, value of 14; pre-morbid 30,

94; temporal lobe epilepsy 93;
traumatic brain injury (Mr Van
Der Merwe, case # 53) 32–35,
37, 38, 39

petit mal attacks 110

Pick's disease 21, 177; see also
Kruger, Blanche (case # 33,
Pick's disease)

Pietersen, Mr (case # 91, traumatic
brain injury) 18–20

Poe, Edgar Allan (quotation) 183

Porteus Maze test 19, 34–35, 41,
50, 78, 89, 97, 114, 137, 171,
174, 199

possession 69

post-traumatic amnesia 31, 40

poverty and social deprivation: as a
cause of neurological disability
82, 125–126, 154, 176; formal
test performance 210; parasite-
induced brain infection 74–75;
patient histories 18–19, 20,
68–69, 71, 72, 81, 92, 96, 117

Pretorius, Klaas (case # 72,
epilepsy) 112–115

Prins, Jannie (case # 34,
schizophrenia) 147–151

procedures, importance of 115–117

progressive supranuclear palsy
(Julio Adriato, case # 103) 21,
190–192

pseudo-seizures 121, 123

psychiatric aspects of neurological
injury: diagnostic groupings 21;
genetic disorders 91; Jakobs,
Elsie (case # 54, alcoholism)
159–161; and the limits of
science 152–154; neurosyphilis
80; patient on the roof anecdote
73–74; pre-existing conditions
30; Prins, Jannie (case # 34
paranoid schizophrenia) 147–151,
152; reading the medical file
14; referrals 22, 49, 94–95, 135;

Taylor & Francis eBooks

Helping you to choose the right eBooks for your Library

Add Routledge titles to your library's digital collection today. Taylor and Francis ebooks contains over 50,000 titles in the Humanities, Social Sciences, Behavioural Sciences, Built Environment and Law.

Choose from a range of subject packages or create your own!

Benefits for you

>> Free MARC records
>> COUNTER-compliant usage statistics
>> Flexible purchase and pricing options
>> All titles DRM-free.

Benefits for your user

>> Off-site, anytime access via Athens or referring URL
>> Print or copy pages or chapters
>> Full content search
>> Bookmark, highlight and annotate text
>> Access to thousands of pages of quality research at the click of a button.

REQUEST YOUR **FREE** INSTITUTIONAL TRIAL TODAY

Free Trials Available
We offer free trials to qualifying academic, corporate and government customers.

eCollections – Choose from over 30 subject eCollections, including:

Archaeology	Language Learning
Architecture	Law
Asian Studies	Literature
Business & Management	Media & Communication
Classical Studies	Middle East Studies
Construction	Music
Creative & Media Arts	Philosophy
Criminology & Criminal Justice	Planning
Economics	Politics
Education	Psychology & Mental Health
Energy	Religion
Engineering	Security
English Language & Linguistics	Social Work
Environment & Sustainability	Sociology
Geography	Sport
Health Studies	Theatre & Performance
History	Tourism, Hospitality & Events

For more information, pricing enquiries or to order a free trial, please contact your local sales team: www.tandfebooks.com/page/sales